IMAGES
of America

HAMILTON COUNTY PARKS

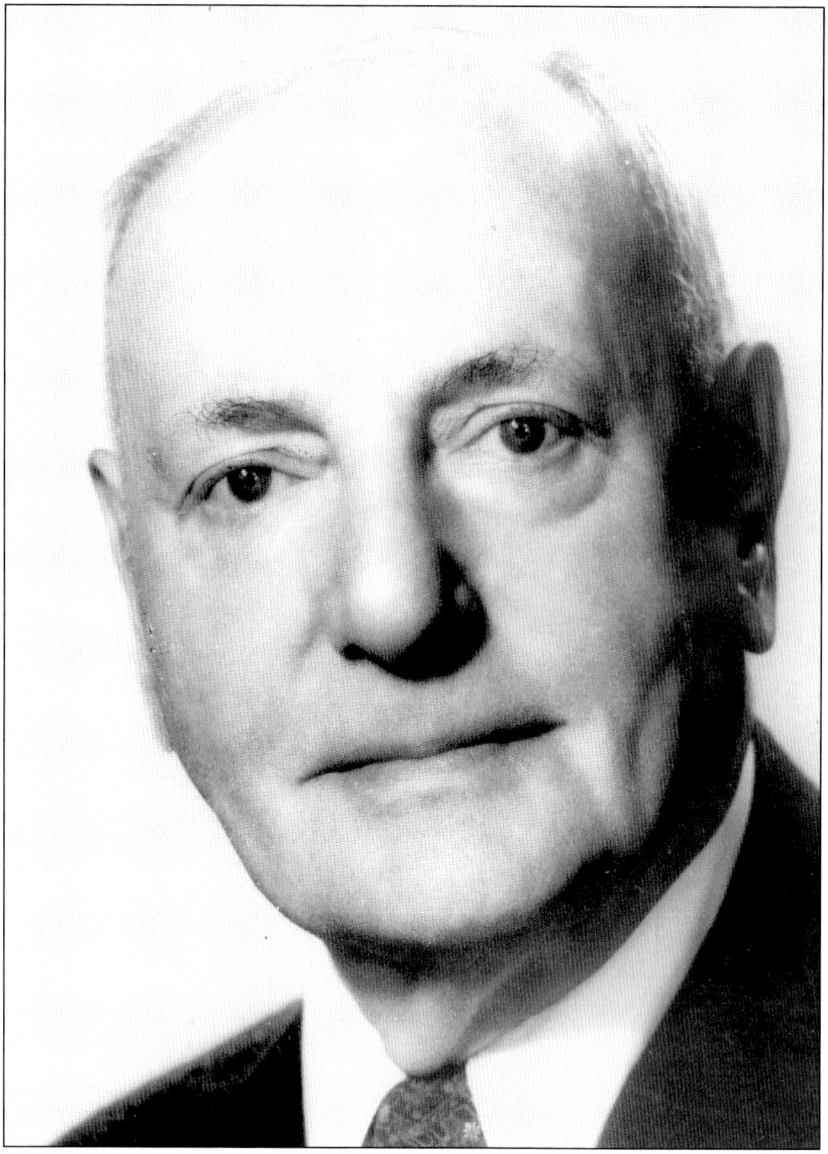

FOUNDING FATHER. Murray P. Seasongood helped chart the course of Cincinnati politics and civic life throughout much of the 20th century. Elected as a reform mayor of the newly created Charterite Party in the 1920s, Seasongood restored the reputation of good government to Cincinnati. During his first term, in 1926, he visited the Cleveland Metropolitan Park District. The mayor returned home dedicated to the proposition of creating a regional park authority that would acquire and manage parklands for the Greater Cincinnati metropolitan area. Four years later, his efforts came to fruition with the creation of the Hamilton County Park District. This photograph was taken in 1975, when the park district presented him with a conservation award.

On the cover: **THE APPEAL OF THE COUNTY PARKS.** This view is of the par-four No. 10 hole at Sharon Woods as it appeared from Sharon Woods Lake. Both the lake and the golf course were constructed by Works Progress Administration workers during the Great Depression. (Courtesy of the Hamilton County Park District.)

IMAGES
of America

HAMILTON COUNTY PARKS

Robert Earnest Miller

ARCADIA
PUBLISHING

ISBN 978-0-7385-4114-3

Published by Arcadia Publishing
Charleston, South Carolina

Printed in the United States of America

Library of Congress Control Number: 2006930904

For all general information, please contact Arcadia Publishing:
Telephone 843-853-2070
Fax 843-853-0044
E-mail sales@arcadiapublishing.com
For customer service and orders:
Toll-Free 1-888-313-2665

Visit us on the Internet at www.arcadiapublishing.com

To my parents, Roger and Mary Jane Miller, who taught me to love the outdoors at an early age. To Frank Tufts, my former scoutmaster, who gave me an appreciation for hiking and camping. To Ed Hall, who taught me the importance of golf etiquette and instilled in me a passion for the game.

CONTENTS

ACKNOWLEDGMENTS

Authors always accumulate many debts in the process of writing. This book has been no exception. First of all, I would like to express sincere thanks for all the cooperation that was extended to me by members of the Hamilton County Park District. Jim Rahtz, visitor services director, was my first contact when I had the notion of writing this book. Jim helped facilitate support for this project among the current board members, and he lent encouragement and expertise along the way. A veteran park employee of 23 years, Jim proved to be a tremendous resource in identifying images and providing information on park history. He arranged for me to have unfettered access to the park district's photograph archives, as well as digitized copies of the park board minutes. I made several trips to the park district headquarters at Winton Woods to scan these vintage photographs. On several of my visits, I sat for hours in the same boardroom where park commissioners have gathered over the years to discuss issues related to park governance and administration. I also owe a debt to Joy Landry, communications specialist for the park district. She made sure that each of my trips to the park office headquarters was a productive visit. Thanks also go out to the civic-minded individuals who have served as park commissioners, and the paid staff, including park rangers and naturalists. Without their collective dedication to conserving and preserving the county's finite natural resources, the book never would have been possible.

Personal debts play an equally important role. My wife and soul mate, Therese, provided much-needed moral support and critical, 11th-hour logistical support. My daughters, Jen and Emma, were patient with all the time-consuming demands of research and writing. At critical junctures, several relatives and friends, including Roger and Mary Jane Miller, Len and Elisa Grammel, Jim and Rita Gayer, Teri Hinkle, and Julie Smith, rescued me by providing much-needed and much-appreciated child care for Emma.

Finally, thank you to Melissa Basilone, my editor at Arcadia. This is my second book with her. She has provided professional guidance and expertise at every step of the production process, shepherding this book to its successful completion.

Introduction

An old adage about one's roots and lineage goes something like this—you can take the boy out of the country, but you can't take the country out of the boy. The same wisdom holds true regarding my connections to Hamilton County. Even though I have lived in Warren County for the past 10 years, I am, at heart, an old west-sider. My ties to Hamilton County and its parks remain integral parts of my childhood and adolescence. As a young boy, I remember piling in the car with my parents and siblings and heading out to Miami Whitewater Forest for family outings. As a member of Boy Scout Troop 288, in Bridgetown, I hiked on trails in the same park in preparation for a two-week backpacking trip out West. Since I was old enough to drive, I have played golf at Sharon Woods. Over the years, the No. 4, straight-up-hill, 460-yard par-four hole has taught me the importance of good humor and humility. Many years later, as a parent, I would return with my children to the newly constructed water recreation areas at Winton Woods and Sharon Woods and the recently opened Highfield Discovery Garden at Glenwood Gardens.

The Hamilton County Park District is one of the region's most treasured resources. It attracts more than seven million visitors per year, surpassing the combined total attendance for such tourist attractions as the Cincinnati Reds, the Bengals, and Kings Island, to name a few. It is easily the area's most popular outdoor attraction. In 2005, the Hamilton County Park District celebrated its 75th anniversary of service to the residents of Hamilton County and Greater Cincinnati. This book will commemorate the hard work of elected officials, park board commissioners and staff, and anonymous volunteers who have ensured that the Hamilton County Park District will flourish in future years.

This book spans the years 1930 to 2006. It traces the park district's history, from its humble beginnings to its present state. The Hamilton County Park District was created in 1930, at a time when the county, like the rest of the nation, was struggling through the hard times of the Great Depression. The park district began with extremely meager resources, including a paltry budget and a skeleton staff. Yet, armed with monumental ambitions, the park district purchased approximately 335 acres of land near Sharonville, the so-called Reading Tract. In 1932, Sharon Woods welcomed its first visitors. Over the next several decades, the park district grew exponentially. It increased its total acreage through outright purchases, long-term leases, and gifts. By the 1970s, parks served residents in every part of the county. Thirty-five years later, the park district comprised 19 different parks and preserves, totaling more than 14,500 acres.

This book is organized chronologically. Chapter 1 covers the early years, in which the park district laid out its ambitious plan to develop a network of parks. Working through the challenges of the Great Depression and World War II, the Hamilton County Park District expanded to three parks within its first 20 years. Chapter 2 explores how the park district continued to acquire new lands. By the time the park district celebrated its 50th anniversary in 1980, the number of parks had increased to 15. Chapter 3 retraces the same chronological period as the previous chapter, and it examines the new directions in programs and services, with particular emphasis on nature education. Chapter 4 offers a composite view of the park district in the past few decades and looks briefly at its current state and plans for the future.

The primary source materials for this book are the actual board minutes of the Hamilton County Park District. These records proved invaluable to me. They offered a window into the world of those individuals who shaped policy for the park district since its inception. Supplemental research of microfilmed issues of the three Cincinnati daily newspapers, the *Enquirer*, the *Post*, and the *Times-Star*, at the University of Cincinnati's Langsam Library, provided important background and contextual information.

Since this book is an illustrated history, it is appropriate to offer a word or two of explanation about the photographs in this book. While there are, indeed, 19 different parks and preserves, most of the images included feature the first three parks: Sharon Woods, Winton Woods, and Miami Whitewater Forest. On occasion, the park board commissioned professional photographers, such as Marsh Studios, to perform photograph shoots of the multitude of activities in the parks. More often, the extant photographs were taken by park rangers and naturalists. One park ranger, J. Herbert Heger, deserves special mention. He is responsible for providing most of the images from the 1950s and 1960s. Because the photograph record is less than comprehensive, this book will not endeavor to retell the story of each and every park. That task would be too daunting and, I fear, more than a little redundant.

While local history is important in its own right, local stories often take on larger meanings when they intersect with or parallel historical trends that are operating simultaneously on a national or global level. On occasion, these types of intersections presented themselves in the course of my research. The inception of the park district happened in the midst of the Great Depression. The lean years of the 1930s played a big role in how the park district first developed. Unemployed workers on relief rolls played a key role in construction projects. Two decades later, at the height of post–World War II prosperity, park commissioners fought to conserve existing parks and to acquire and preserve more lands threatened by the development of suburbs, shopping malls, and highways. During the 1960s and 1970s, a grassroots environmental movement emerged. This growing awareness of the fragility of the earth and its natural resources soon manifested itself through the efforts of the Hamilton County Park District. Today more than 80 percent of the land it administers is land in its natural habitat—wetlands, prairies, and old-growth forests.

What follows, in the chapters ahead, is an amazing story of foresight and vision, coupled with hard work and perseverance.

One

The Early Years 1930–1950

One hot, July day in 1930, three men, William H. Albers, Ralph Rogan, and L. Alvin Kreis, gathered in the downtown Cincinnati chambers of probate judge William H. Leubbers. One year earlier, Cincinnati City Council had passed a resolution calling for the establishment of a county-wide park district. When Hamilton County Park District began, the commissioners had no staff and, more importantly, no parks. In 1931, they hired Alfred M. Husted, who would serve as the board's director-secretary until 1959. Under Husted's direction, the commissioners purchased a 335-acre tract of land near Sharonville. By 1932, the first curious visitors streamed through the front entrance of the county's first park, Sharon Woods.

What is remarkable about the early history of the park district is when it started. During the Great Depression, when most economic initiatives ground to a halt, the park district managed to become a stakeholder in the future development of Hamilton County. As part of the law of unintended consequences, the park district actually benefited from the lean years of the Depression. New Deal relief agencies, such as the Federal Emergency Relief Administration (FERA) and the Works Progress Administration (WPA), supplied construction crews who enhanced the infrastructure and ascetics of Sharon Woods. In 1939, as the demand for relief work lessened, the federal government leased more than 900 acres of land, south of Greenhills, to the park district. Greenhills was one of three so-called greenbelt communities developed by the Resettlement Administration in the 1930s. The park district pledged to develop a second golf course and other recreational facilities on this newly acquired land.

When the United States entered World War II on December 8, 1941, those plans were put on hold for the duration. When peace finally returned in 1945, the park commissioners revived plans to develop Winton Woods and acquire new properties. That same year, voters passed a tax levy to sustain the park district over the next five years. By 1949, the park district purchased 709 additional acres in the western part of the county and acquired its third park, Miami Whitewater Forest.

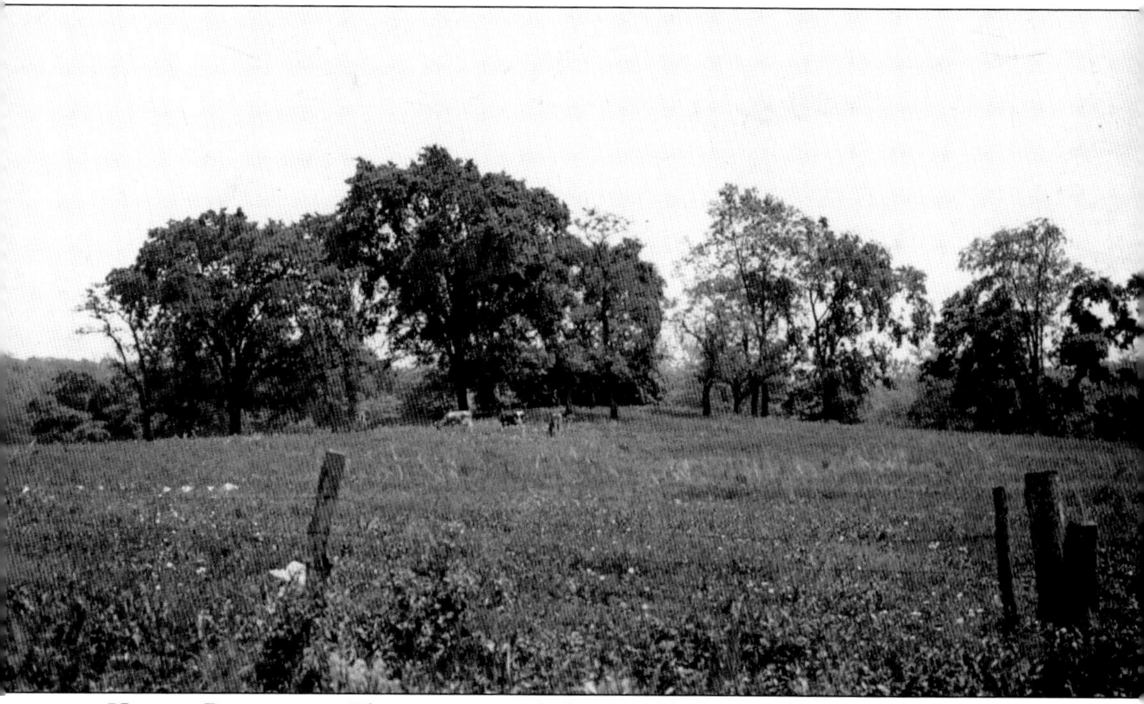

Humble Beginnings. The two posts mark the site of the proposed park entrance of the Reading Tract, which would become Sharon Woods, the first park to be developed by the Hamilton County Park District.

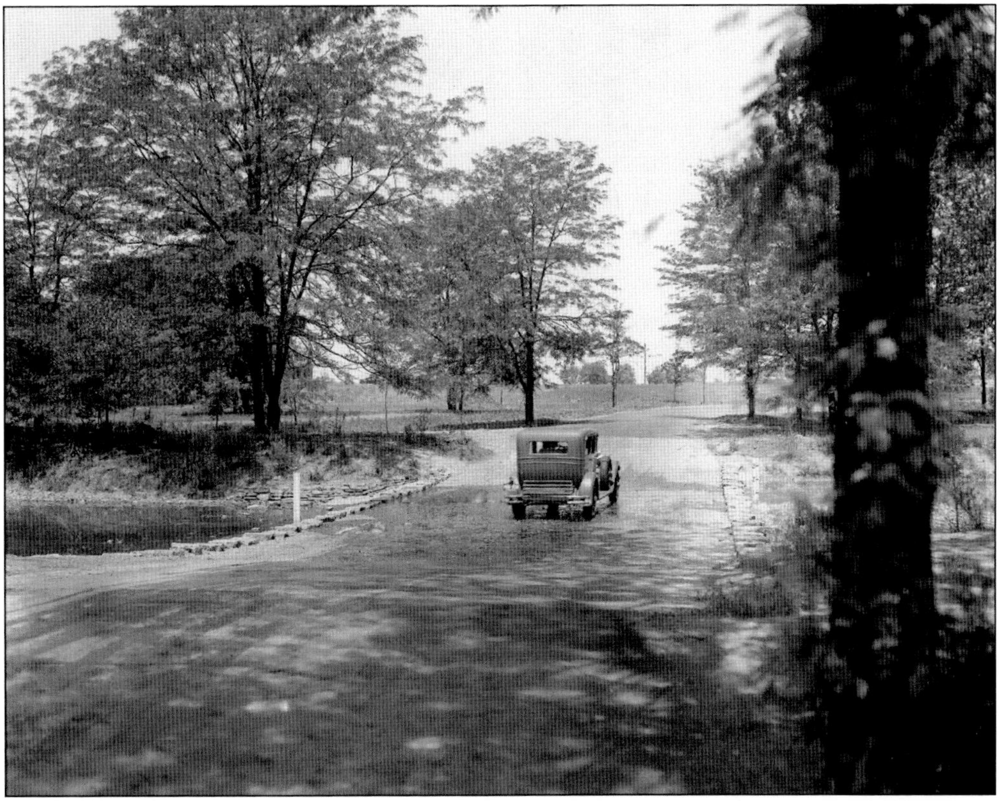

First Visitors. A car enters through the Sharon Woods park entrance off Reading Road (above). Even during the depths of the Depression, most visitors arrived at Sharon Woods via automobile (below). When the park opened in 1932, there were no available parking areas, only 3,000 feet of paved roads, and no designated areas for parking. One year later, park workers had constructed 12 parking lots and completed more than 14,000 linear feet of paved roads.

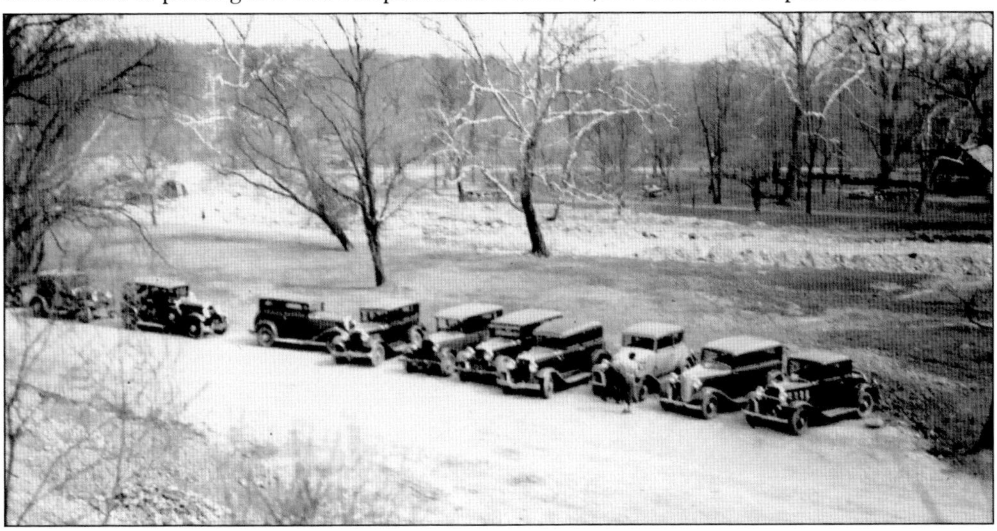

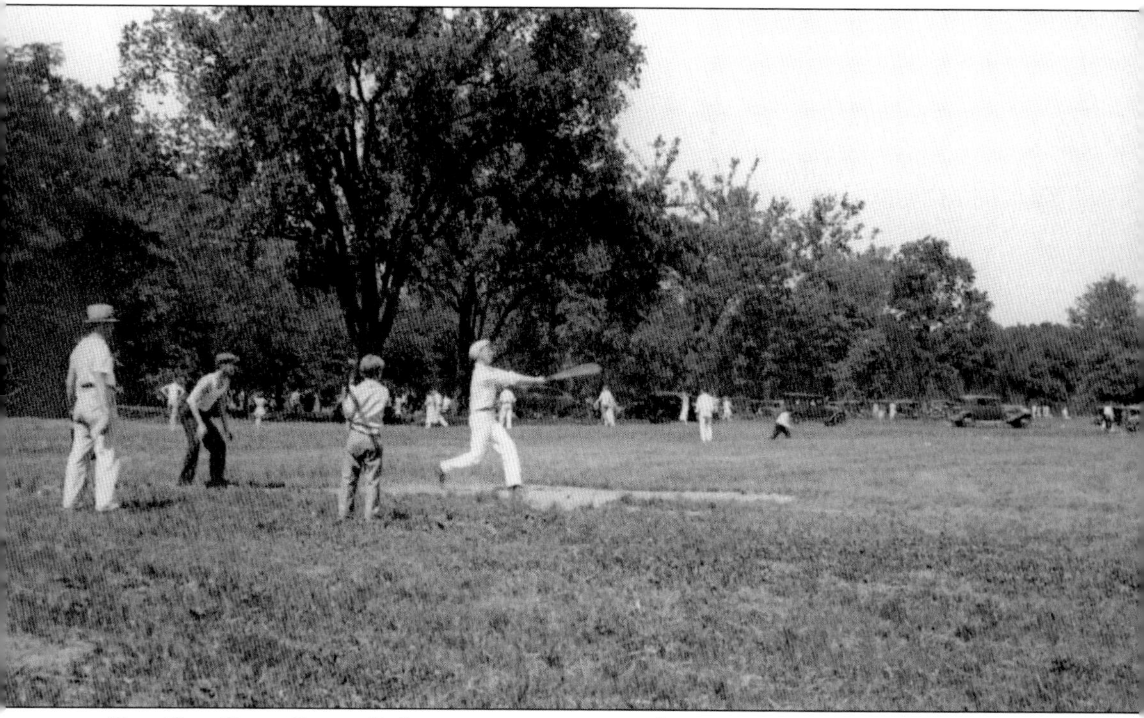

THE OLD BALL GAME. Park commissioners wanted to create an attractive environment for visitors that afforded them a variety of recreational opportunities. Softball and baseball fields with backstops were constructed in the early 1930s.

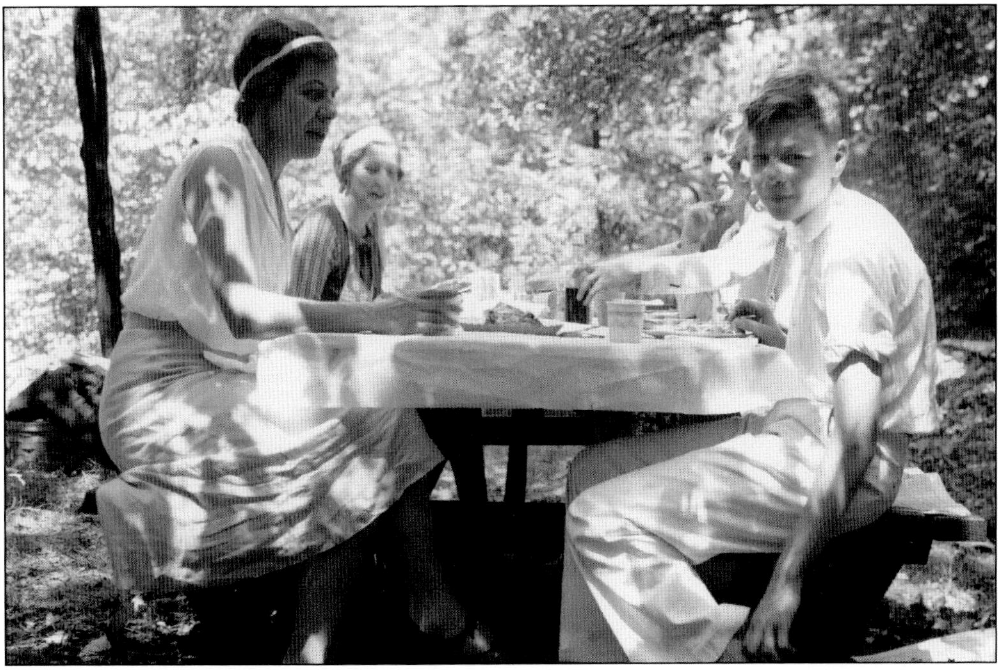

A Flood of Picnickers. It is well documented that movie attendance actually increased during the lean years of the Great Depression. People craved the escapist films to take their minds off the drudgery of real-life woes. Perhaps the same parallel argument could be made regarding the appeal of Sharon Woods. Original estimates for park attendance in 1932 proved to be way off the mark. Instead of the projected 80,000 visitors, Sharon Woods claimed more than 200,000 attendees. Alfred M. Husted informed the commissioners that "the development of Sharon Woods has unquestionably aroused the residents of Hamilton County to the possibility of a new type of outdoor re-creation—the outdoor picnic."

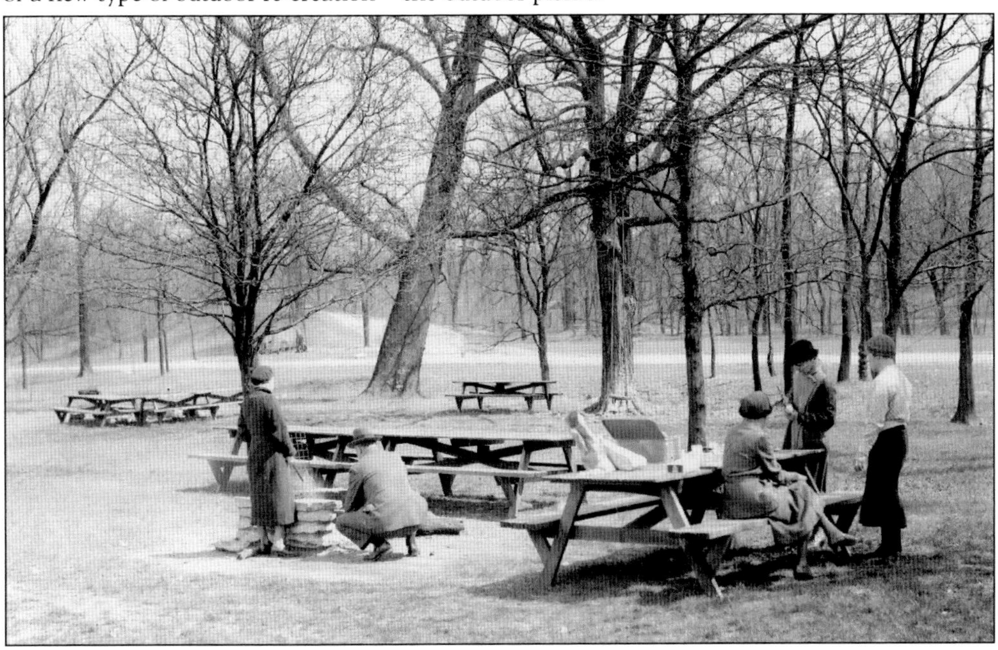

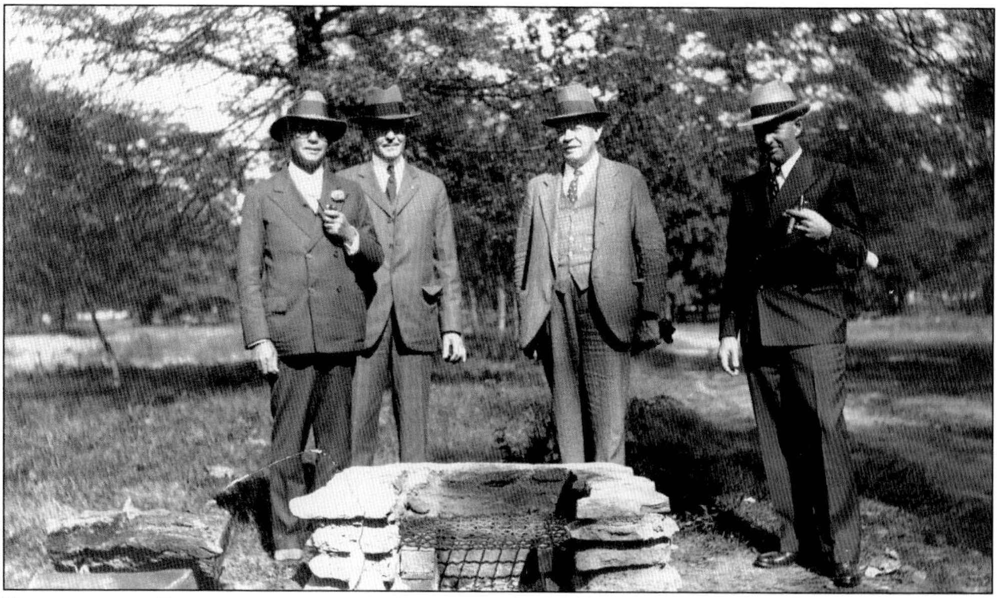

Keeping the Customer Satisfied. During its first full season of operation, the park's limited picnic facilities included only 47 picnic tables and 14 fireplaces. By the 1933 season, Alfred M. Husted reported a significant increase in picnic equipment. More than 450 picnic tables had been added to the grounds, and 200 additional tables were still under construction. In addition, some 85 fireplaces were installed. A group of well-dressed unidentified men (above) pose next to a newly constructed fireplace. Two women (below) prepare a hot meal for their families.

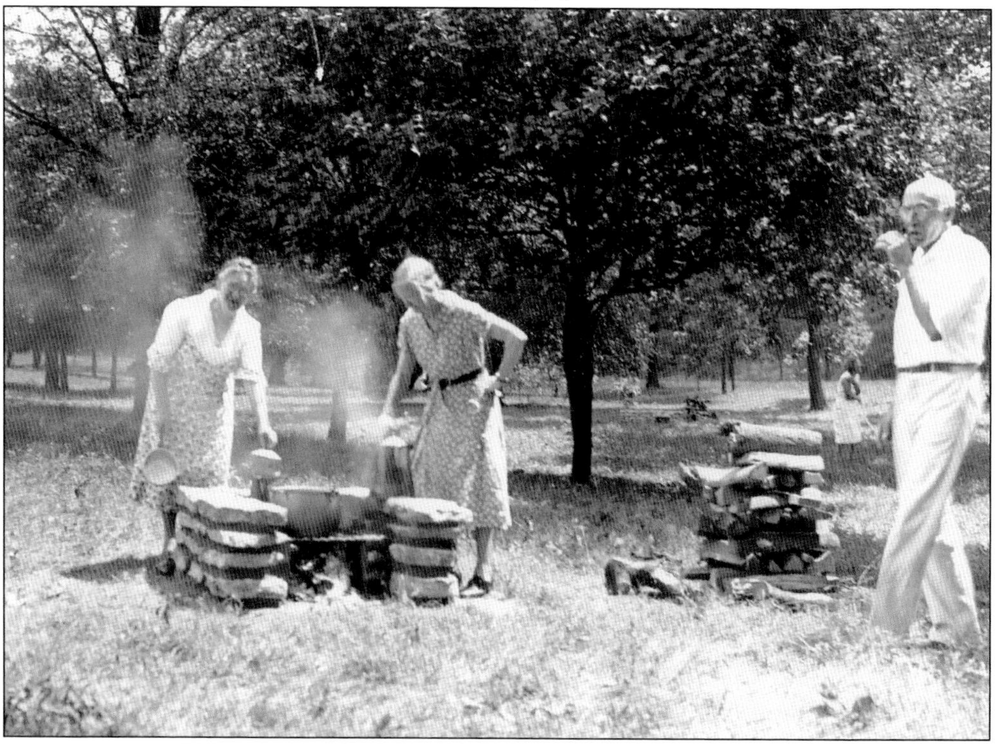

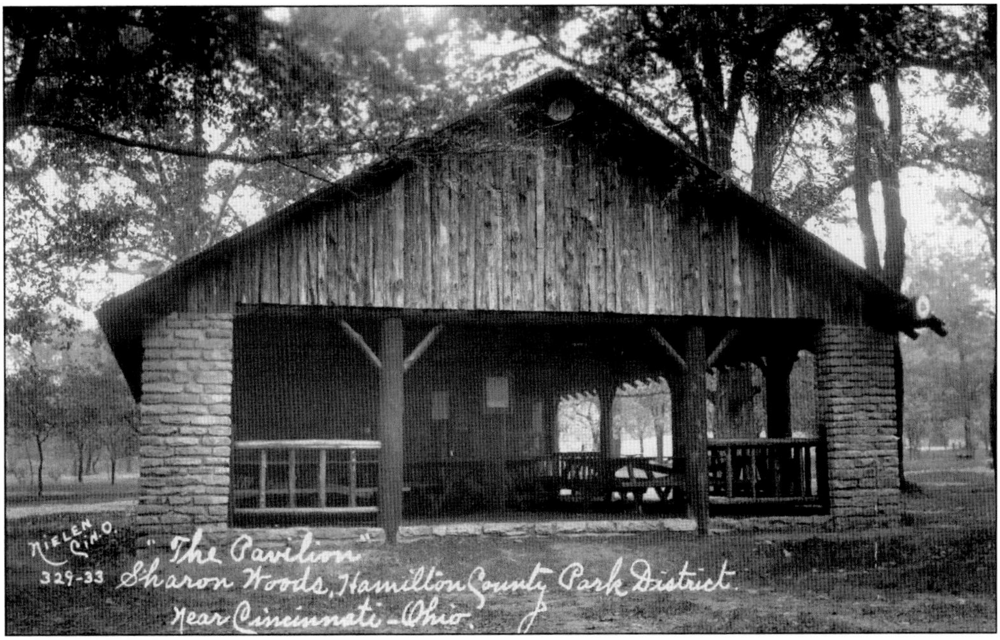

STILL STANDING. To accommodate picnic groups on a nearly year-round basis, a pavilion was constructed in the spring of 1933. The pavilion is the oldest structure still standing on Hamilton County Park District grounds. Later on, a concession area was added, and four toilets were constructed. A family (below) seeks out the shade provided by the pavilion on a warm summer afternoon.

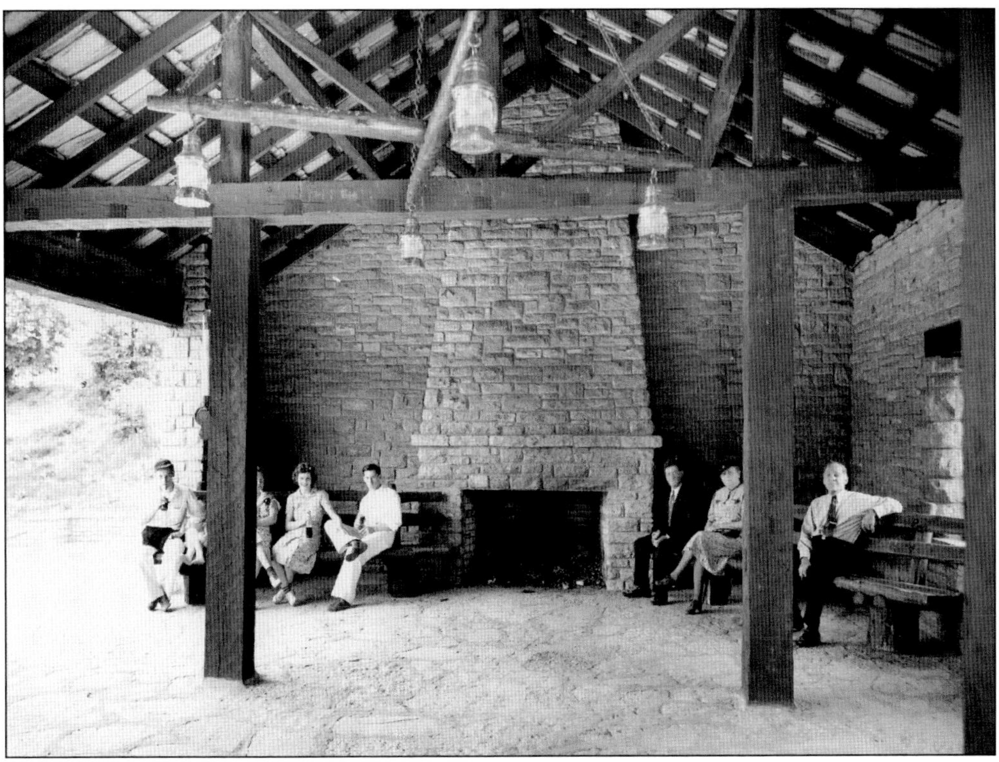

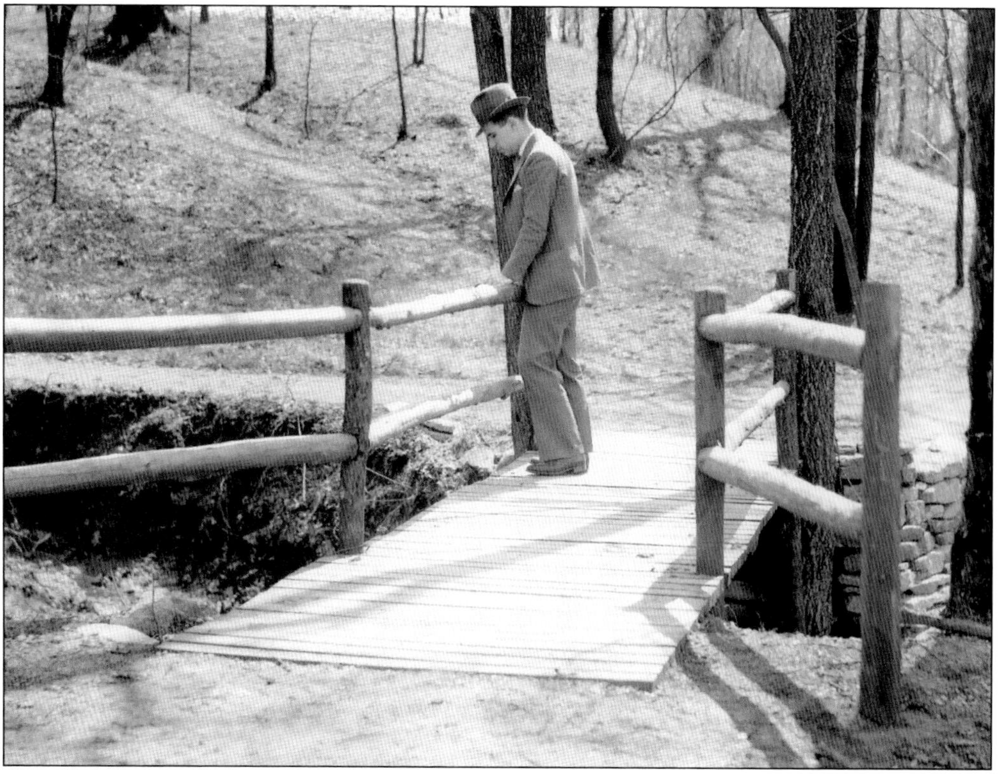

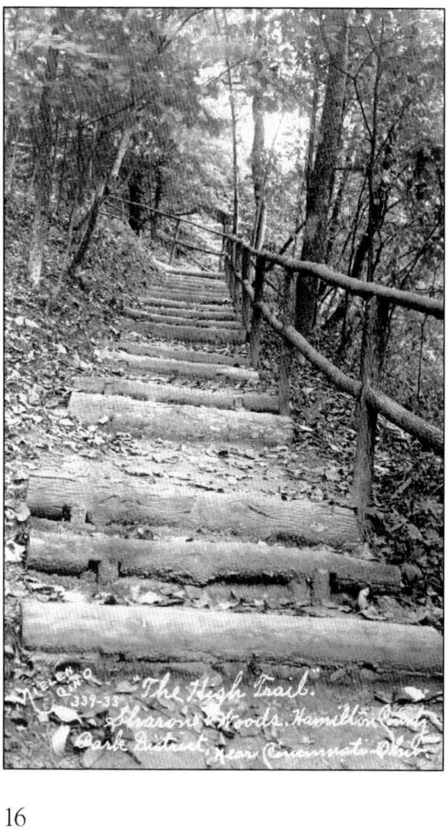

TRAILS GALORE! A network of footbridges and trails were constructed to make navigating the park more accessible. A visitor (above) surveys the workmanship of one of these bridges. Crews worked to blaze and mark trails such as the High Trail (left), complete with steps. At the same time, other workers cleared out brush and debris in forested areas, to enhance the hikers' experience, while still others sowed grass in meadow areas.

Natural Wonders. Intrepid explorers at Sharon Woods were rewarded with beautiful vistas and impressive sights. This unique overhead photograph of a waterfall was taken from a bluff along one of the park's trails.

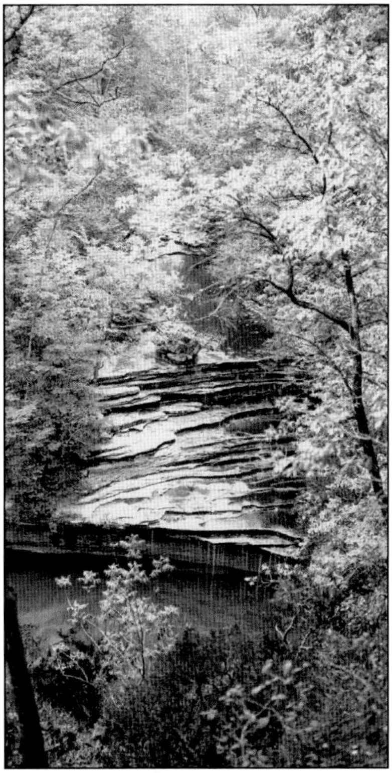

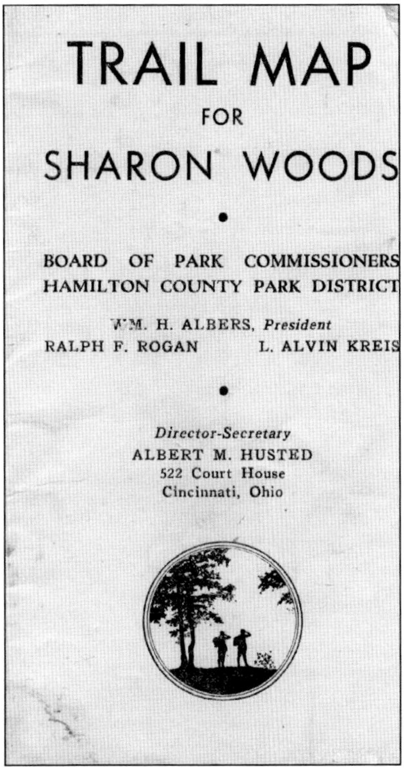

TRAIL MAP
FOR
SHARON WOODS

BOARD OF PARK COMMISSIONERS
HAMILTON COUNTY PARK DISTRICT

WM. H. ALBERS, *President*
RALPH F. ROGAN L. ALVIN KREIS

Director-Secretary
ALBERT M. HUSTED
522 Court House
Cincinnati, Ohio

Hiking 101. By the late 1930s, the park board felt justified in commissioning a map of the hiking trails at Sharon Woods. Along with descriptions of each trail, the commissioners included the following invitation to Hamilton County residents: "The County Parks are maintained for the use and enjoyment of the people that they may find release from the tension of the over-crowded daily existence and that contact with nature will result in a better, healthier and happier life for all."

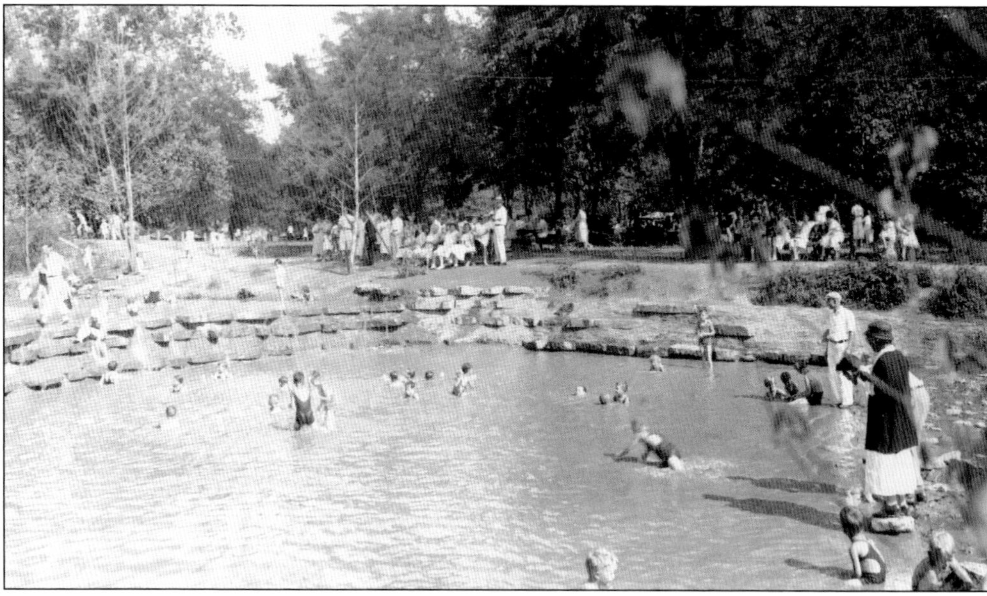

BUCKEYE POOL, BEFORE AND AFTER. During the Great Depression, the FERA assembled work crews who performed vital tasks for the park district. Most of the improvements took place at Sharon Woods. FERA workers dredged the silt and gravel from the Buckeye Pool and constructed a stone bridge, providing visitors better access to the swimming area.

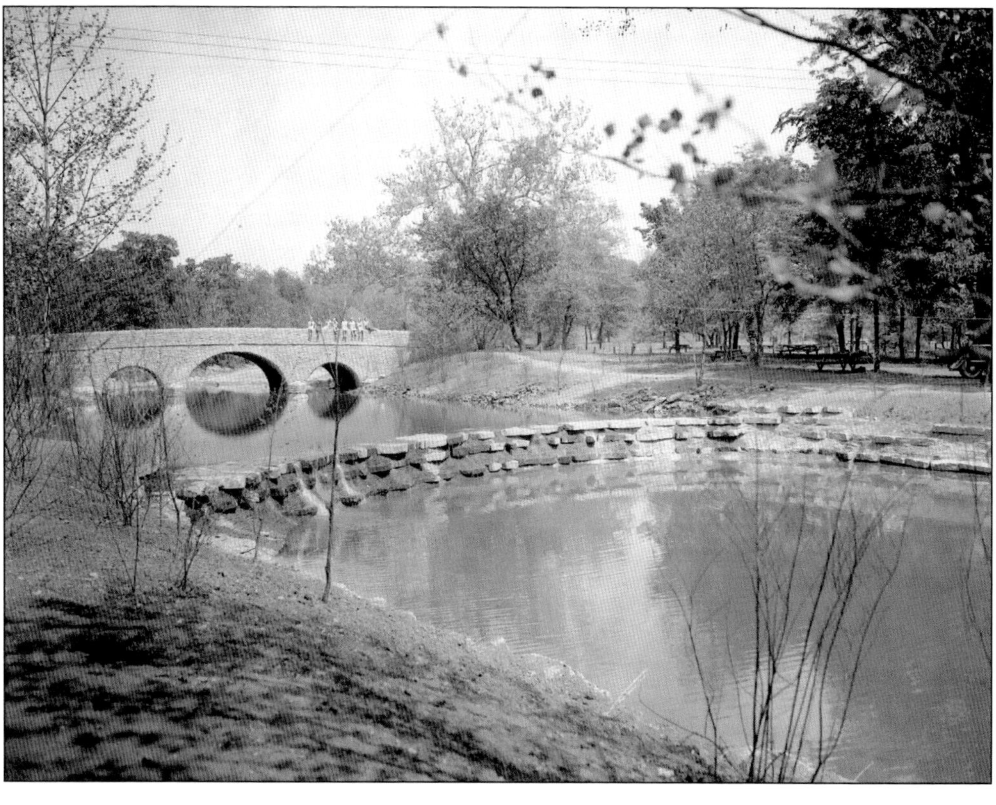

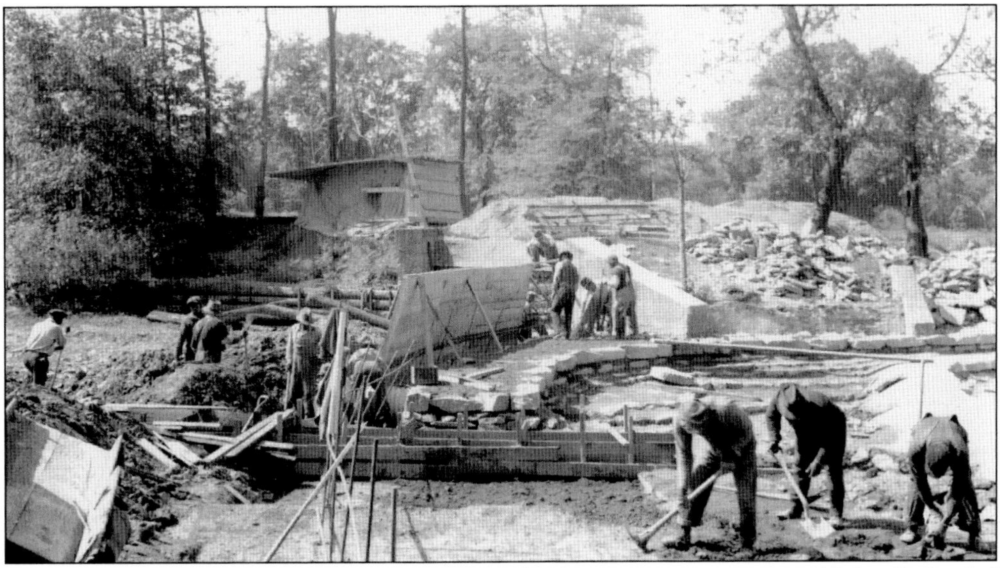

The WPA Takes Over. By 1935, the WPA had taken over management of federally funded public works projects from the FERA. These photographs show the labor-intensive nature of road construction within Sharon Woods.

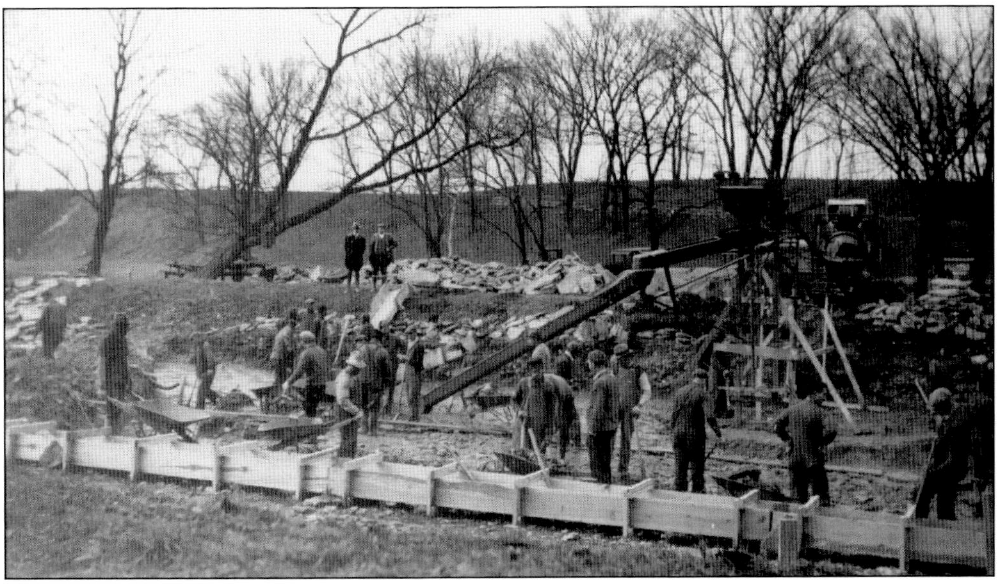

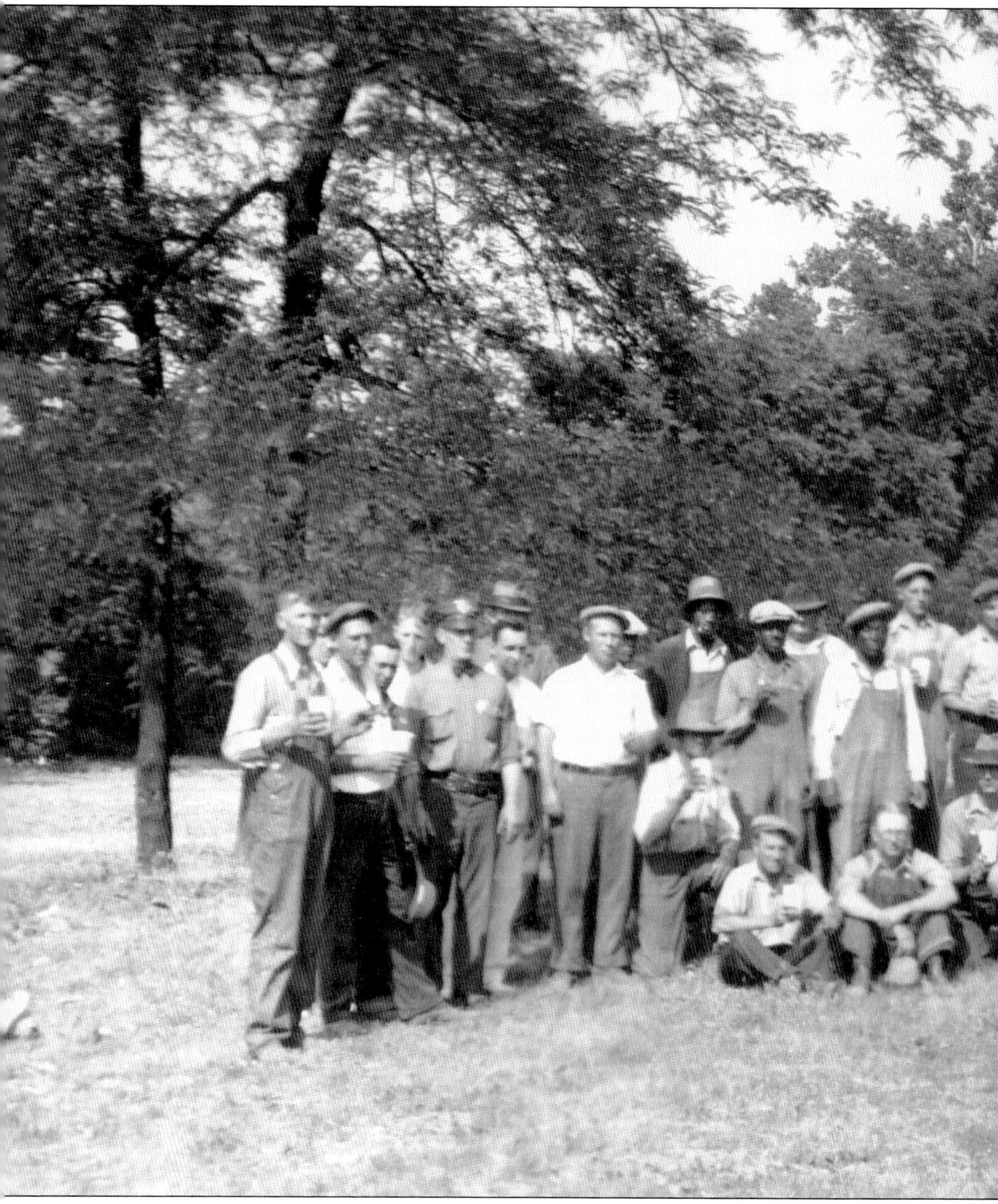

Proud Workers. WPA workers took great pride in the work they performed. Since profit motives did not necessarily factor into Depression-era public works projects, these laborers were not compelled to do fast or shoddy work. The crews had the luxury of making sure that quality was a part of each job they performed. As many as 500 WPA workers participated in projects at Sharon

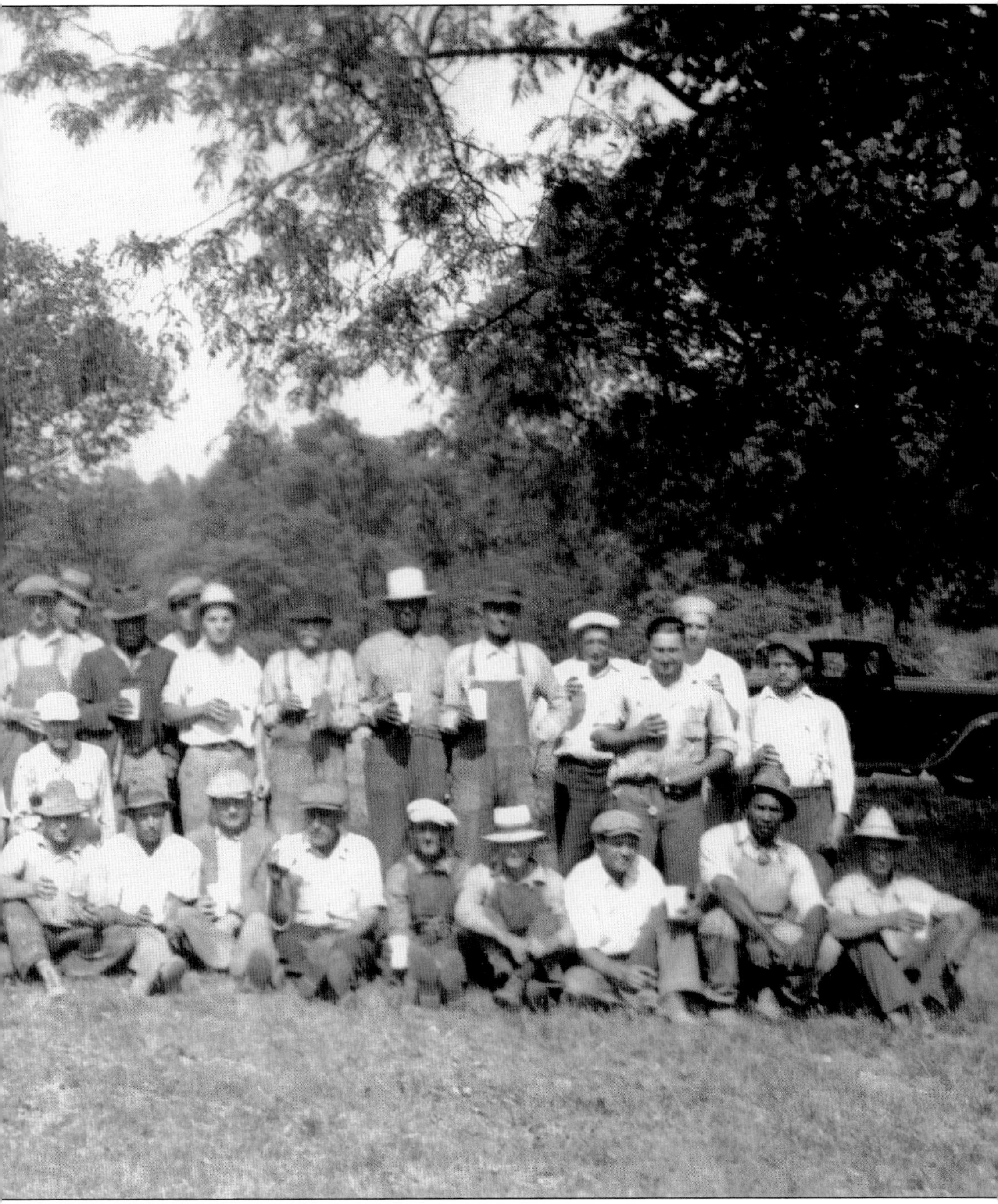

Woods between 1935 and 1936. A few of the workers are even buried in an old pioneer cemetery located in the northwest corner of the park. These workers poured their hearts and souls into the work they performed for the park district. They could take pride in the fact that they had left several lasting legacies at Sharon Woods for future generations of park visitors to enjoy.

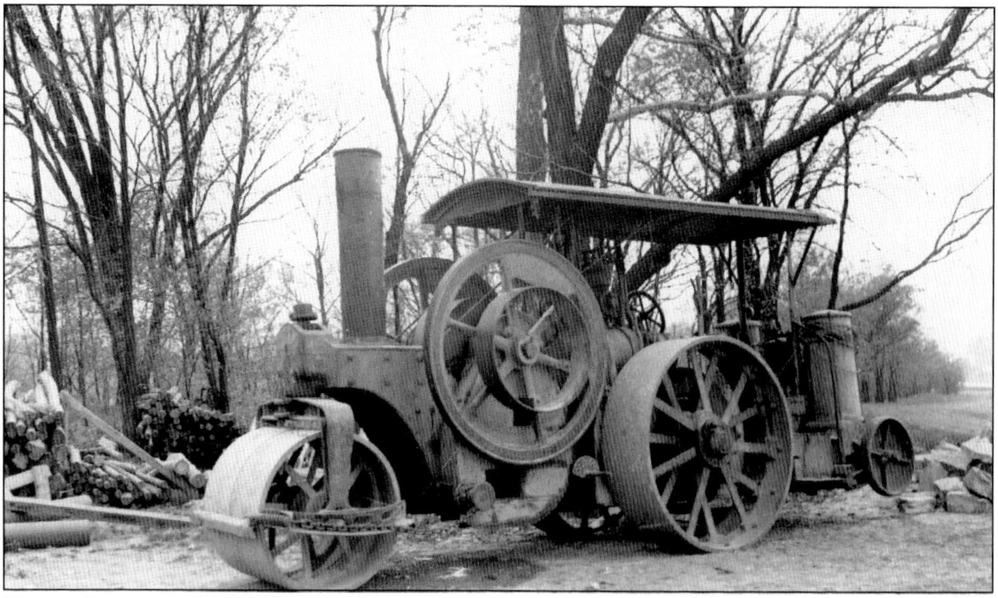

HEAVY LIFTING. Of course, not all construction work at the park was done by hand. Heavy machinery, including tractors and bulldozers, were used by road construction crews. Large tractors were also used for reforestation projects. Reforestation of parklands represented an ongoing project. Beginning in 1933, the park district received a $50 donation from members of the Cincinnati branch of the Daughters of the American Revolution for the purchase of seedlings. This first gift helped start the George Washington Memorial Forest located in Sharon Woods. Over the years, the park district has received generous donations of cash and seedlings from civic organizations, neighboring cities, and commercial nurseries. Hundreds of thousands of seedlings have been planted as part of this ongoing process to maintain and perpetuate wooded areas in Hamilton County parks.

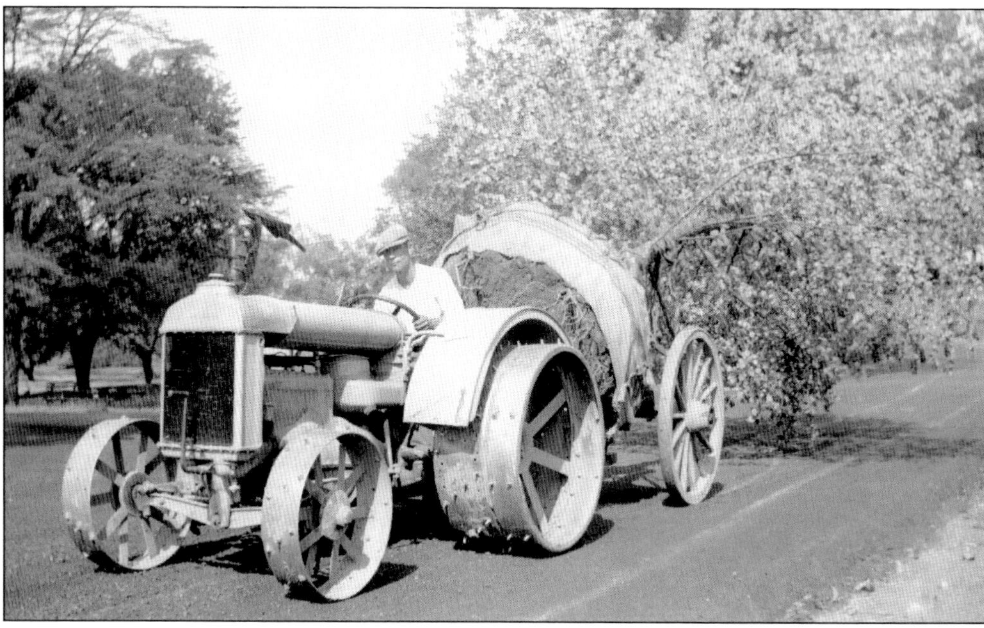

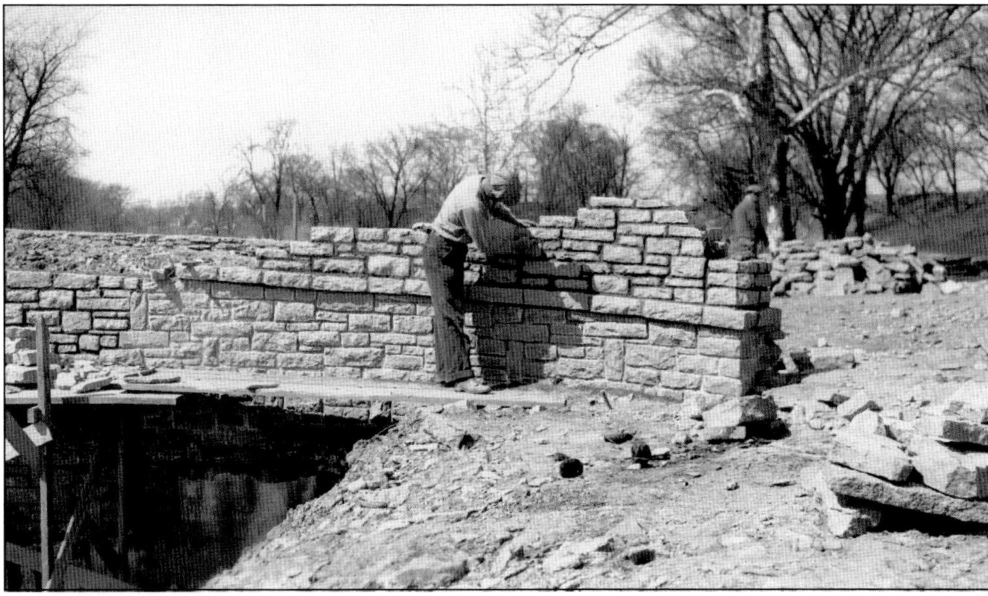

STONE BRIDGES. Like the FERA workers before them, WPA crews constructed stone bridges to help facilitate traffic flow in Sharon Woods. The close-up photograph above highlights the level of craftsmanship involved in such projects.

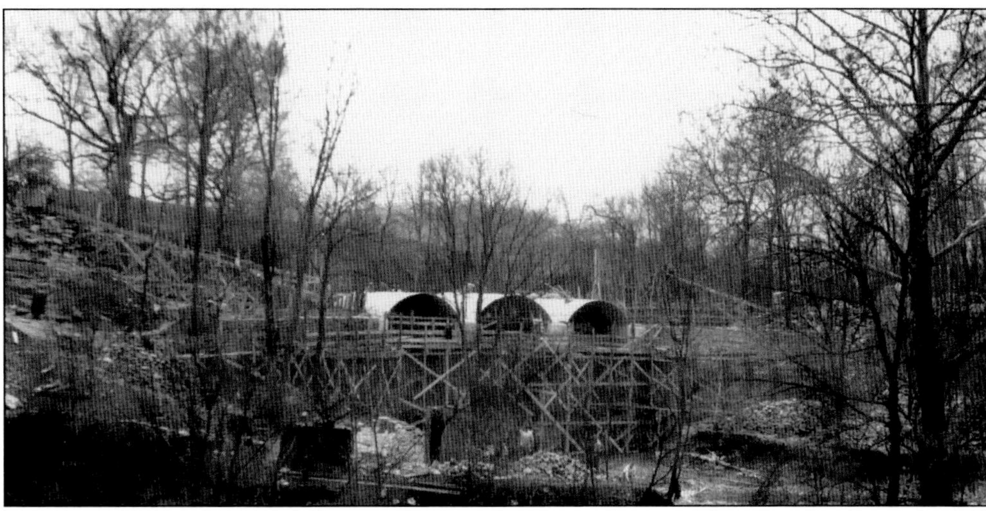

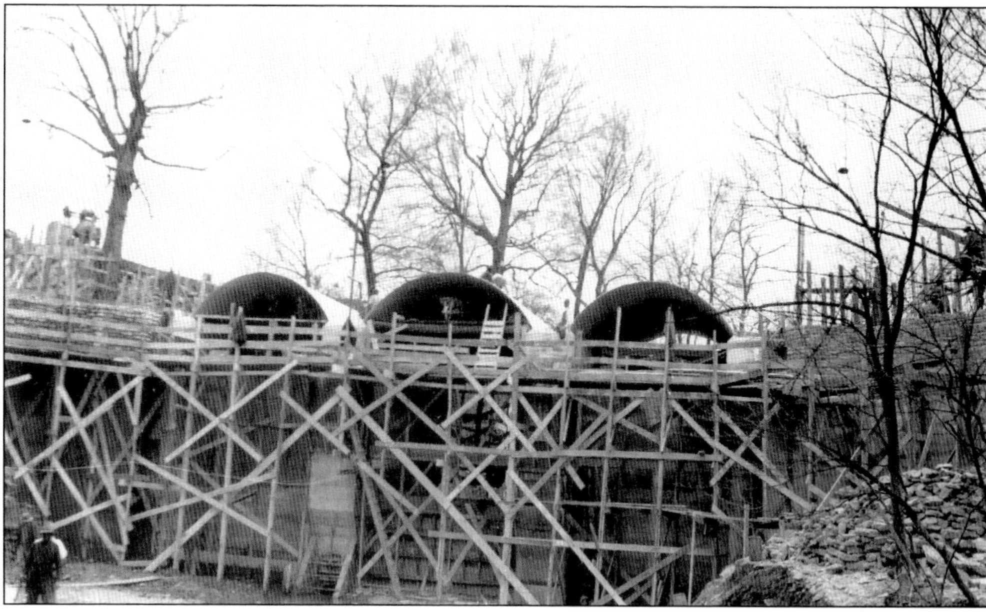

HAZARDOUS DUTY. Construction of the Stone Arch Bridge was completed in 1936. The erection of the support scaffolding proved to be one of the most arduous tasks associated with this project.

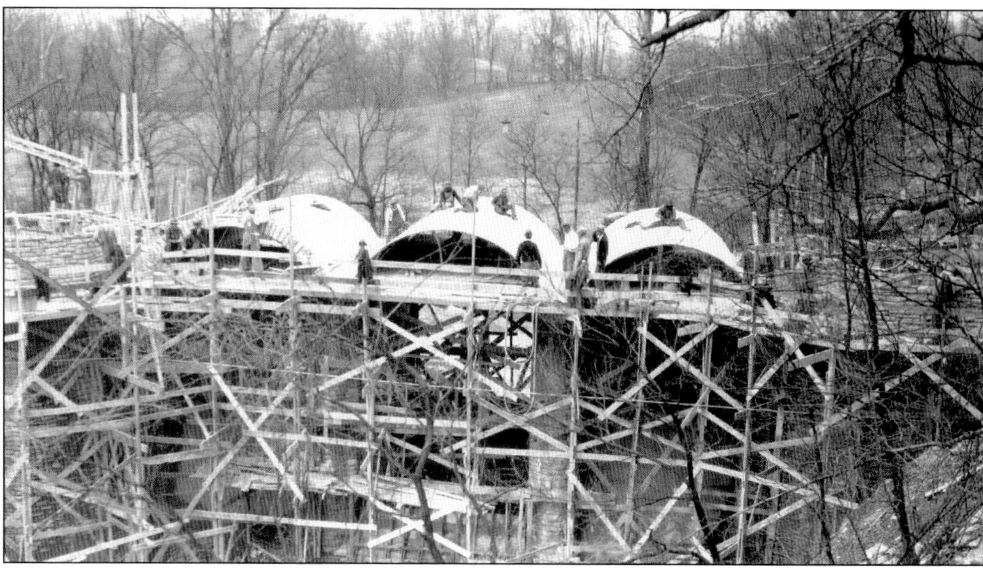

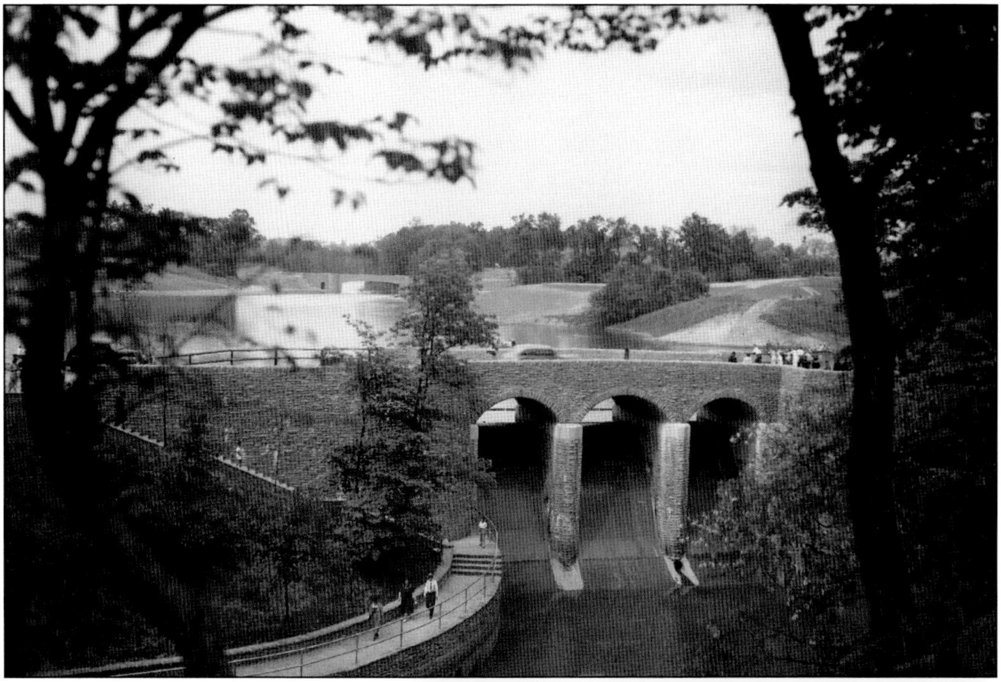

SHARON WOODS DAM. As early as 1934, park commissioners had planned to construct a man-made lake at Sharon Woods. Work on the dam was not completed until 1937. On Halloween Day, more than 600 people attended the dedication of the L. Alvin Kreis Memorial Dam. Kreis, one of the three original park commissioners, had died a year earlier. Among those in attendance paying tribute to Kreis were Cincinnati mayor Russell Wilson and Dr. C. R. Campbell, representing the Hamilton County commissioners. The dam created a 30-acre lake that had an average depth of six feet and contained three and a half miles of shoreline.

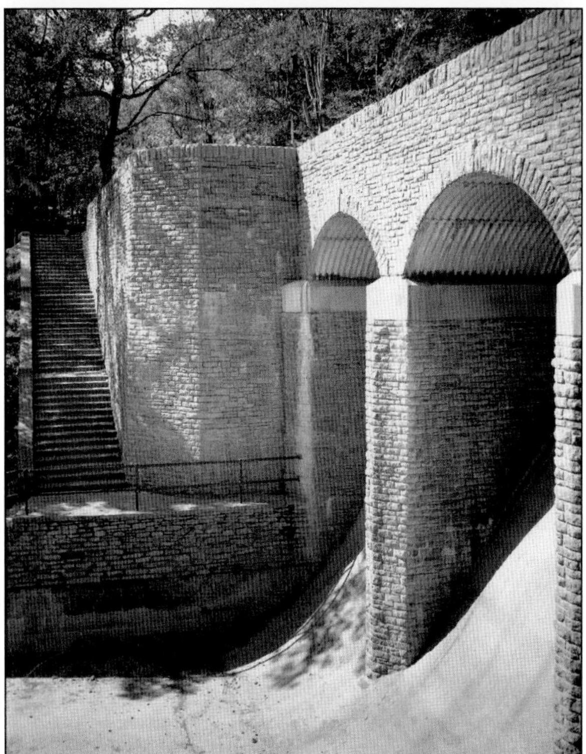

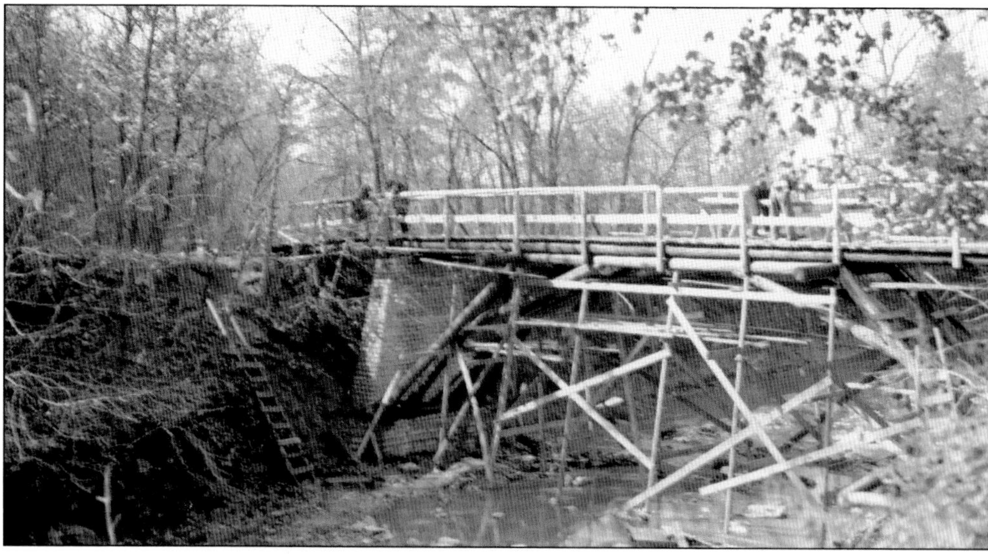

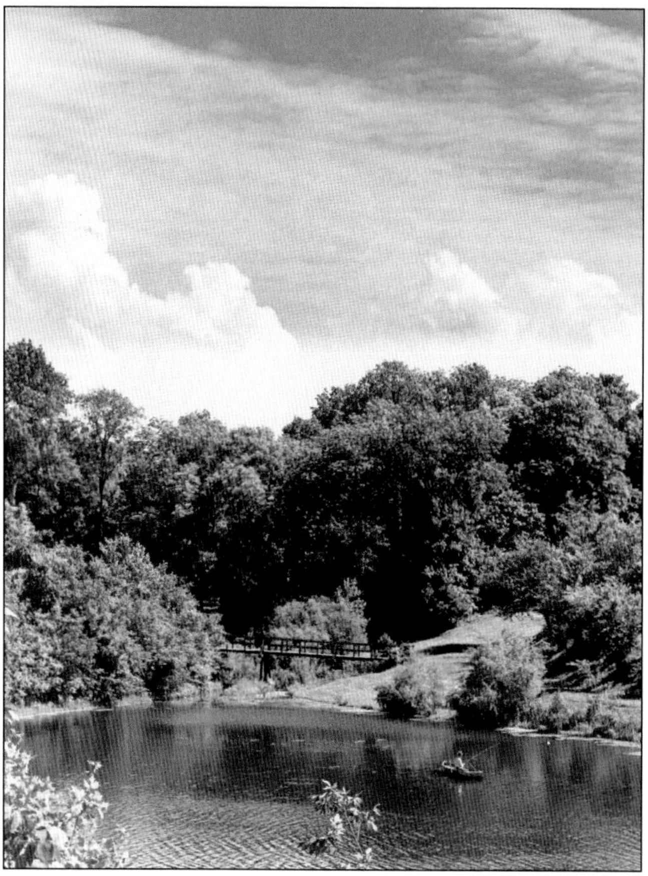

ANATOMY OF A FOOTBRIDGE. With the completion of the lake at Sharon Woods, it became necessary to construct footbridges for hiking trails that circumnavigated that body of water. These photographs show the East Finger Bridge in both its beginning stages of construction and its final stages of completion.

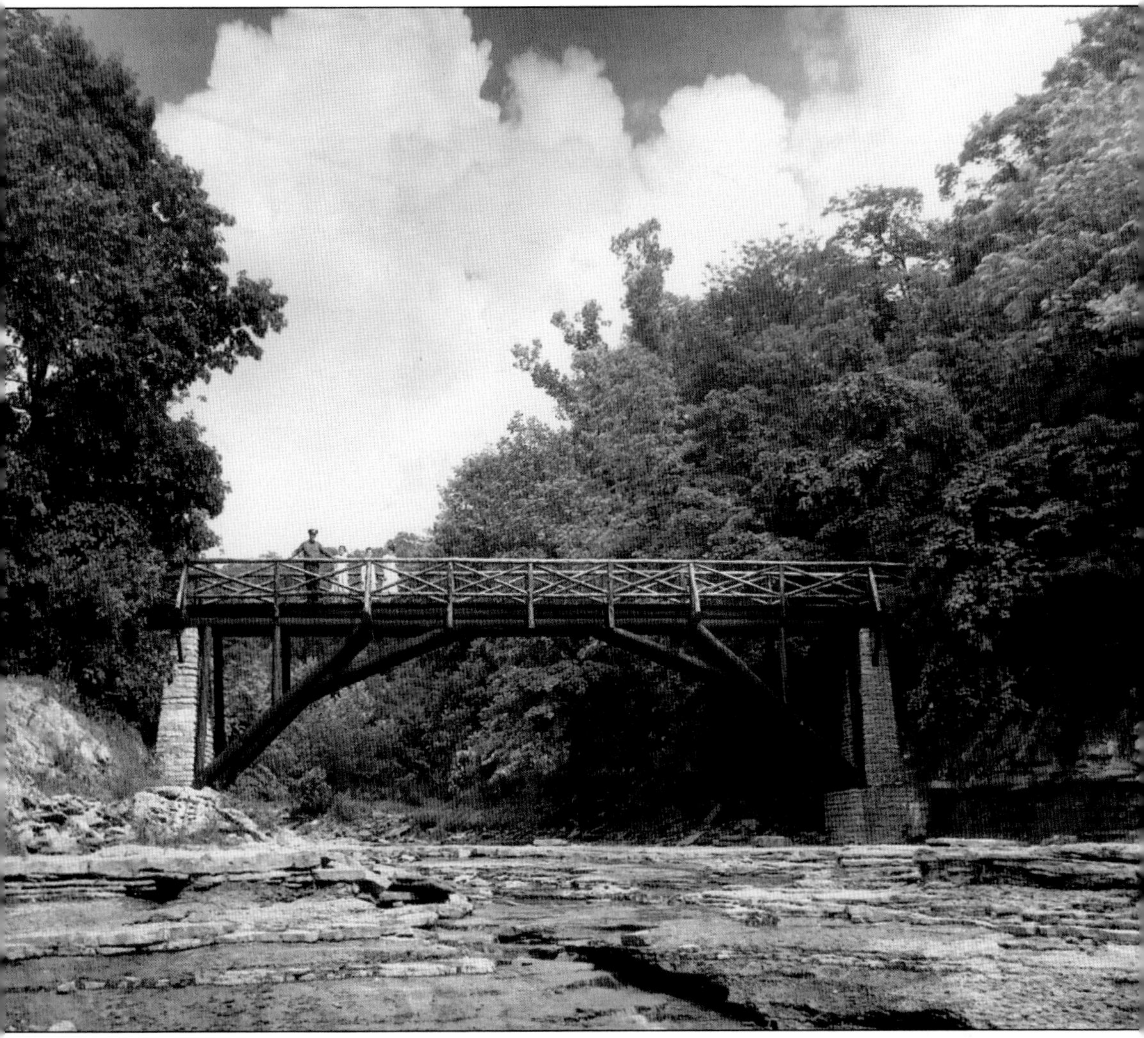

GORGE BRIDGE. This impressive footbridge spanned the Sharon Woods Gorge. This arduous terrain included a 90-foot cliff that was carved by glaciers. Over the years, this area has been a favorite spot for amateur and professional paleontologists, geologists, and fossil collectors.

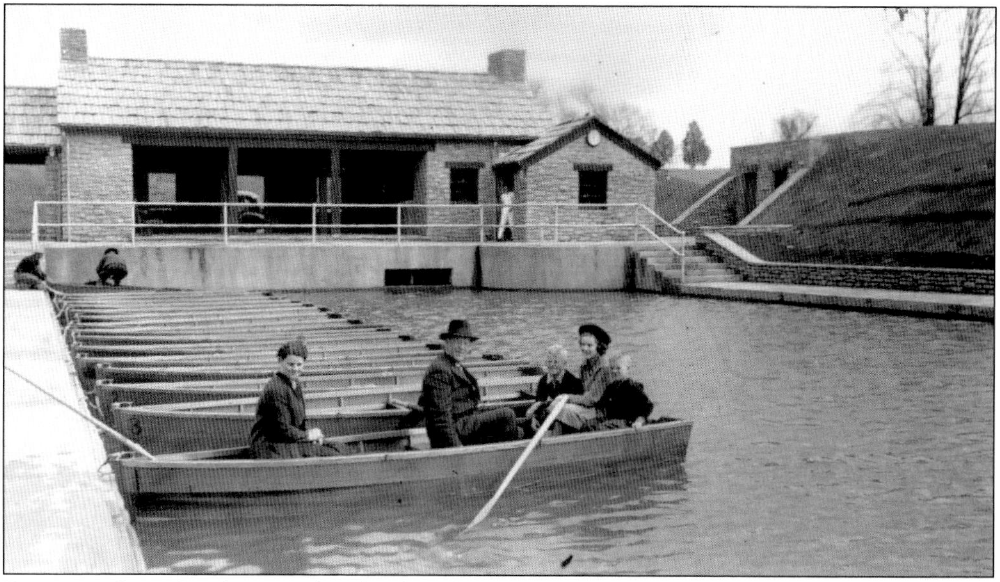

Boating Gets Its Start. Shortly after the dam was dedicated, and the lake opened to the public, a boathouse and docking area were constructed. Since the park did not charge admission fees, it relied on the sale of food concessions and rental of recreational equipment, such as boat and bicycle rentals, to generate profits. Park commissioners announced that within two years, the lake would be stocked and fishing would become a regular pastime at Sharon Woods.

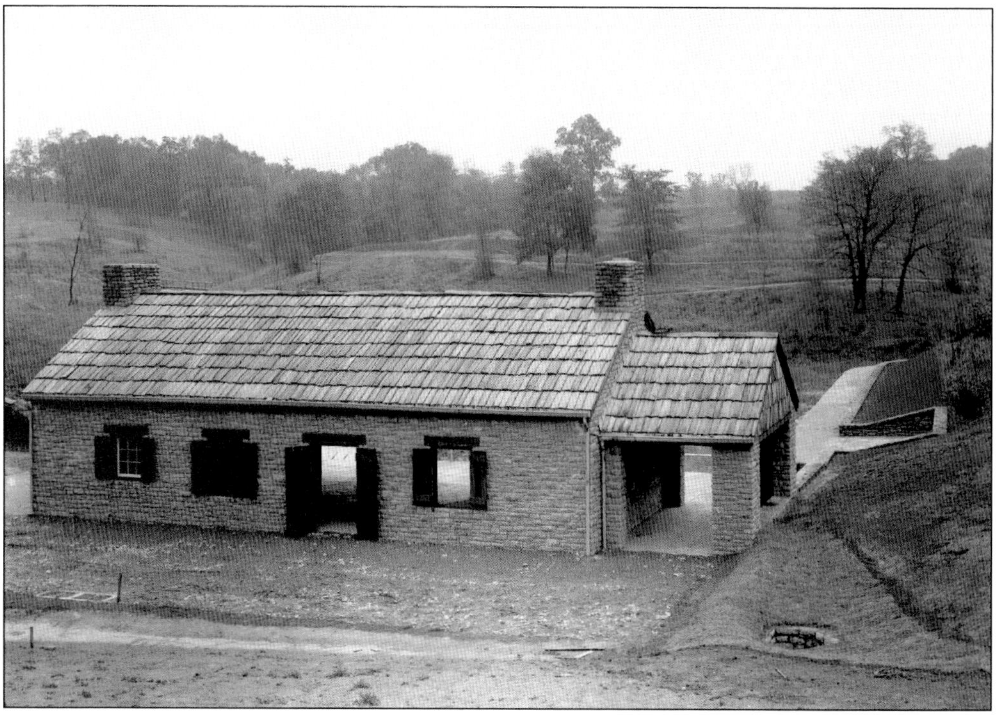

Lakeside Lodge. In 1936, WPA workers also completed construction of the Lakeside Lodge. Overlooking the eastern side of the lake, the site proved appealing to both picnic groups and recreational boaters.

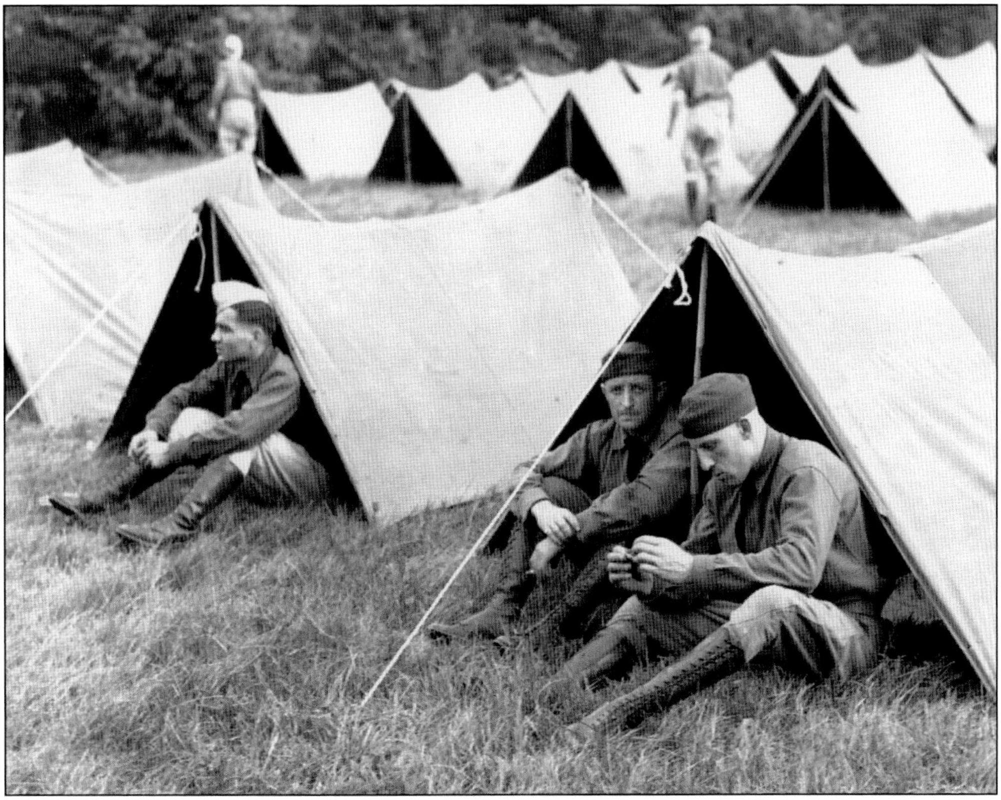

The Army Comes to Town. In August 1937, members of the 134th U.S. Army Infantry spent two days and one night bivouacked at Sharon Woods. The unit also practiced military drills.

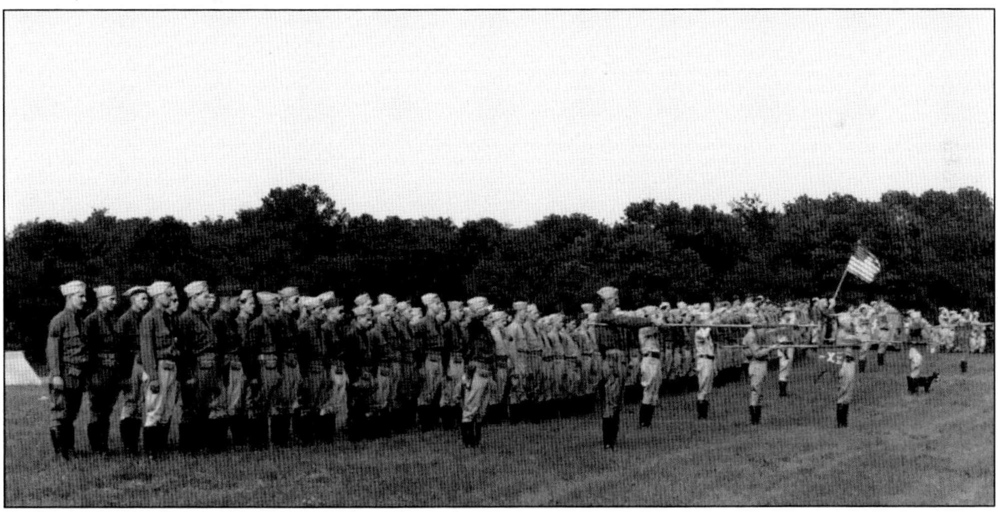

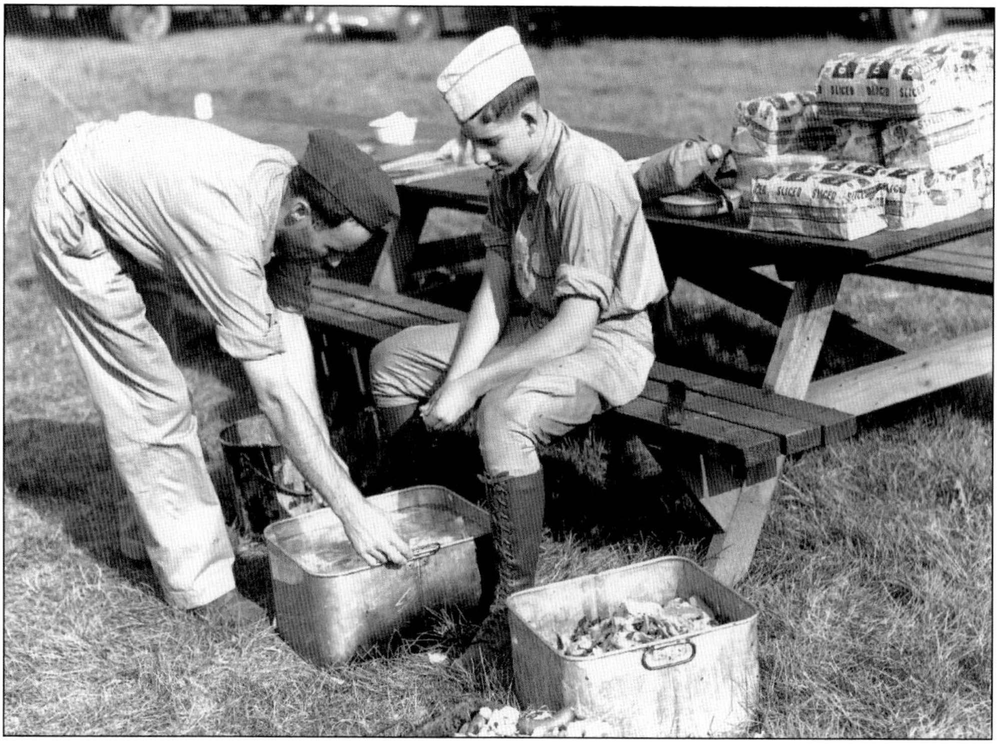

KP DUTY. Henry Cooke (left) and Clyde Shorkwiler, both of Portsmouth, Ohio, prepare food for the troops. Over the decades, the park district received numerous requests from army and National Guard units, requesting the use of park grounds for layover stops or for training drills such as the 134th U.S. Army Infantry's.

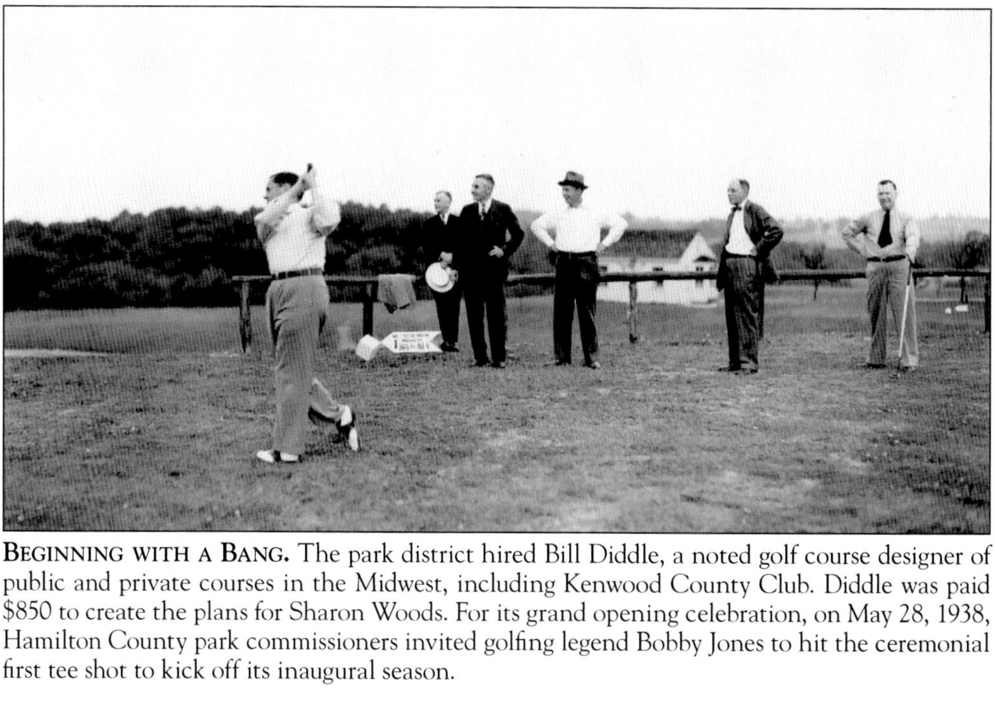

BEGINNING WITH A BANG. The park district hired Bill Diddle, a noted golf course designer of public and private courses in the Midwest, including Kenwood County Club. Diddle was paid $850 to create the plans for Sharon Woods. For its grand opening celebration, on May 28, 1938, Hamilton County park commissioners invited golfing legend Bobby Jones to hit the ceremonial first tee shot to kick off its inaugural season.

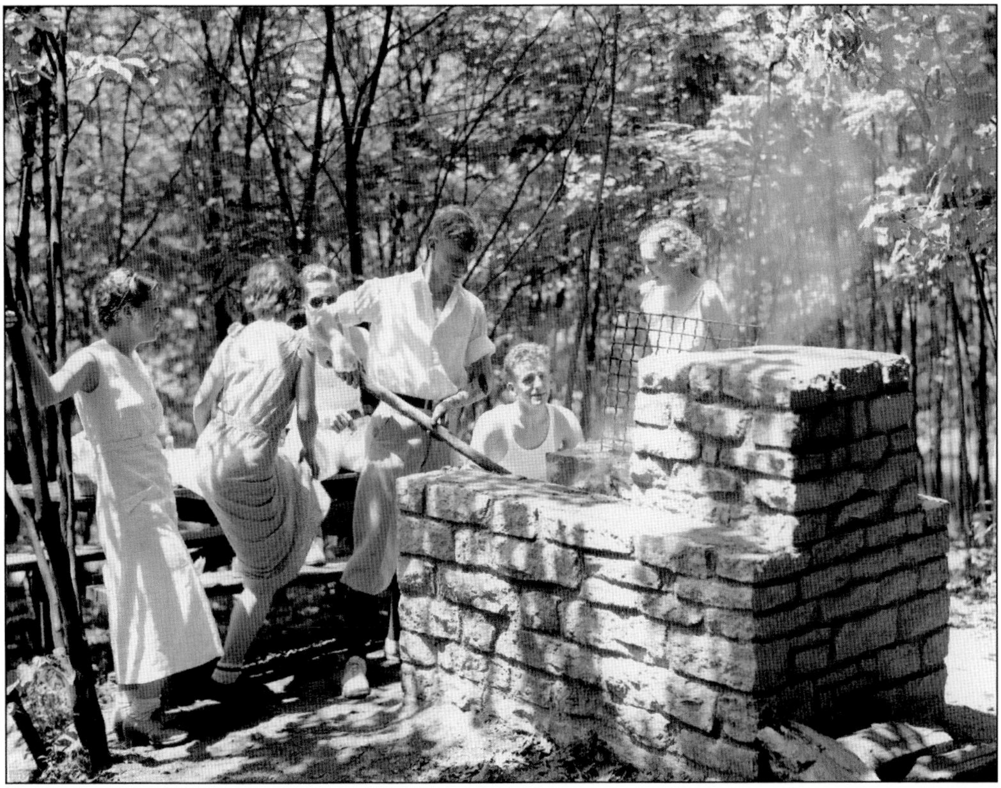

TEEN SCENE. During the late 1930s and early 1940s, teenagers participated in group outings at Sharon Woods. Overall, during the war years, park attendance dropped off, but teen attendance was less affected. Couples make use of the picnic facilities (above). Girls chat and sun themselves near the boathouse, while the boys show off their Y chromosomes on the boats (below).

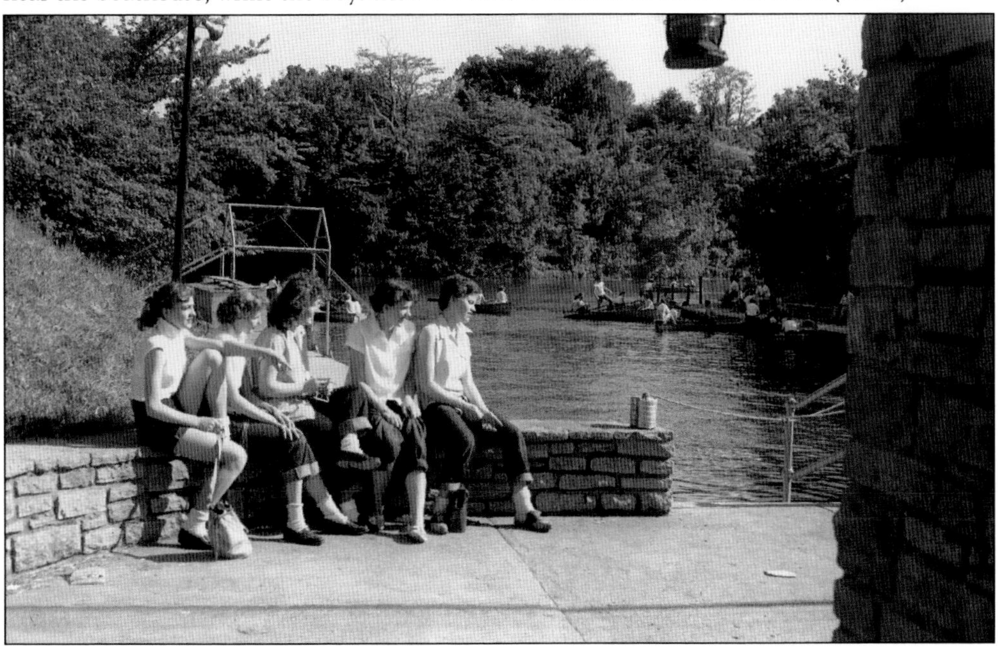

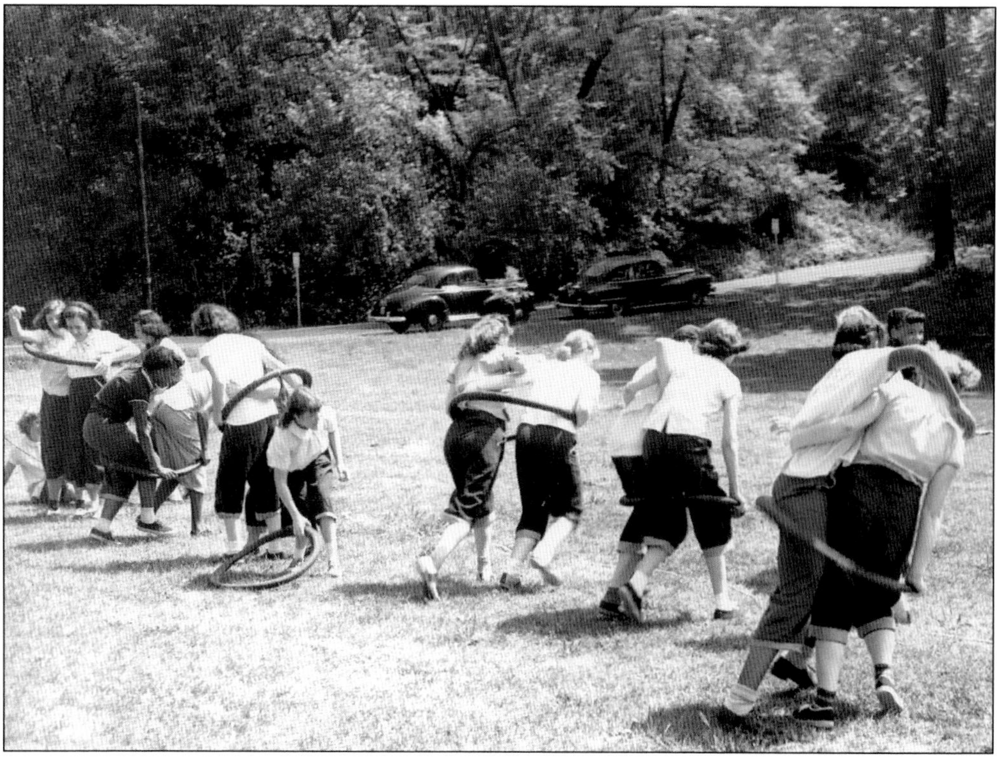

GIRLS, GIRLS, GIRLS! As the war continued, teenage girls developed strong relationships with other girls when more and more young men were drafted or enlisted in the armed forces. These girls engage in a relay race on one of the athletic fields in Sharon Woods (above). Other girls take advantage of a sunny day to rent bicycles from a park concessionaire (below).

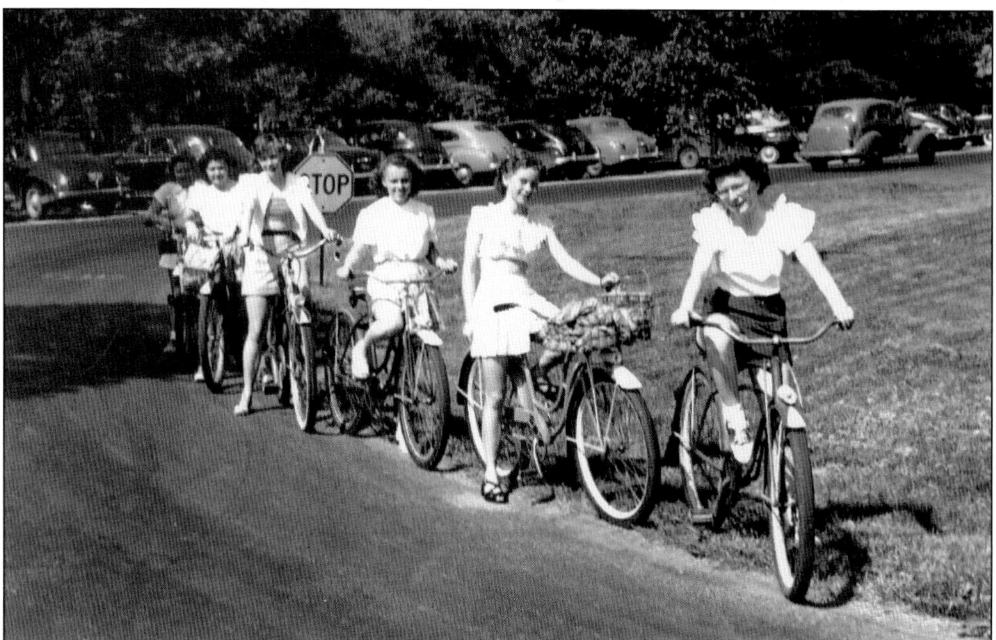

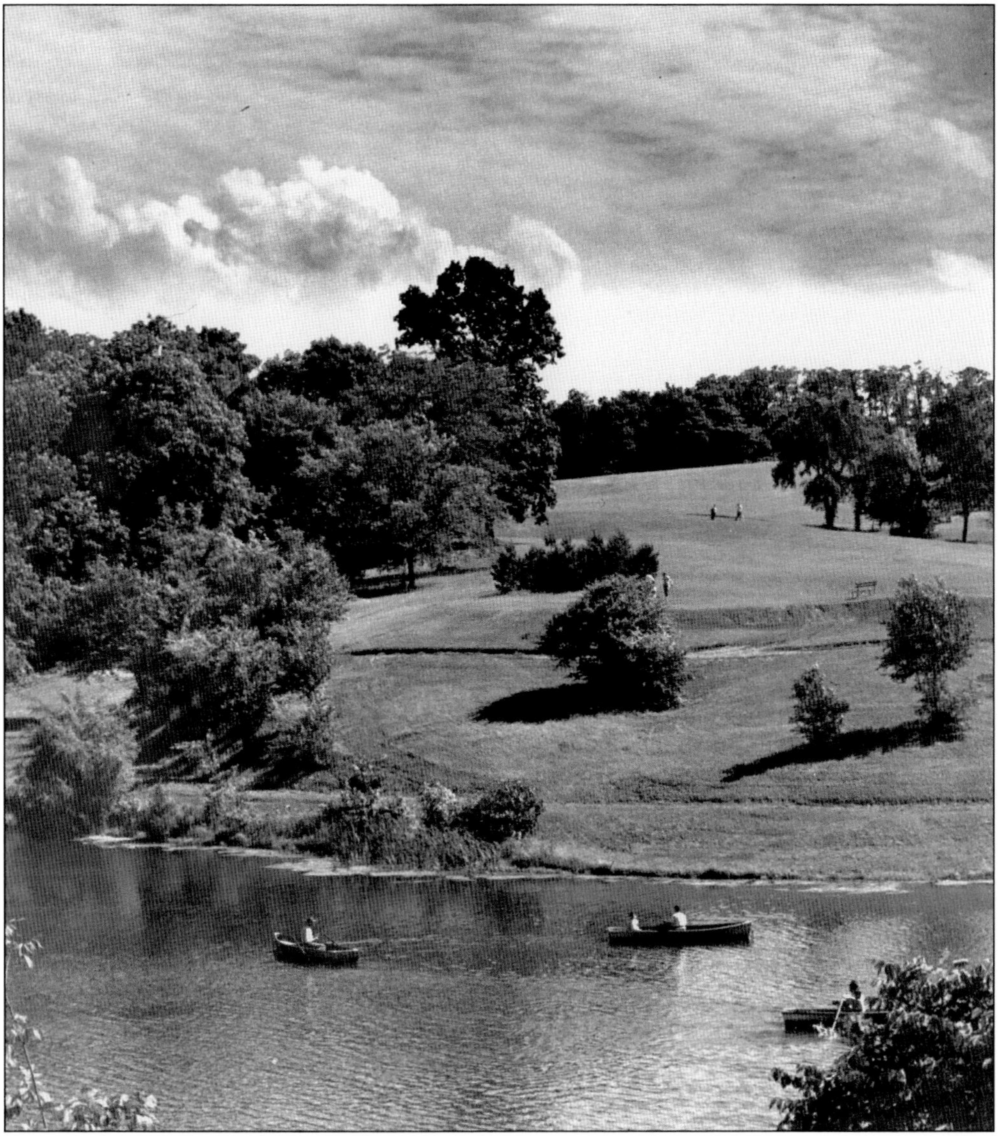

WORTH THE WAIT. The construction of Sharon Woods Golf Course began in 1936. WPA crews did most of the groundwork on this project. Tons of topsoil was dredged from the East Finger of the lake for the purpose of constructing greens. More than 31,000 feet of tile and more than 18,500 feet of pipe were laid to provide for adequate drainage of the course. Despite a lag in overall park attendance during the war years, golf manager Marty Kavanaugh reported an annual average of 35,000 rounds of golf. In 1942, Kavanaugh, a natural promoter, offered husband-and-wife season memberships for a mere $27, about the price of a round of golf for one adult today. Kavanaugh also allowed active servicemen who were passing through town the chance to play for free. This practice was revived in the early 1950s during the Korean conflict.

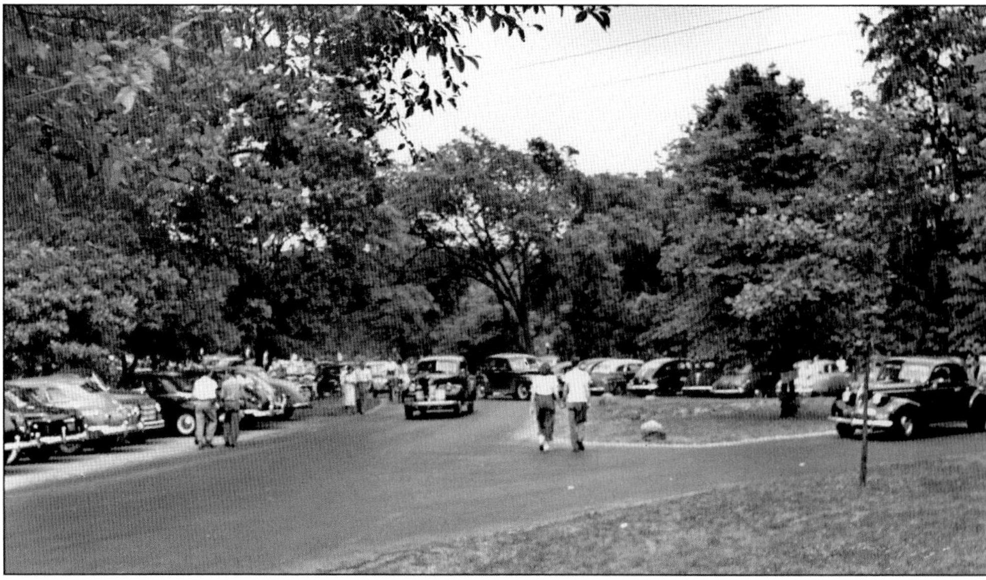

The Return of Peace. Without question, the war years pulled people who were left on the home front in many directions. Outdoor recreation became a luxury. Until the war ended and the troops came home, larger issues loomed in people's lives. In addition, gas rationing, which began in 1942 and continued through the duration of the war, limited people's mobility. Pleasure drives were viewed as unpatriotic acts. All of this changed, of course, with the return of peace. During the late 1940s, automobile traffic once again became a familiar sight at Sharon Woods.

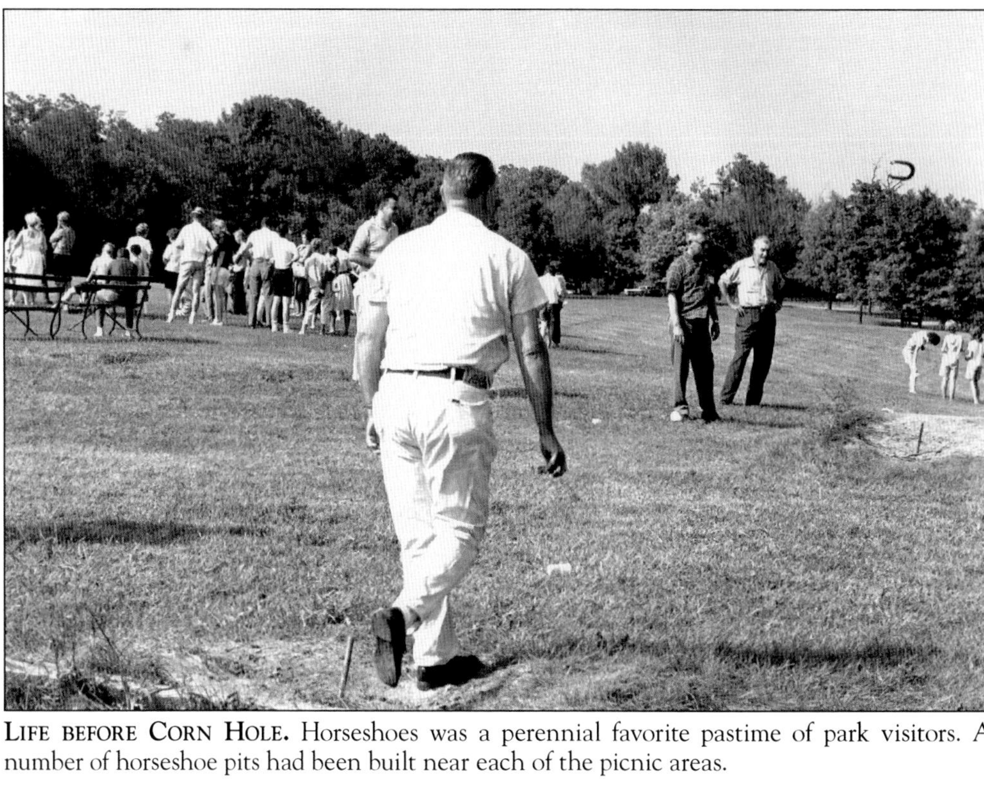

Life before Corn Hole. Horseshoes was a perennial favorite pastime of park visitors. A number of horseshoe pits had been built near each of the picnic areas.

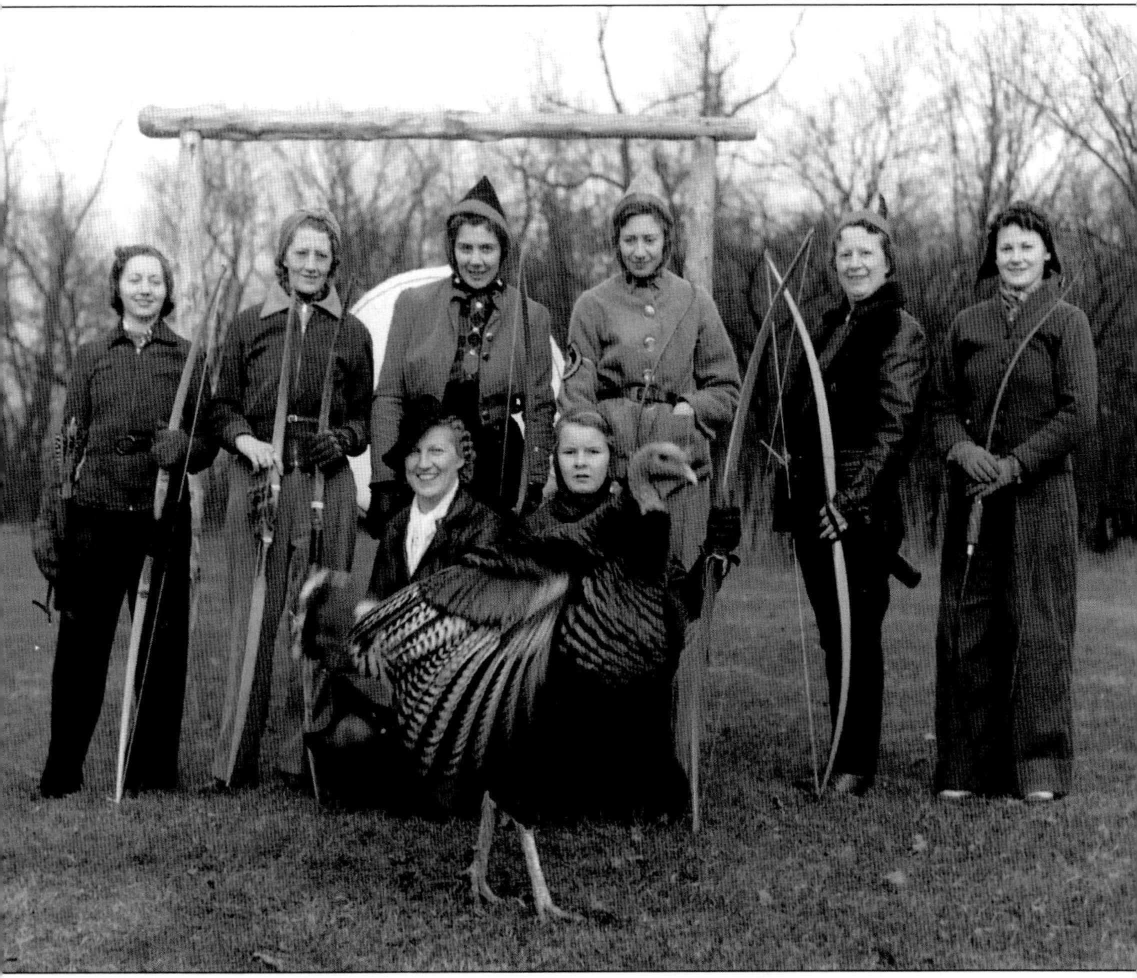

DON'T MESS WITH THESE WOMEN. Beginning in the late 1940s, the Winton Bowmen, a local archery club, operated a target archery range at Winton Woods. These women posed for this 1947 picture before that year's Thanksgiving turkey met its maker. Archery continued to grow in popularity in the 1950s.

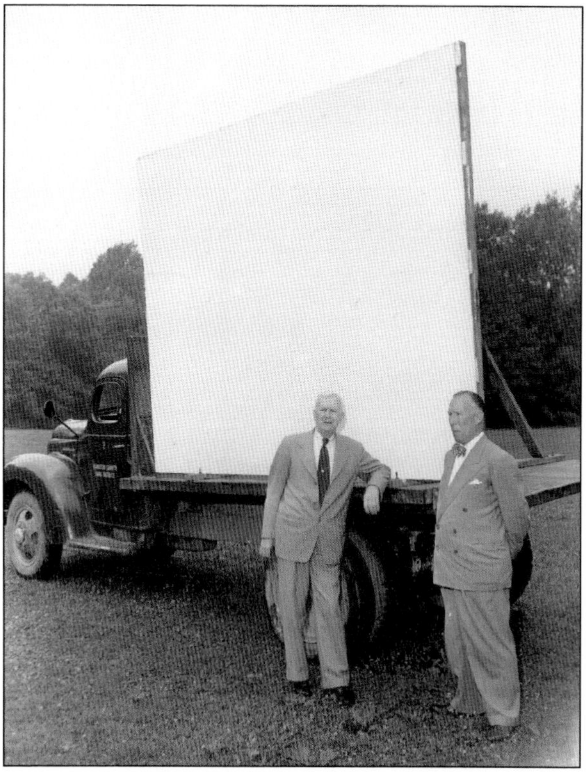

OUTDOOR MOVIES AT THE PARK. Beginning in July 1948, park officials began showing nature films at Sharon Woods. More than 400 people attended the first screening. By the end of 1949, attendance for the series of 12 films reached more than 5,300 people. The park board borrowed the films from the Cincinnati Public Library and rented a projector and speakers. Crowds viewed the films on a 12-by-12-foot screen. On a related note, in the late 1940s, the park district created a film called *Acres of Fun at Sharon Woods*, which circulated to hundreds of community and civic organizations in Hamilton County. By the end of the decade, the park district, which now included Sharon Woods, Winton Woods, and Miami Whitewater Forest, topped one million visitors for the first time in its history.

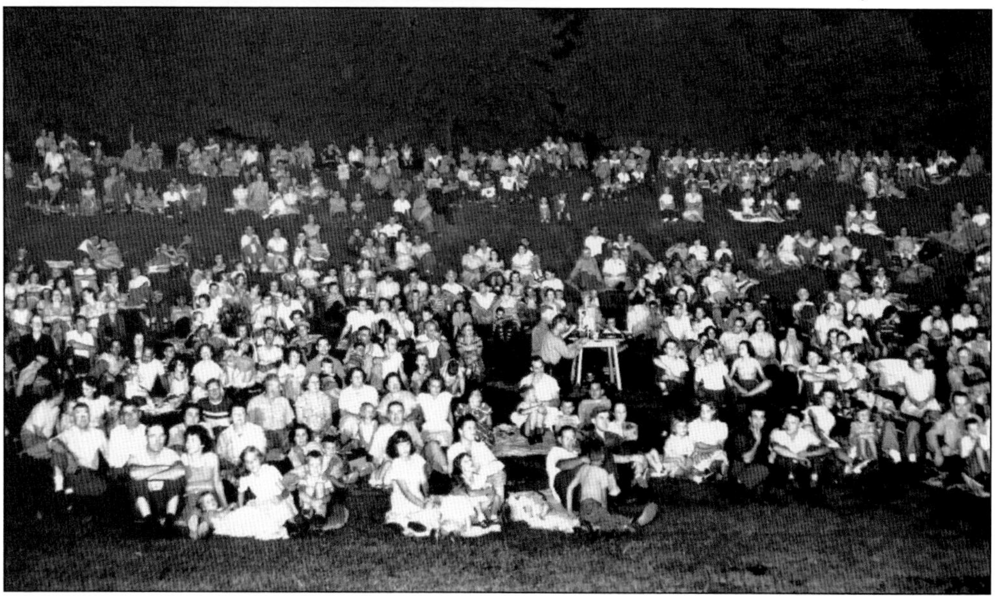

Two

POSTWAR GROWTH AND EXPANSION 1951–1980

Just recently, Americans observed the 50th anniversary of the interstate highway system. On June 29, 1956, Pres. Dwight D. Eisenhower signed the Interstate Highway Act into law. The new law would appropriate $25 billion of federal funds over the next 13 years to construct a network of highways totaling some 41,000 miles. The secretary of commerce called it "the greatest public works project in the history of the world." Highways were merely one tangible symbol of the United States' economic standing relative to other countries after World War II. During the late 1940s and early 1950s, landscapes of most major cities were transformed by the baby boom and the new wave of suburbanization that accompanied it. These national trends were reflected throughout Hamilton County. The postwar housing market boomed as young families eagerly trekked to new suburban developments. Manufacturers, white-collar businesses, and new shopping malls moved into outlying areas of the county.

Within this context, the Hamilton County park commissioners felt compelled to preserve as much county land for the park district as possible. They stood vigilant and determined in their watch over road projects that threatened parklands. Each time highway construction projects threatened parklands, commissioners lobbied state officials to reroute the highways.

In addition to protecting lands from overdevelopment, park commissioners oversaw the growth and development of its parks. Winton Woods and Miami Whitewater Forest were brought up to par with Sharon Woods. By the end of the 1960s, both parks featured fully stocked 18-hole golf courses, lakes for fishing, picnic areas, and overnight camping. In 1968, the park district expanded again when it acquired lands west of Cincinnati along the Ohio River from the Cincinnati Park Board and the Cincinnati Gas and Electric Company. Together these lands would comprise the county's fourth park, along the banks of the Ohio and Great Miami Rivers, called Shawnee Lookout. Over the next few decades, private citizens gifted smaller tracts of land to be used as parks. By the time the park district celebrated its 50th anniversary in 1980, residents had access to 15 county parks.

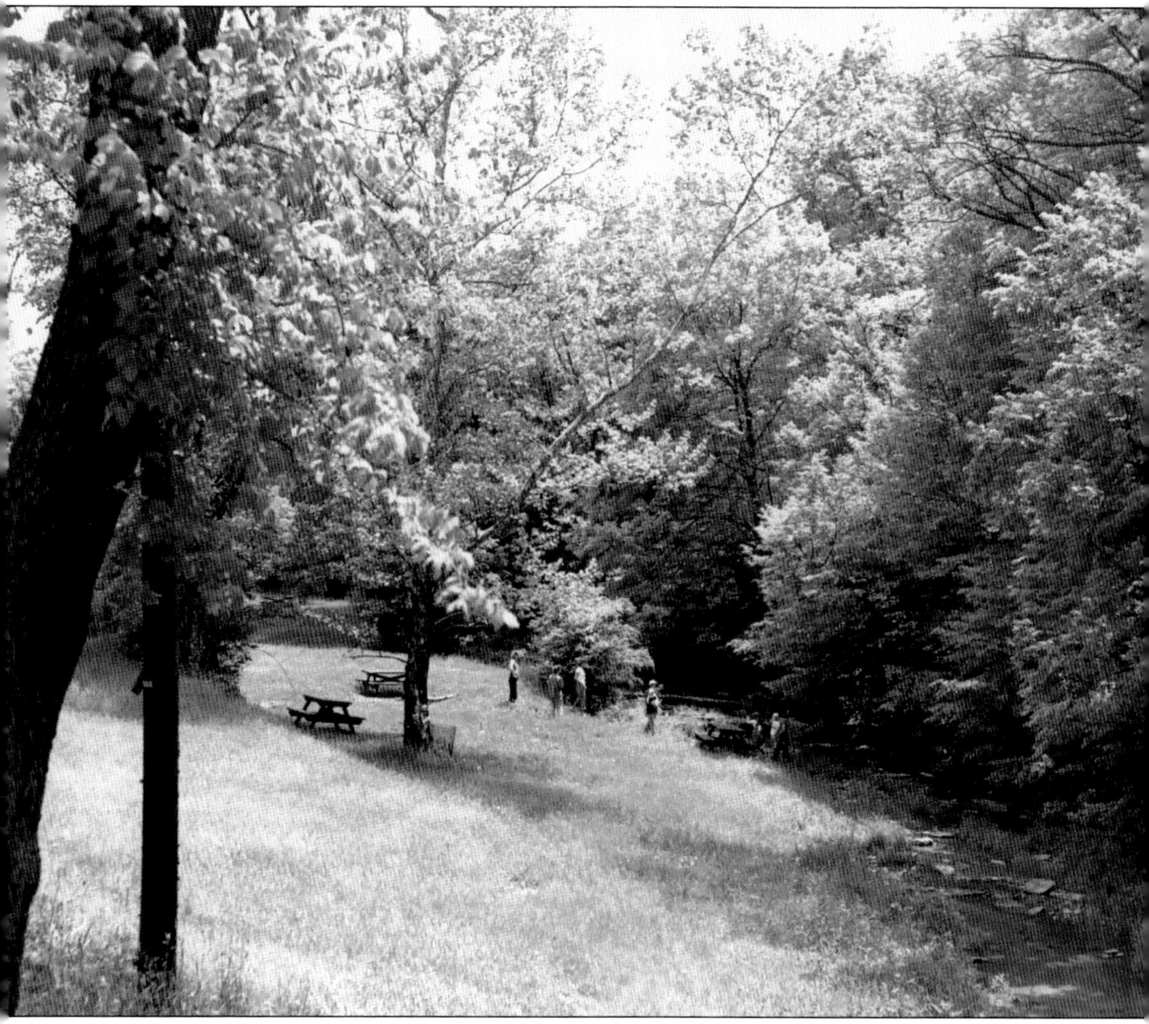

PASTORAL SETTINGS. Picnic sites in the remote corners of Winton Woods attracted visitors to the park in the early 1950s.

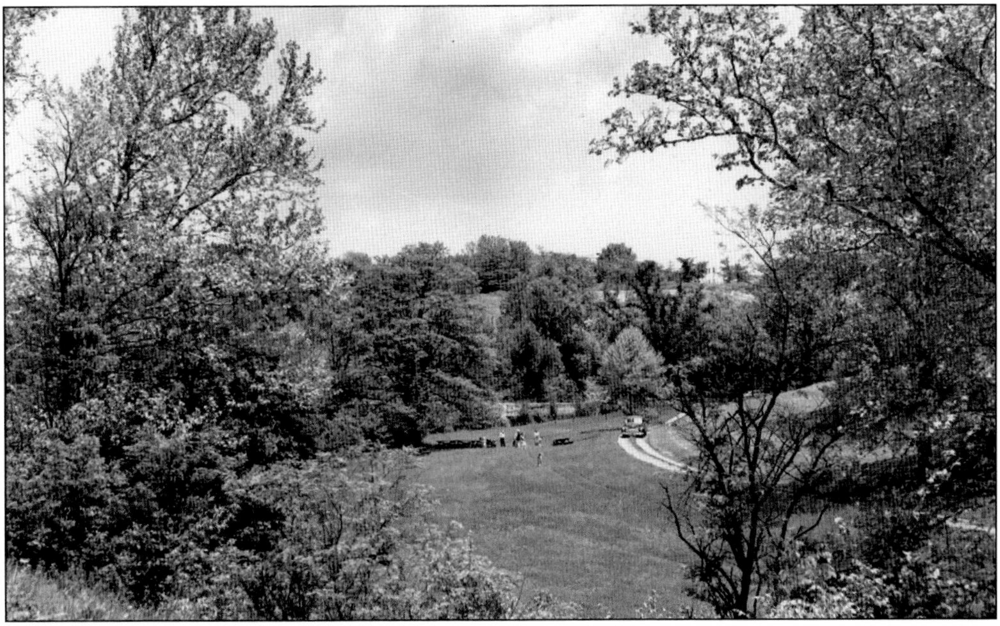

IDEAL GETAWAYS. Lush forested lands provided suitable havens of escape from the pressures of the work week. In the 1950s, the park district maintained its commitment to an ongoing reforestation program. In 1955 alone, 10,000 seedlings were planted, including 1,000 white oak, 6,000 red pine, and 3,000 white pine. Each fall, winter, and spring, maintenance crews transplanted these young trees to the areas in the parks that attracted visitors.

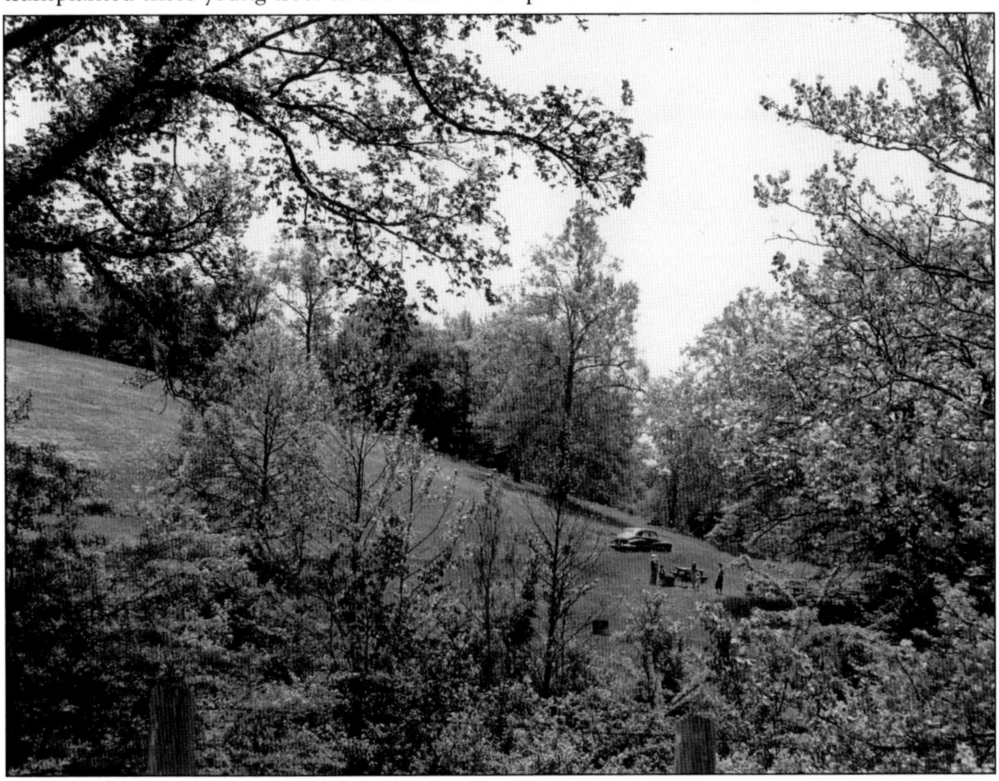

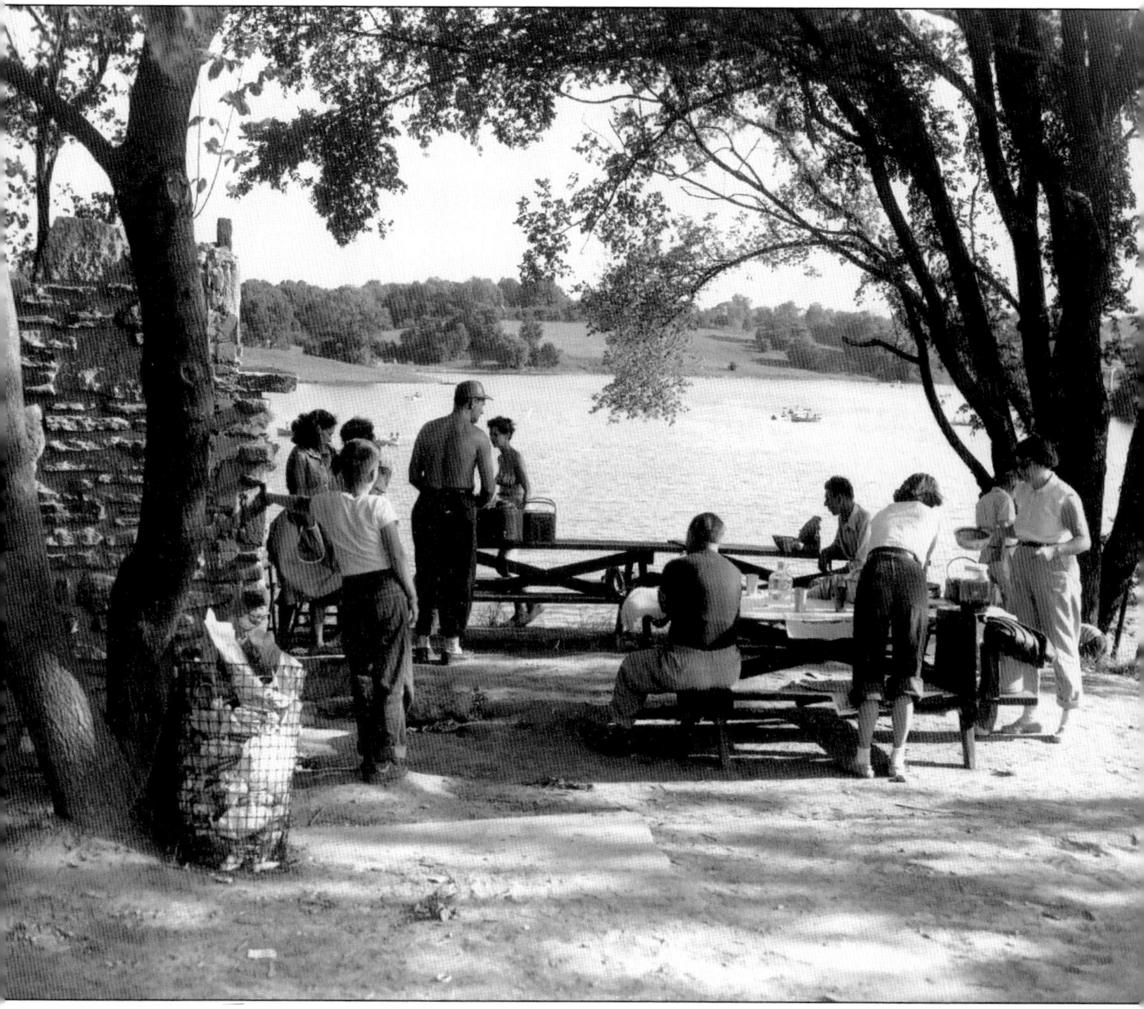

SCENIC OVERLOOK. Once the Winton Woods Lake was completed in the mid-1950s, picnic groups took advantage of new sites at which to gather. This scenic overlook, on the shores of the lake, is framed elegantly by a canopy of nearby trees.

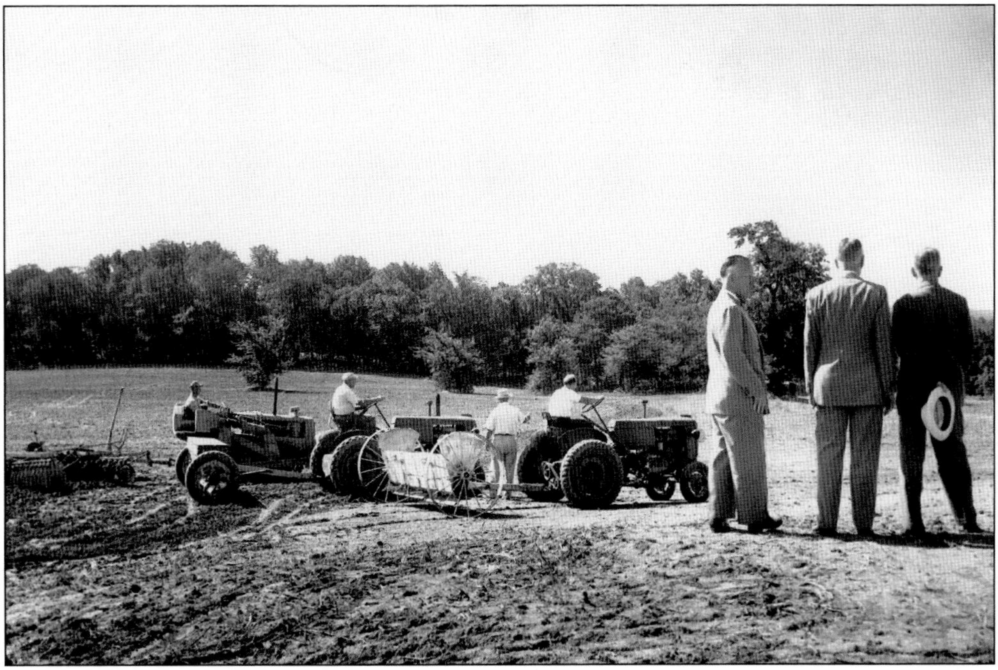

GOLF ARRIVES AT WINTON WOODS. Park commissioners had every intention of developing a second golf course at Winton Woods once they took control of the property. The board hired Bill Diddle to design the new golf course, but plans stalled during the war years. Much of the present golf course was sown with soy beans, hay, and corn during the war. Crops were used as feed for livestock that was also maintained on parklands. The crops also protected the soil from erosion until the construction on the course began. The park commissioners (above) inspect the site, just prior to its opening for the 1951 season. By the mid-1950s, Winton Woods Golf Course exceeded the annual attendance record of the more established course at Sharon Woods. An unidentified foursome (below) prepares to tee off from the No. 2 tee.

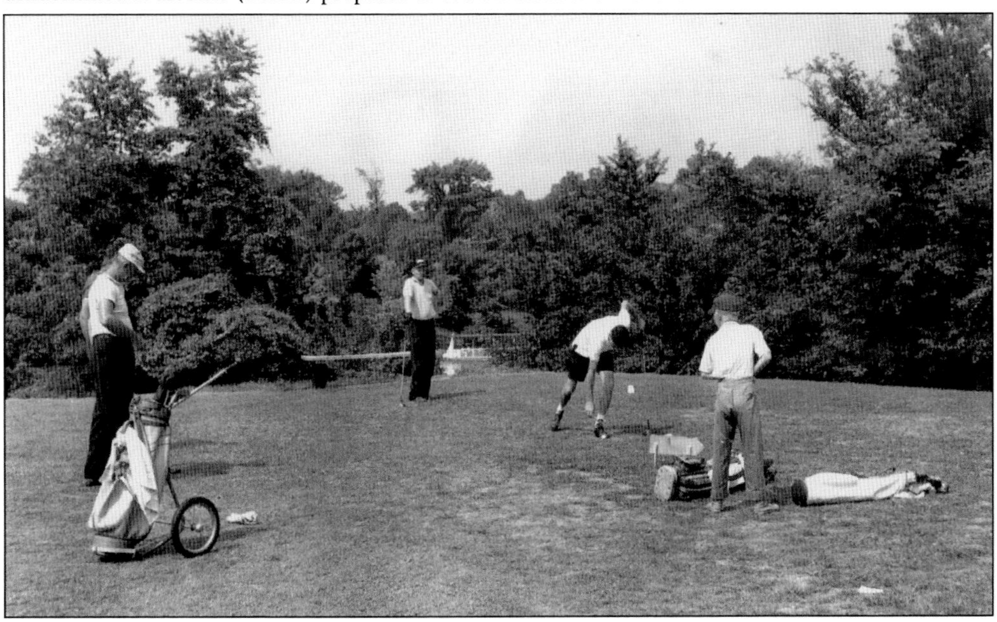

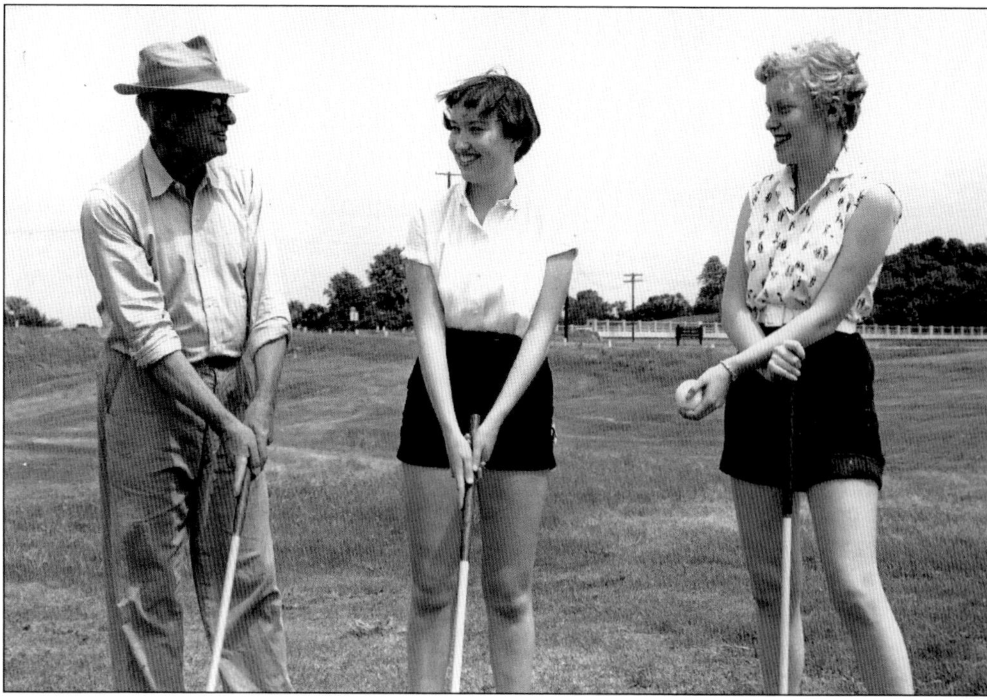

A Short-Lived Craze. During the mid-1950s, Sharon Woods and Winton Woods hired an outside concessionaire to construct and operate lawn golf courses. The new attraction proved to have a limited appeal.

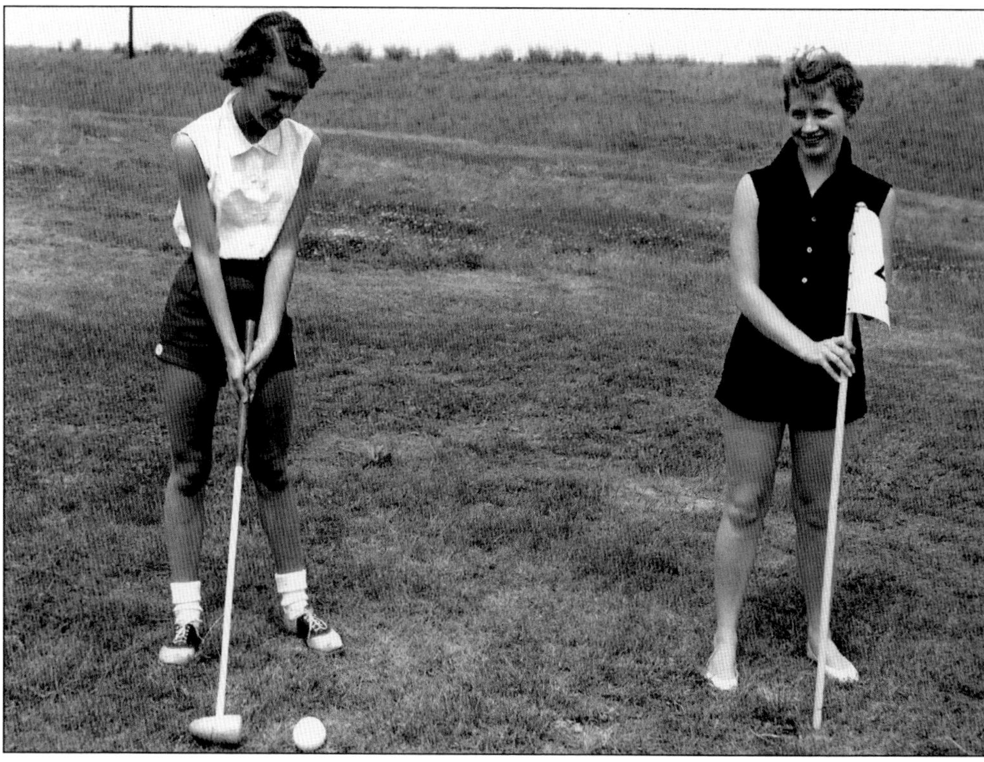

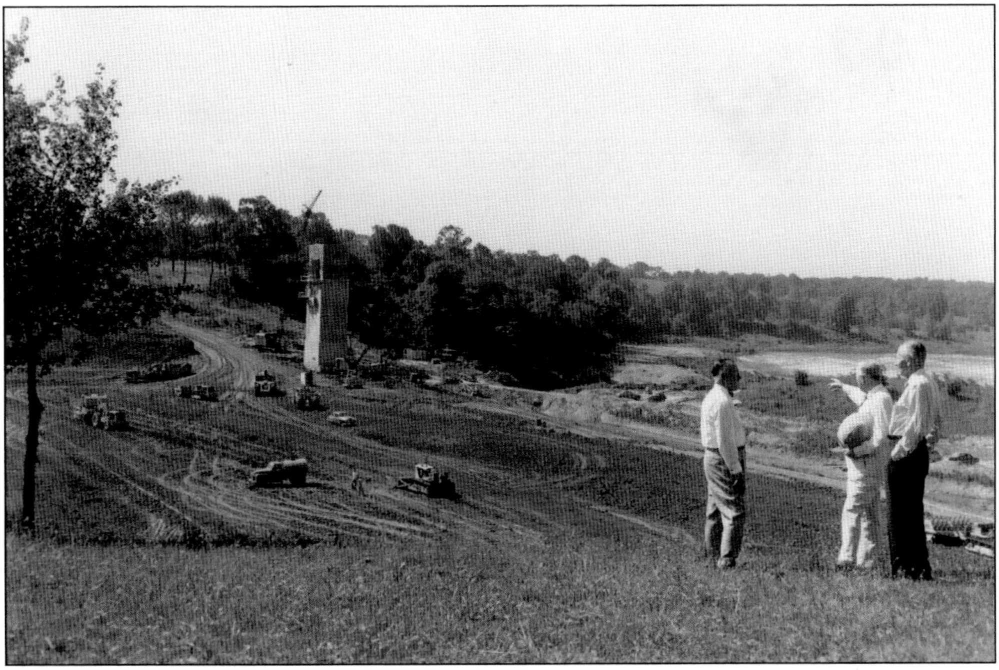

THE MAIN ATTRACTION. In many respects, the addition of the lake at Winton Woods provided a focal point for park visitors. Park officials entered into discussions with the U.S. Army Corps of Engineers about the idea of creating a lake for flood-control purposes. The Great Flood of 1937, the worst in the history of Cincinnati and Hamilton County, still resonated in the minds of policy makers. A sizeable portion of Winton Woods was low-lying land near the West Fork of the Mill Creek. In 1951, park commissioners (above and below) inspect the progress of the construction site. On June 20, 1953, park officials dedicated the West Fork Dam.

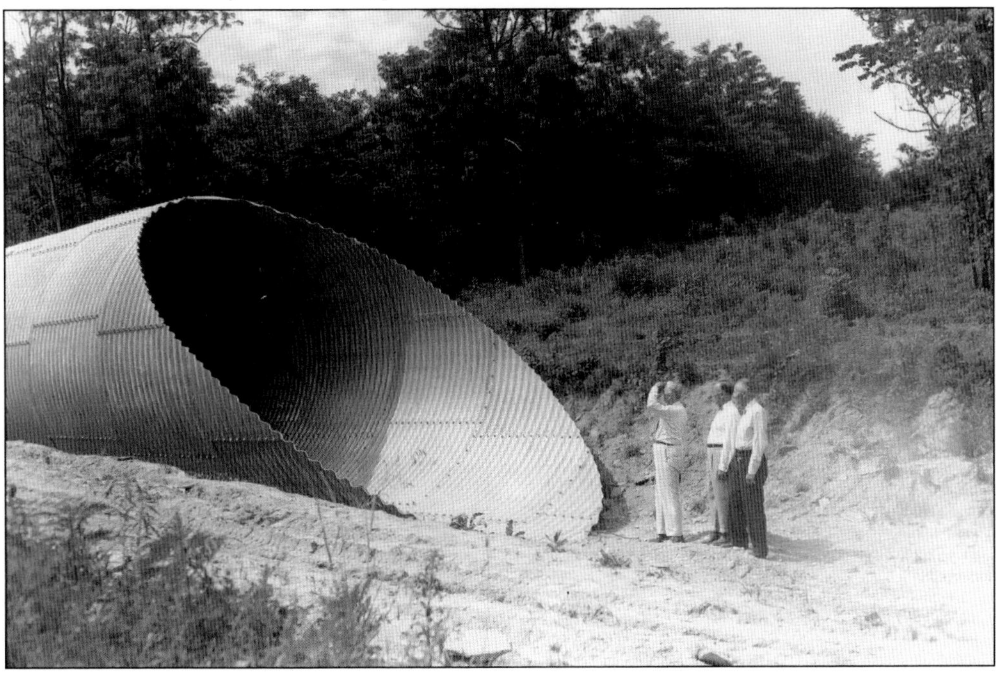

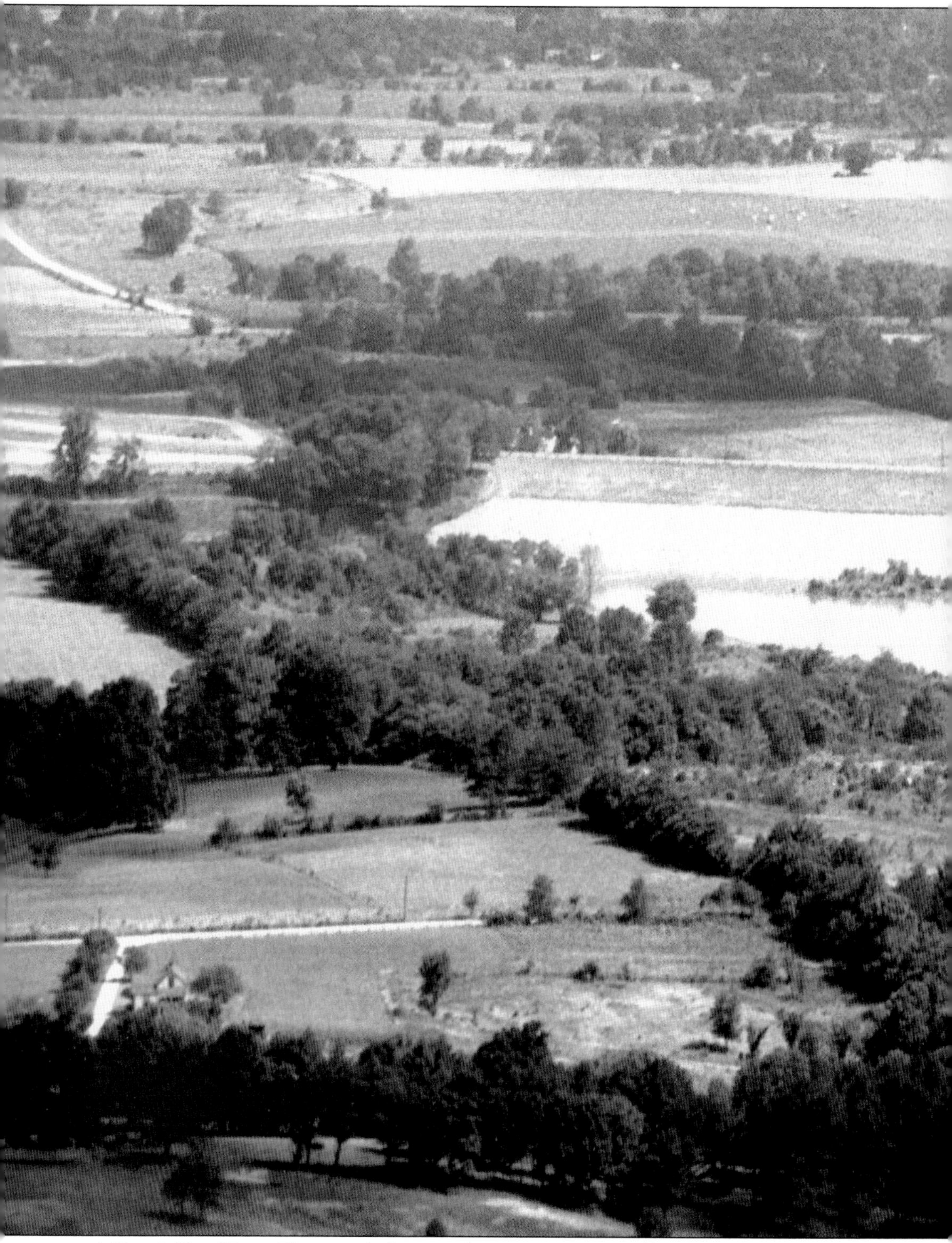

A Bird's-Eye View. This aerial photograph was commissioned by the park board. It provides a good view of the 188-acre lake and the surrounding parklands. The lake became a source

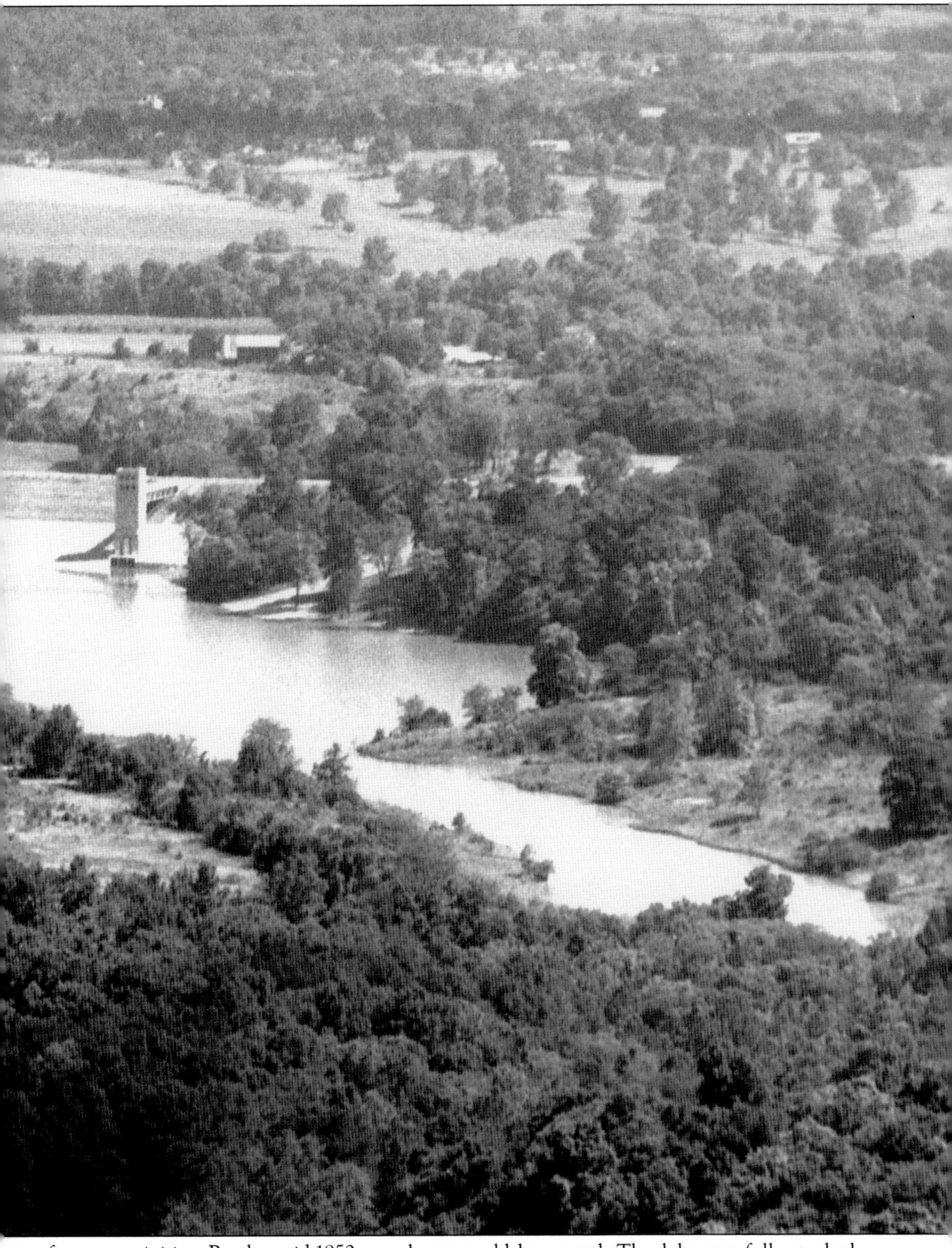

of many activities. By the mid-1950s, rowboats could be rented. The lake was fully stocked. Recreational fishers were catching an average of two fish per person.

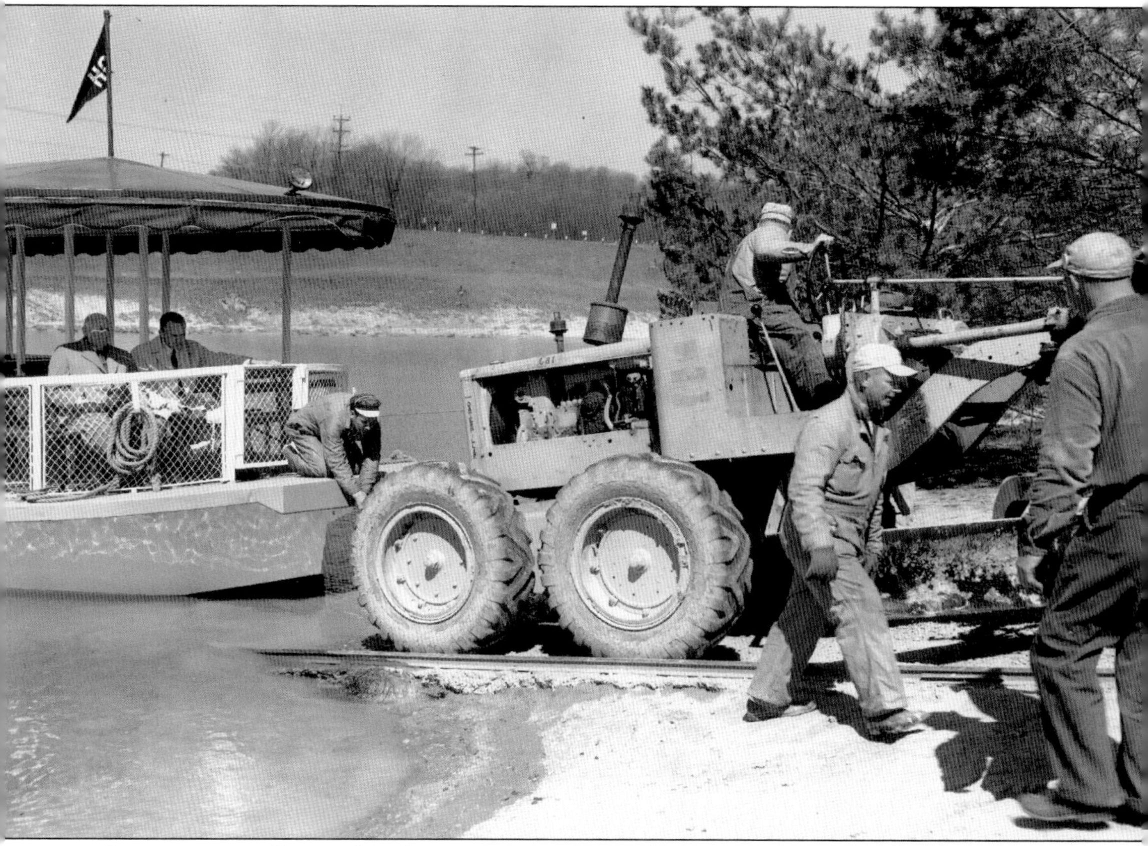

LAUNCHING A QUEEN. Much interest was generated at Winton Woods Lake when park officials decided to purchase a paddleboat, the *Winton Queen*, which could be used for group tours around the lake. In 1954, the board opted to schedule rotating tours of the large lake. One week the boat explored the eastern side; the following week it toured the western banks and environs. The initial cruise was reserved for county commissioners. With each new attraction that was added to Winton Woods in the 1950s, its annual attendance gradually outpaced the number of visitors going to Sharon Woods. A similar boat, dubbed the *Sharon Queen*, was commissioned for Sharon Woods Lake. On more than one occasion the boat was transported to Winton Woods to handle the surplus riders at that location.

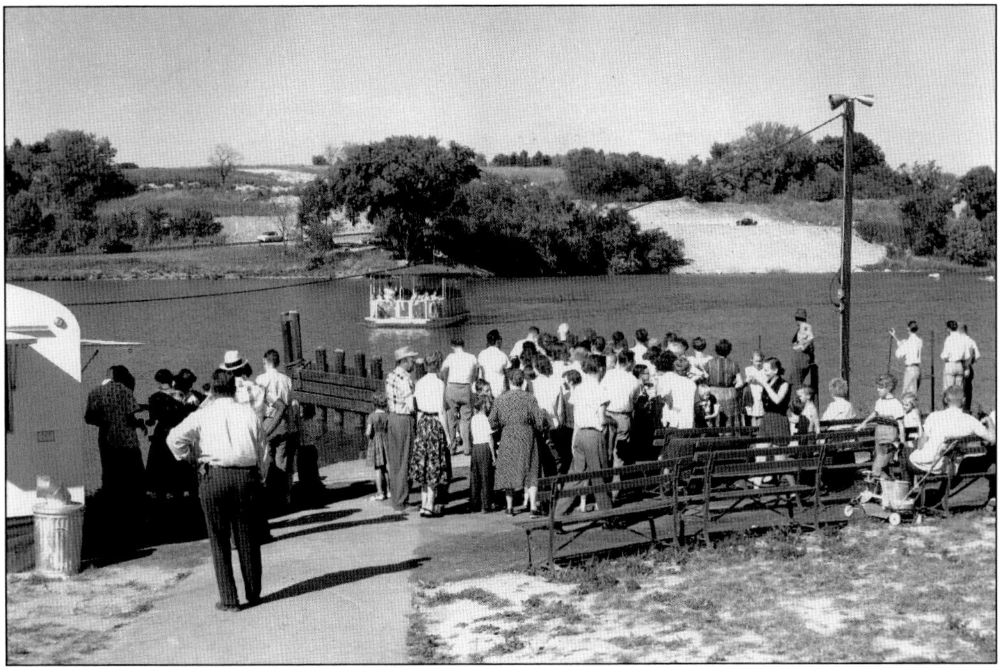

The Winton Queen. Given Cincinnati's rich history as a river city, the attraction to paddleboats and tall stacks seems quite natural. A crowded boat on a sunny day was a familiar sight on Winton Woods Lake. Within a few years, a second boat, the *Winton Princess*, was added.

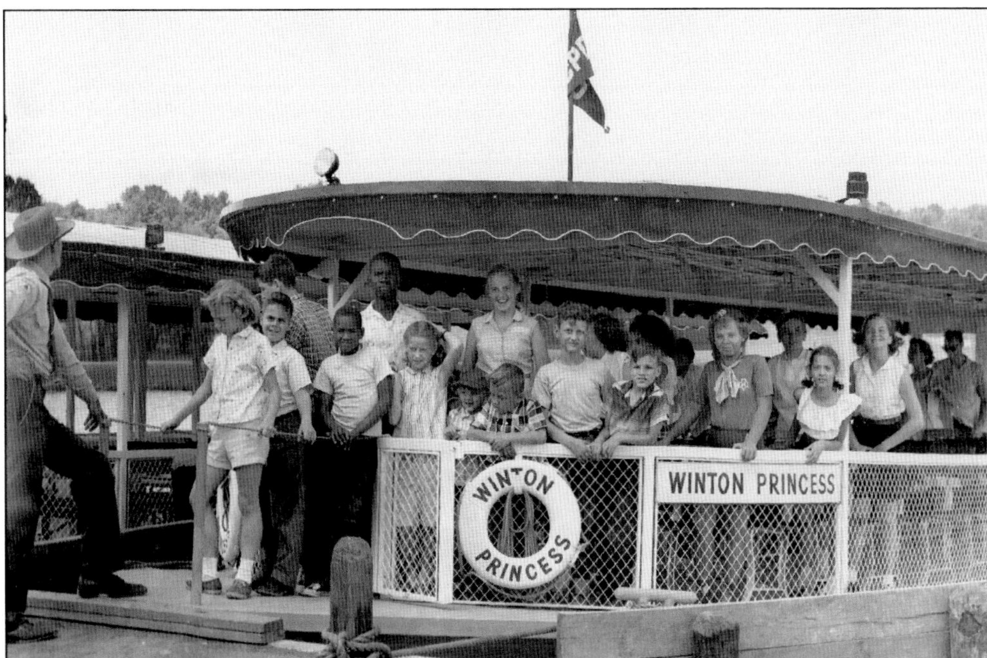

The Ride of Their Lives. Each year, the park board invited underprivileged children to spend a day at the park. These children, from a local school for the hearing impaired, were treated to a boat ride, a picnic lunch, and other activities.

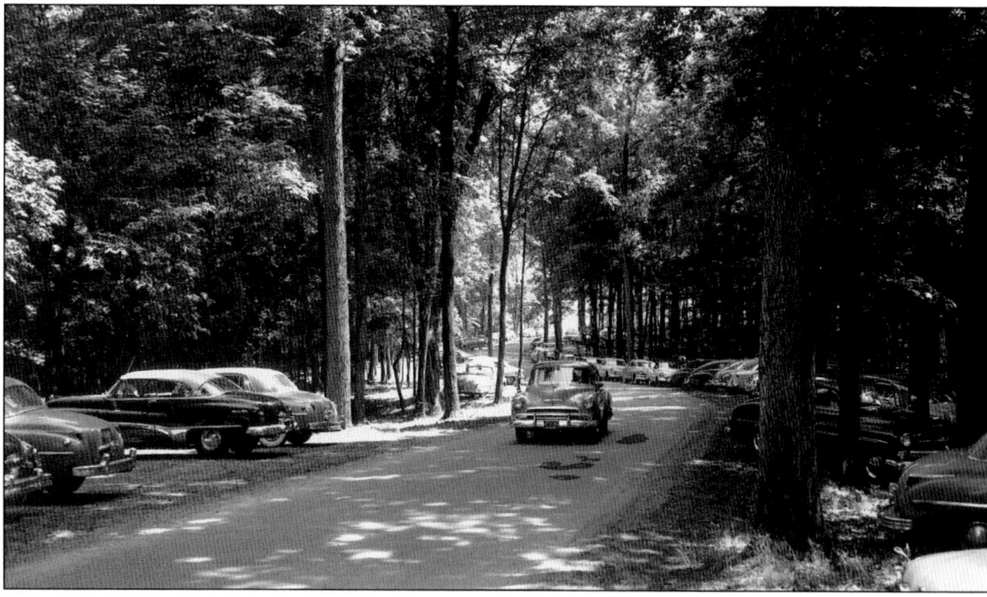

WEST-SIDERS TAKE TO THE PARKS. During much of 1950s, Winton Woods received the majority of attention from park officials. At the same time, however, park officials were also striving to generate interest in their third park, Miami Whitewater Forest (above). The Hamilton County Park District inherited an already developed fishing area in the Timberlake region of the new park. Poor roads and limited parking, however, were disincentives for potential visitors. Cars were forced to crowd along the sides of narrow park roads.

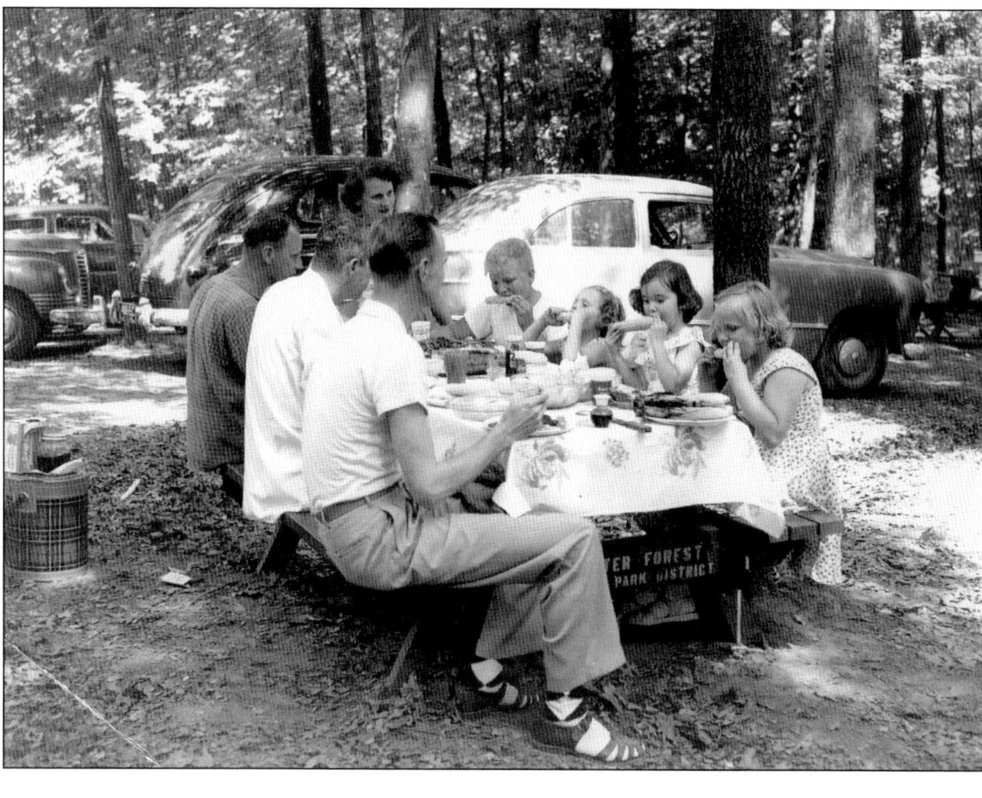

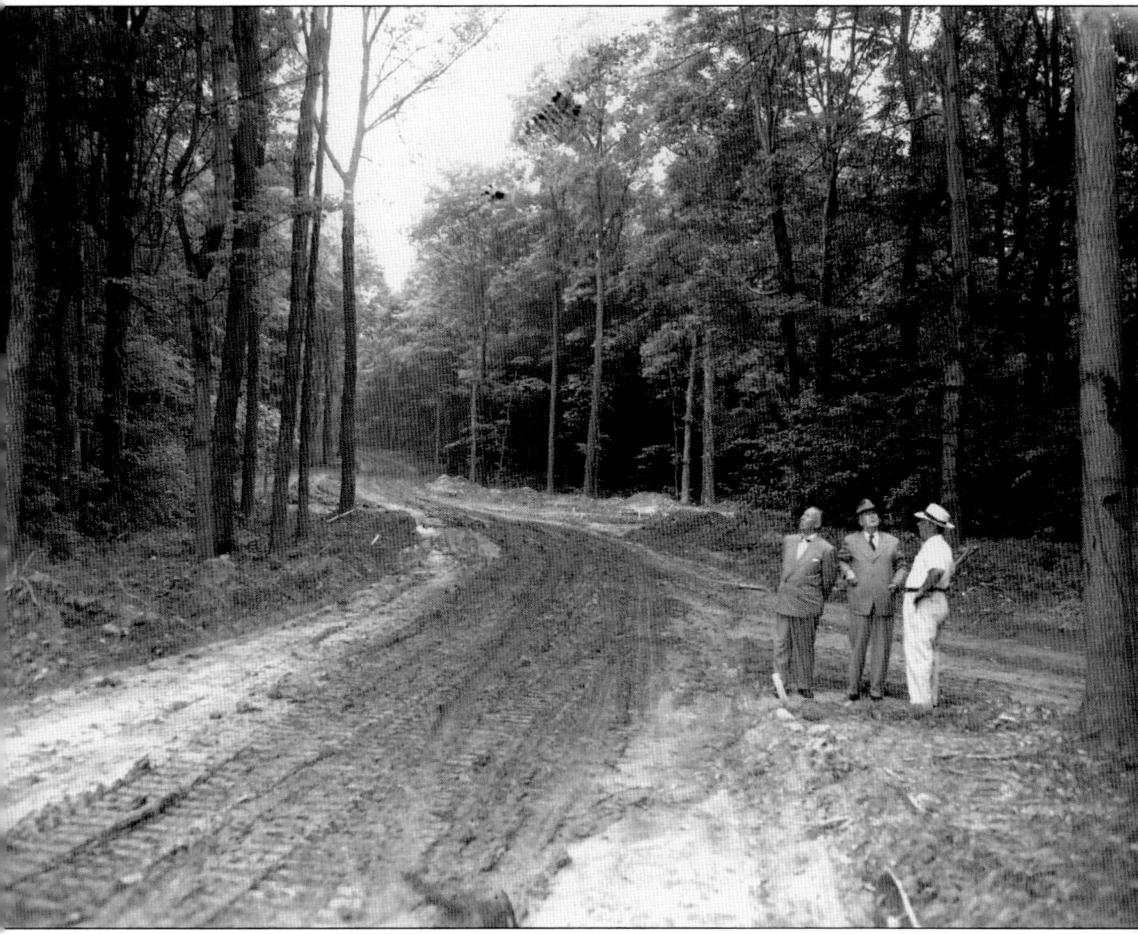

MAKING ROADS AND MAKING WAVES. Improvements in roads were more challenging at Miami Whitewater Forest due to the heavily wooded terrain. Ironically, at the same time Hamilton County park commissioners were authorizing the construction of roads within the park, they found themselves embroiled in a controversy over a highway project that threatened to encroach upon parklands. The State Highway Commission had tentatively approved the route of the Northwestern Expressway (U. S. Route 52, which parallels the modern Interstate 74 today) through the southern portion of Miami Whitewater Forest. Elmer Uhlmansiek, who took over as director-secretary when Alfred M. Husted retired in 1959, urged the commissioners to take a stand against the proposed construction. "In this day of rapid population growth and expanse of urban areas," Uhlmansiek warned, "we face the critical problem of keeping in existence for our children all possible natural green areas that can be acquired and saved. The defense of all natural areas that are now available to our people, is one of the greatest services that we of today can render for the future welfare of Hamilton County." In 1960, the park commissioners sent a letter of protest to Ohio governor Michael DiSalle. Despite their efforts, the highway project proceeded as planned.

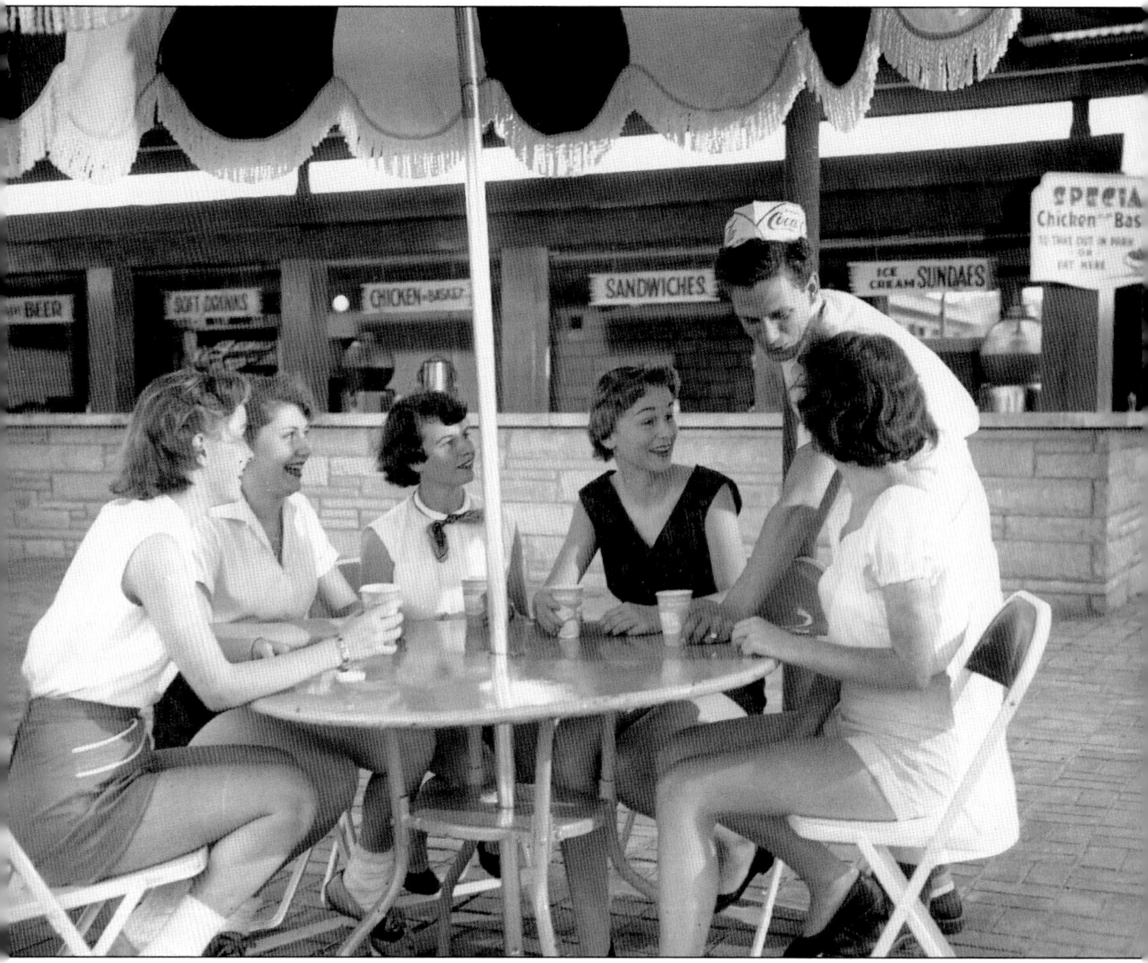

Harbor Point. Clearly this young man enjoys his work. The concession stand at Harbor Point opened in 1953 to receptive crowds. During a decade that was defined by the invention of fast food, when Ray Kroc opened his first McDonald's in 1955 in Des Plaines, Illinois, the appeal of this lunch stand is understandable. Much to the delight of park visitors, soft-serve ice cream was introduced to the menu in the mid-1950s.

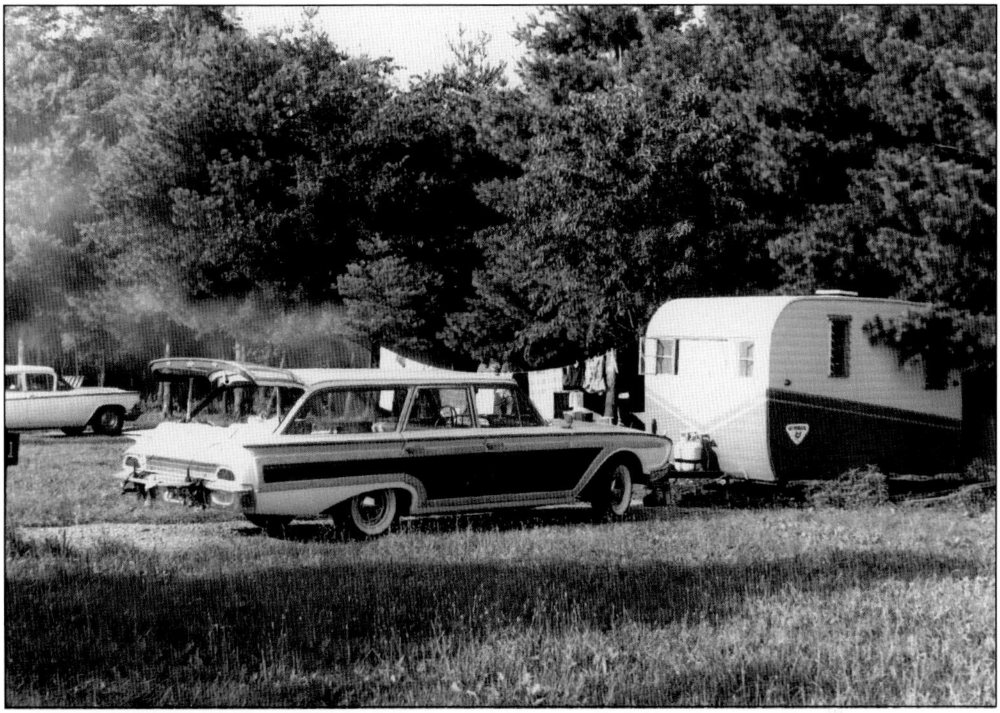

FAMILY CAMPING. Winton Woods made overnight camping an option in 1957. Spacious, wooded campsites attracted many families for overnight and weekend visits to the park.

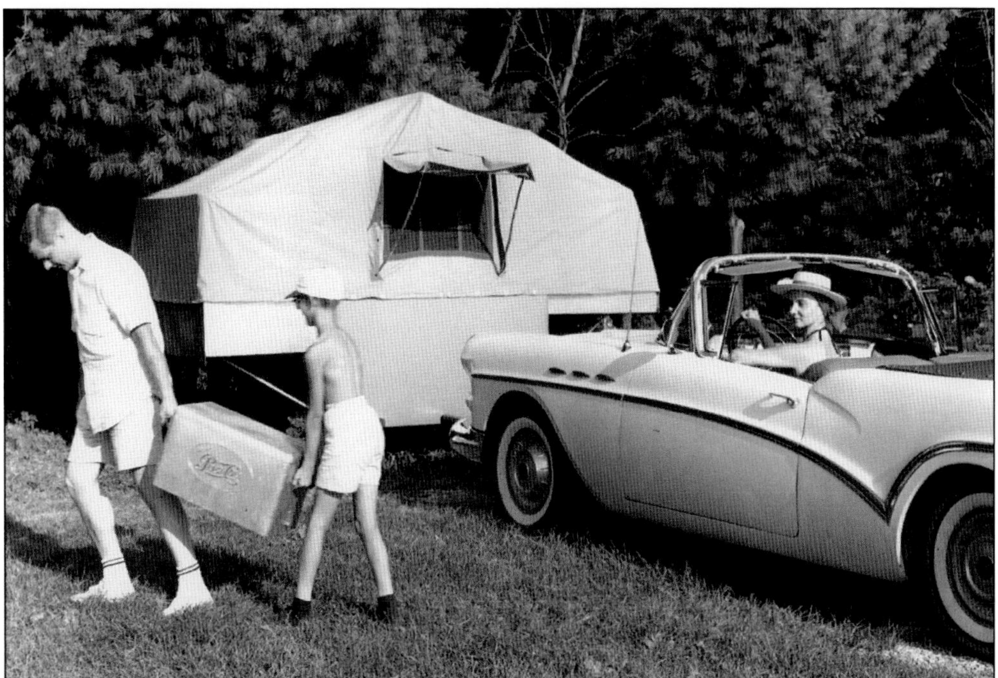

DIVISION OF LABOR. From the comfort of her padded leather seat, this mother supervises the efforts of her brood as they unpack for an overnight camping experience at Winton Woods.

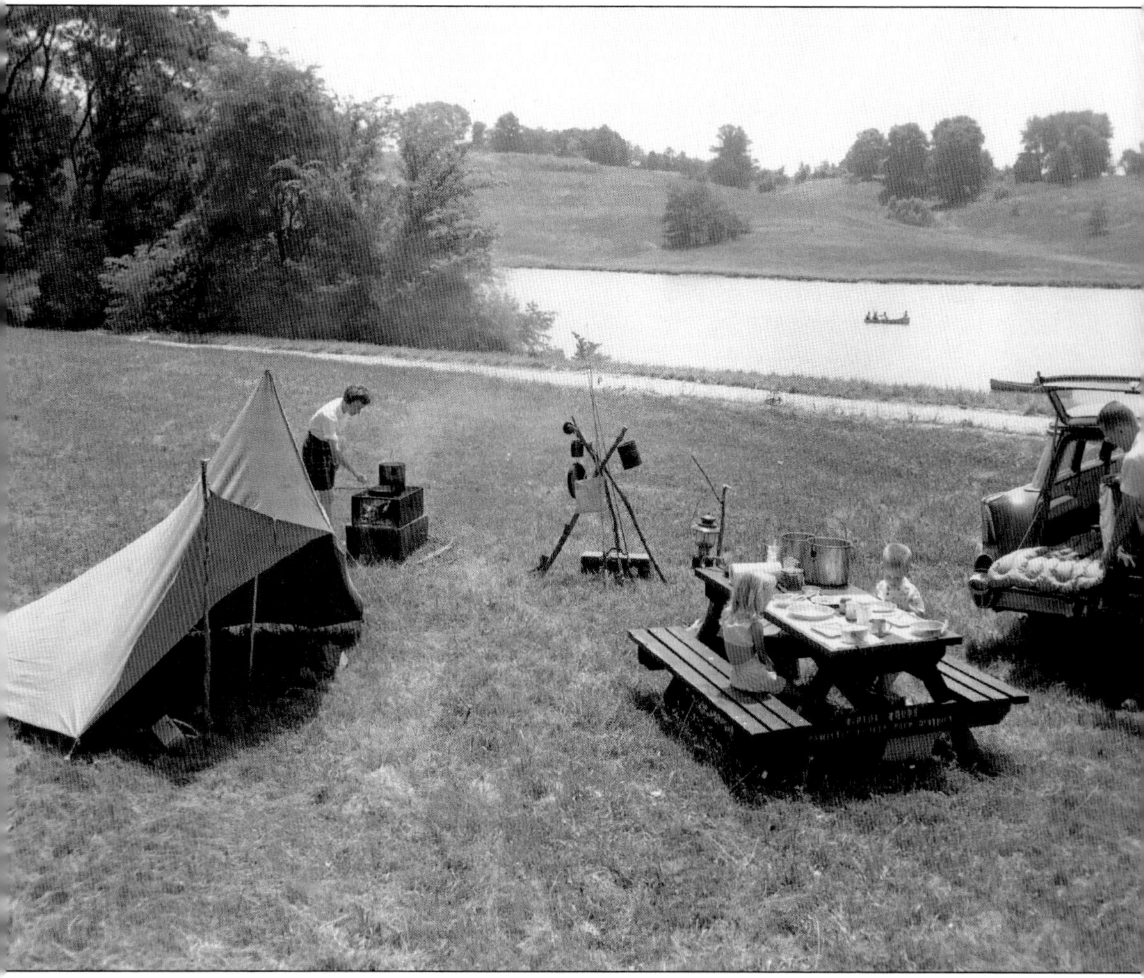

Fresh Fish for Dinner? Several campsites surrounded the newly formed lake, giving campers easy access to offshore fishing. These campers enjoy a meal cooked over open flames.

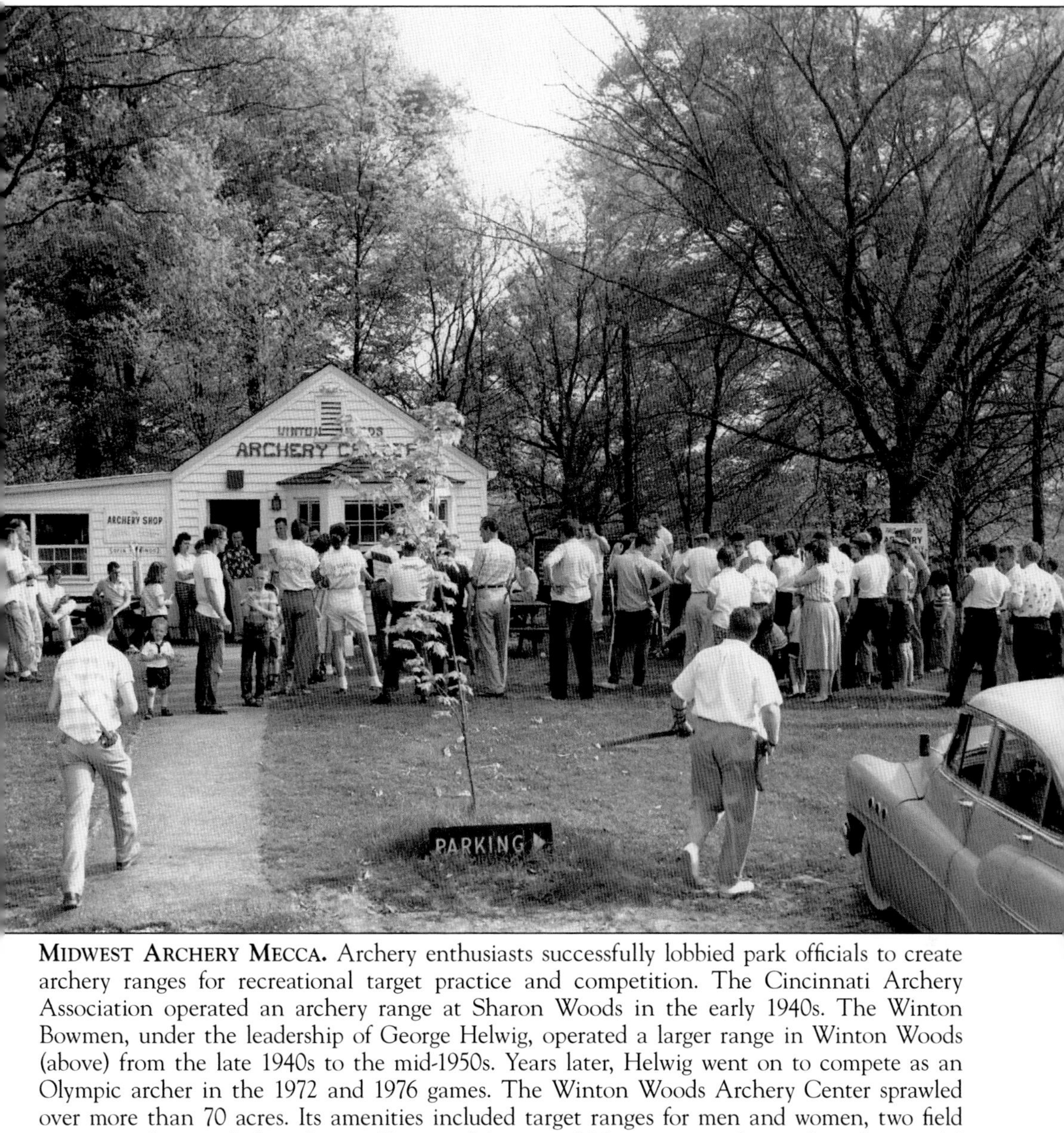

MIDWEST ARCHERY MECCA. Archery enthusiasts successfully lobbied park officials to create archery ranges for recreational target practice and competition. The Cincinnati Archery Association operated an archery range at Sharon Woods in the early 1940s. The Winton Bowmen, under the leadership of George Helwig, operated a larger range in Winton Woods (above) from the late 1940s to the mid-1950s. Years later, Helwig went on to compete as an Olympic archer in the 1972 and 1976 games. The Winton Woods Archery Center sprawled over more than 70 acres. Its amenities included target ranges for men and women, two field courses, and a nine-hole archery golf course. Moreover, Helwig organized a number of successful archery tournaments for the Midwestern Archery Association. Competitors from 17 different states attended. In 1955, the National Archery Association asked Helwig to host its tournament. Unfortunately, the archery range at Winton Woods was not large enough to accommodate such a large gathering, and it was held at Miami University, in Oxford, Ohio.

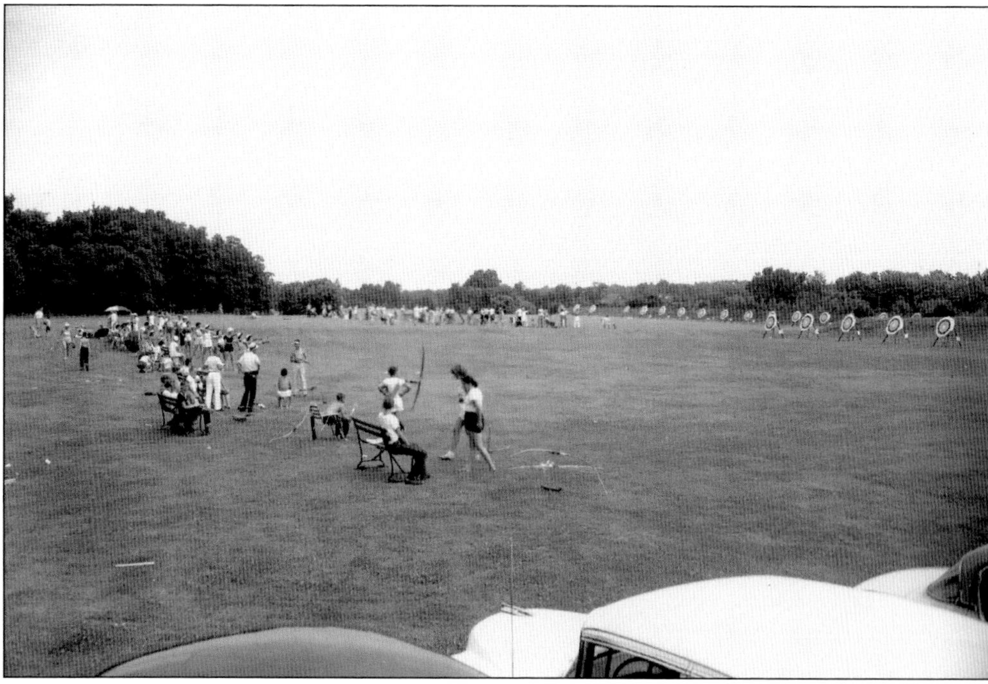

FUN FOR THE ENTIRE FAMILY. The archery range offered free lessons to novice archers as well as children. Newcomers gained experience with stationery targets (above) before advancing to field courses. Range employee Harold Allen assists the Russell Buchman family (below). Using a system of pulleys and ropes, Allen moves the target for the archers.

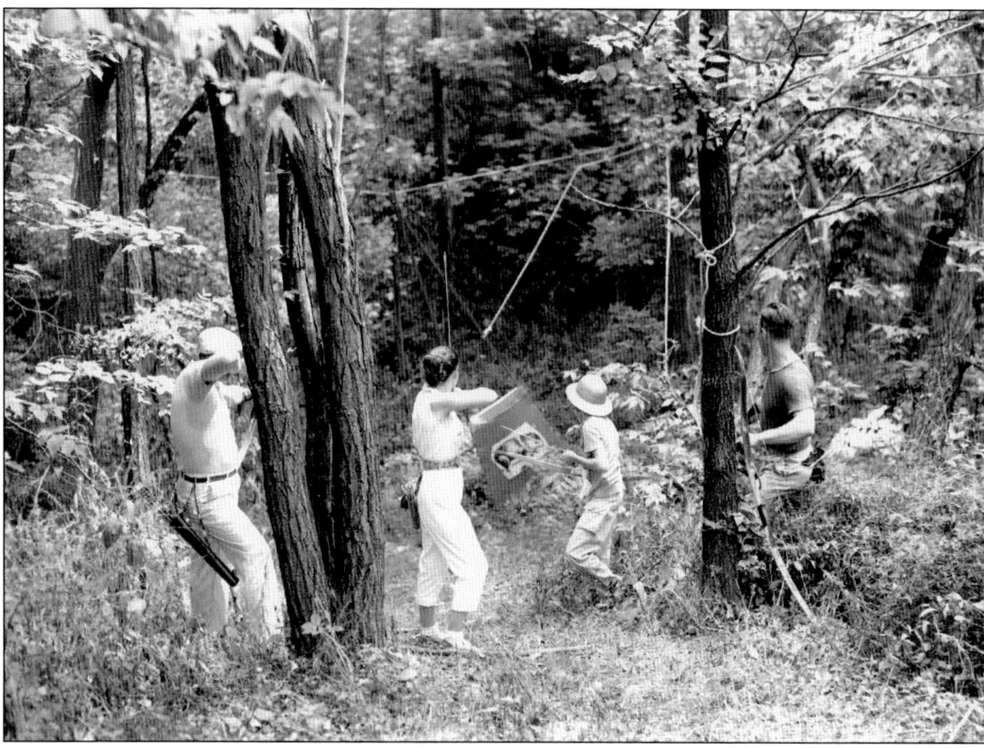

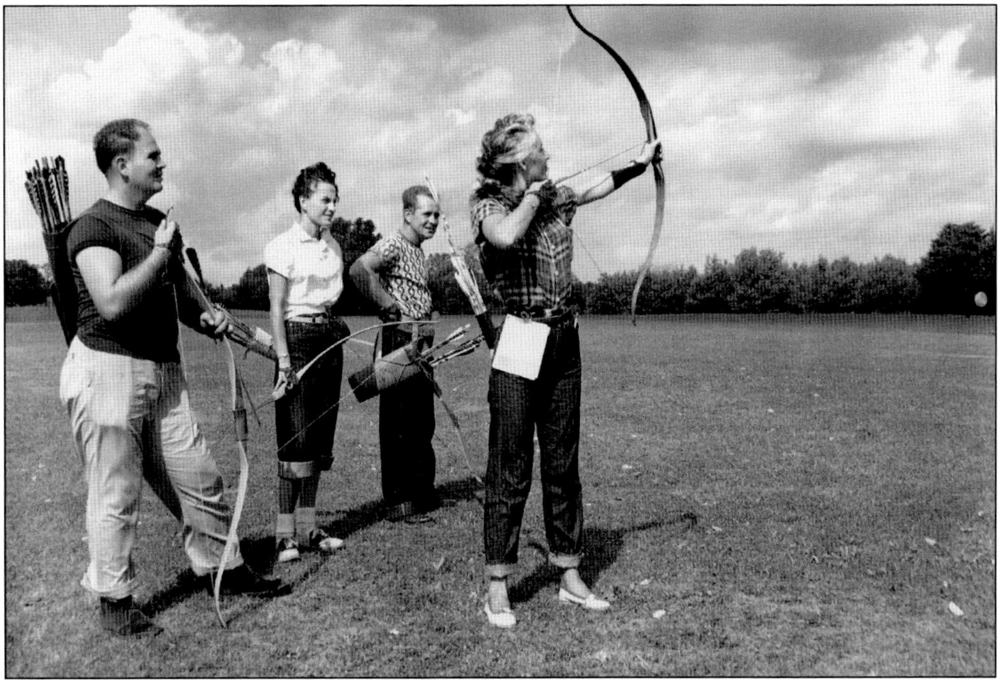

MIXED COUPLES. Target ranges at Winton Woods were segregated by gender. Tournaments were gender-coded events as well. On occasion, however, men and women would pair off for some recreational archery.

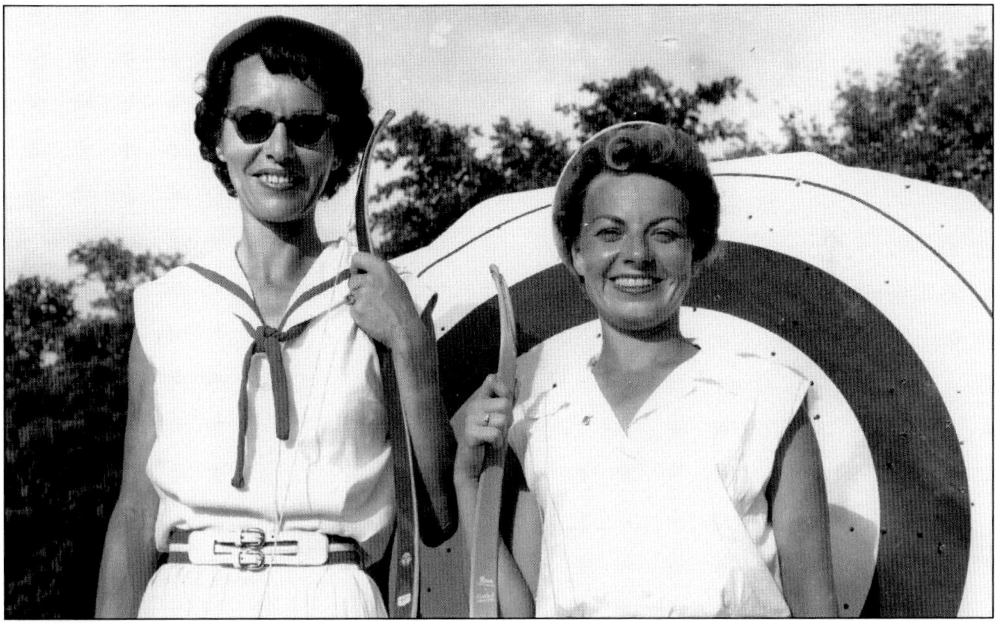

THE CHAMPIONS. On the weekend of July 6 and 7, 1957, Betty Schmidt, of Chicago, and Ann Clark, of Cincinnati, won first- and second-place honors, respectively, in target shooting, at the Midwestern Archery Tournament at the Winton Woods Archery Center. The two women would go on to represent the United States at the World Championship Archery Tournament at Prague, Czechoslovakia.

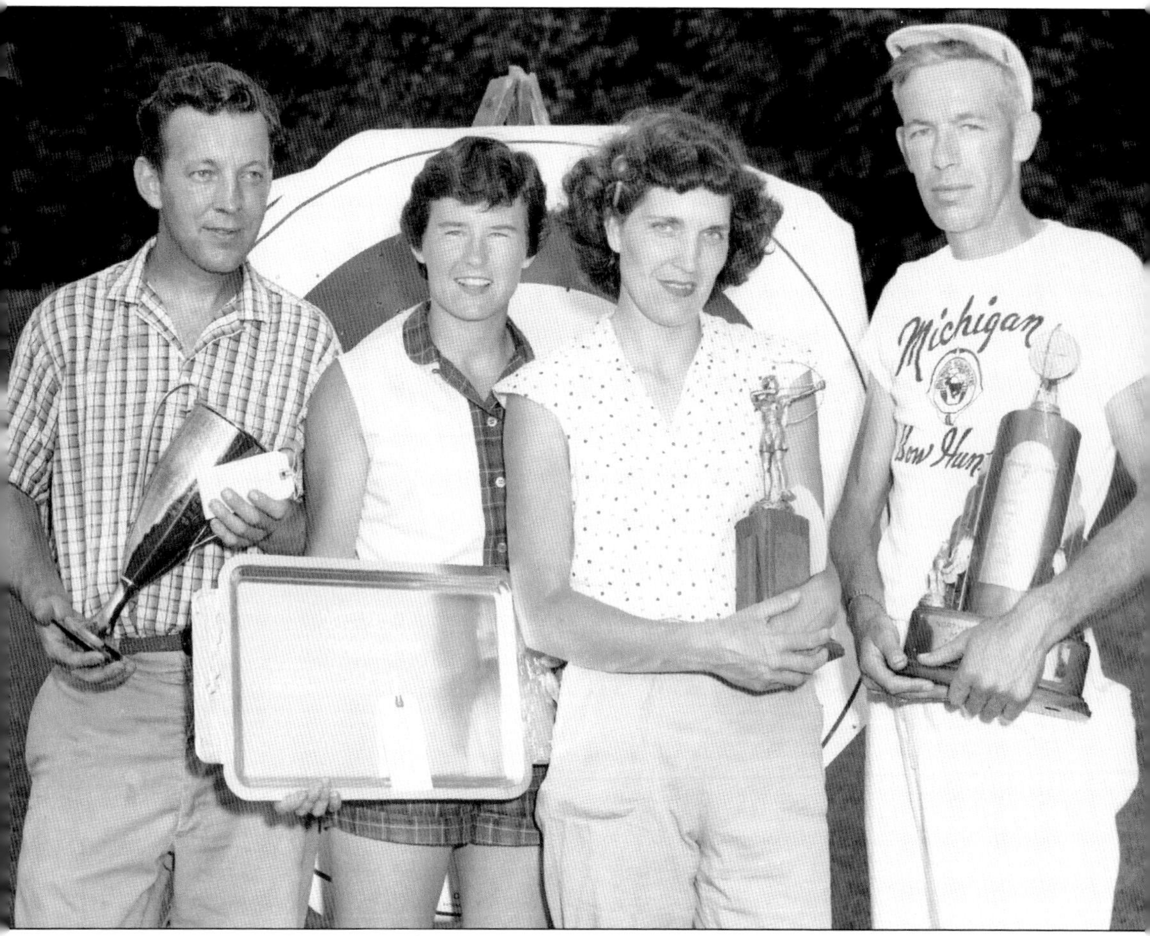

THE WINNER'S CIRCLE. At the same tournament, George Wright (left), from Detroit, and Jean Brown (second from left), from Lakewood, won top honors in the men's and women's division for instinctive field shoot. Cleo Roberson (second from right), of Samaria, Michigan, and Cliff McGrean (right), of Muskingum, Michigan, registered the highest scores in the women's and men's freestyle field shoot.

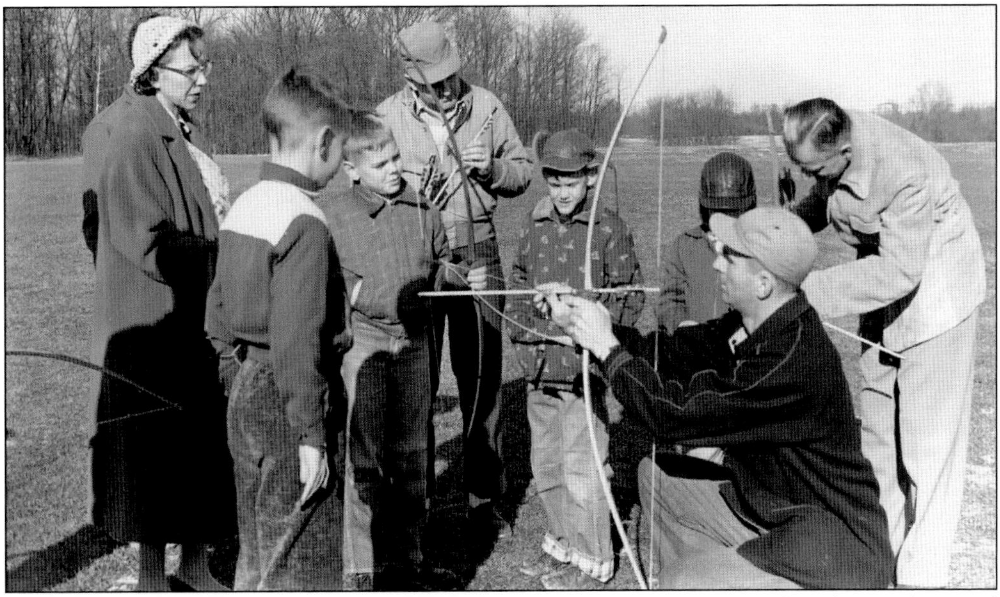

STARTING THEM YOUNG. If parents had second thoughts about giving their boys a bow and arrow for Christmas, the park district helped calm at least some of their buyer's remorse. On a cold December morning, just after Christmas in 1956, children gather at the Winton Woods Archery Center for some free instructions offered by the Winton Bowmen.

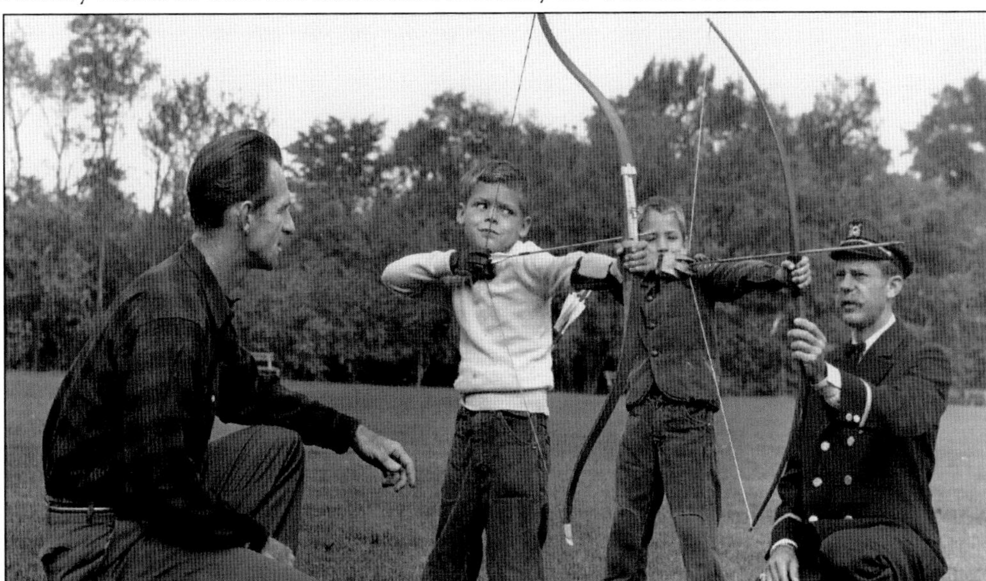

UNDER NEW MANAGEMENT. The park district took over management of the archery range in 1957. Jim Blackburn (left) became the new manager. Attendance dropped off significantly when George Helwig departed. In 1955, Helwig had coordinated the National Archery Association's tournament at Miami University, in Oxford. For the next three decades, Miami hosted most regional and national archery tournaments. Helwig would go on to become a professor of archery at Miami. Meanwhile, Blackburn joined forces with Glenn "Skipper" Ryle (right), a well-known host of a children's television show on WKRC-TV. Terry Leder (second from left) and Dave Sargent (second from right) receive instruction at a Saturday morning session.

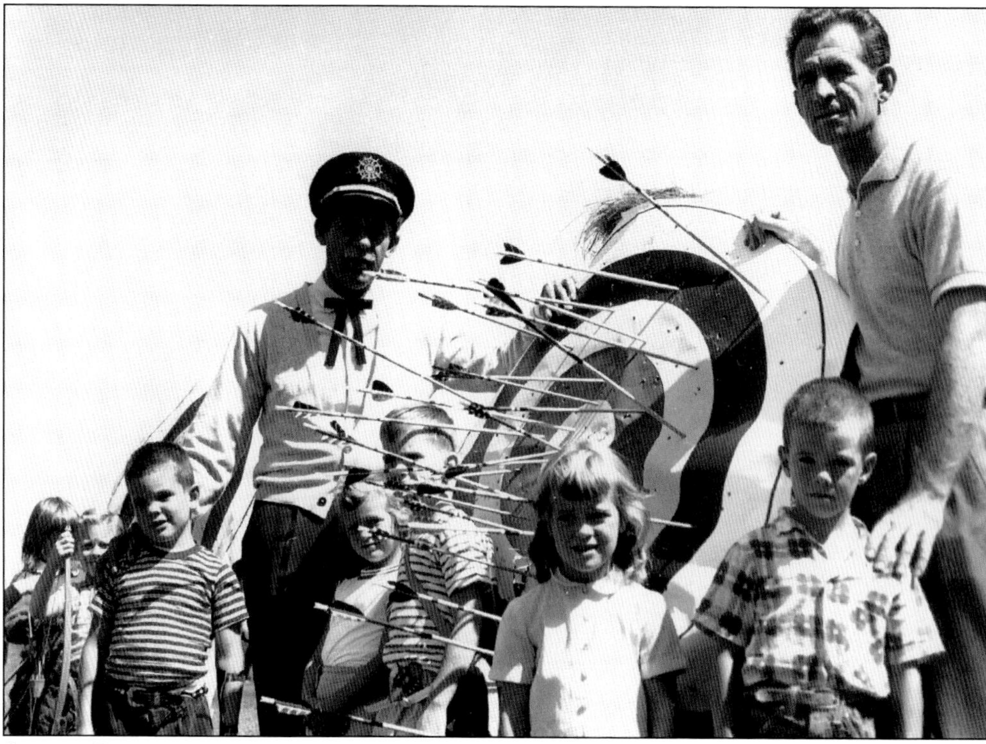

GIVING BACK TO THE COMMUNITY. Glenn "Skipper" Ryle generously gave of his time and energy to promote archery among young people. Besides showing up regularly for instructional sessions and tournaments, Ryle would invite Jim Blackburn and others on his television show to promote upcoming archery events.

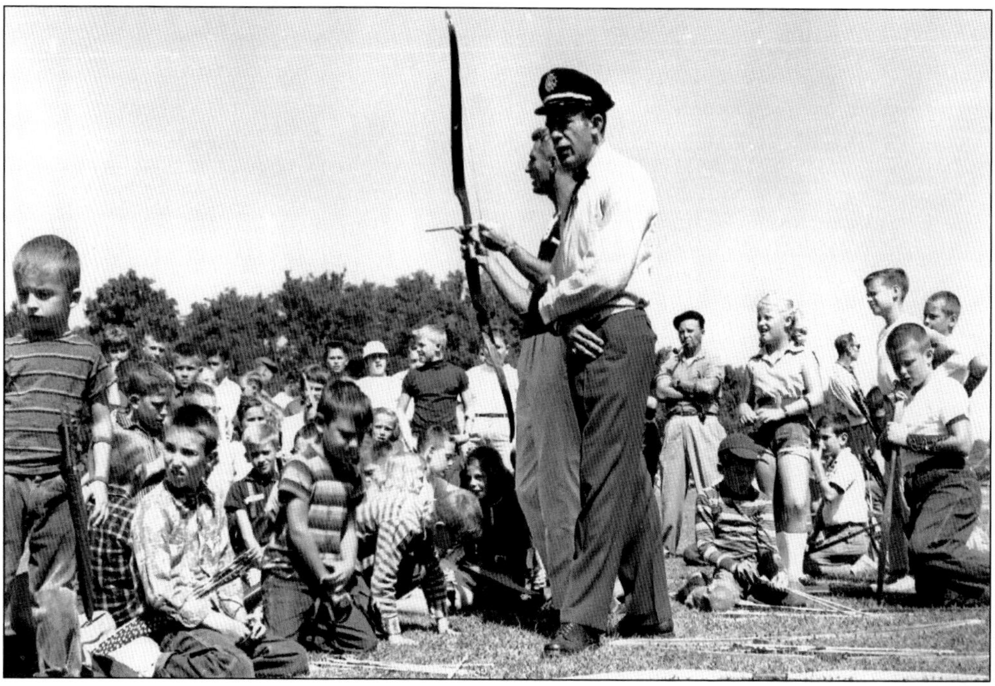

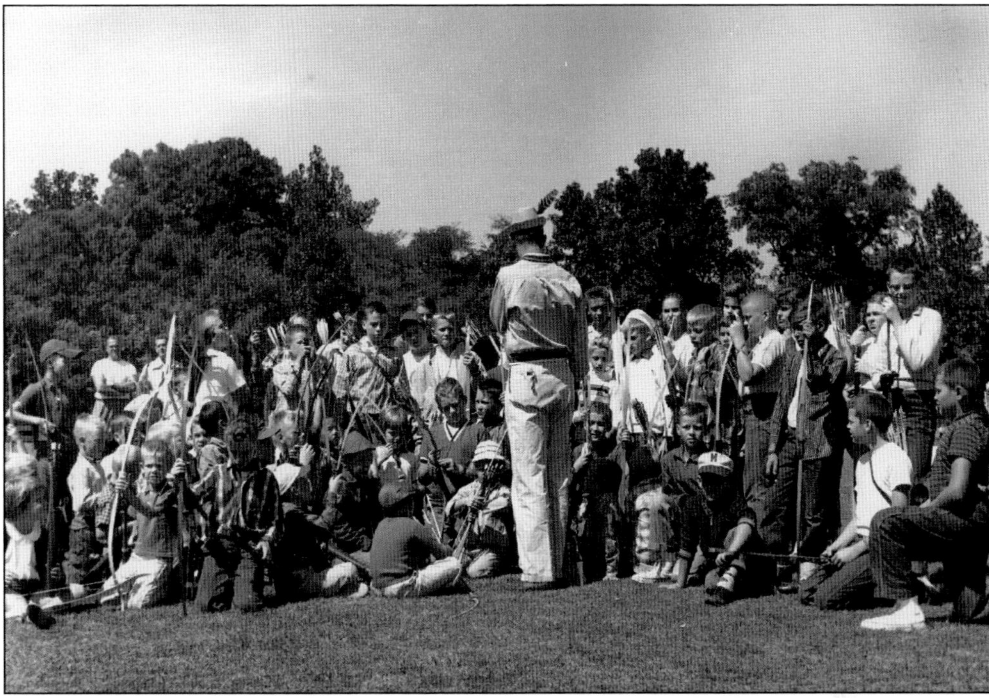

ROBIN HOOD AND HIS CREW. More than 200 children attended the Robin Hood Tournament, sponsored by Valleydale Athletic Club and the Hamilton County Park District. Blackburn donned a Robin Hood costume for the event. Based on the number of arrows in the target (below), the tournament was judged a success. Despite Blackburn's efforts to maintain the vibrancy of the archery program, it fell victim to budget cuts in the early 1960s, after a series of tax levies were voted down.

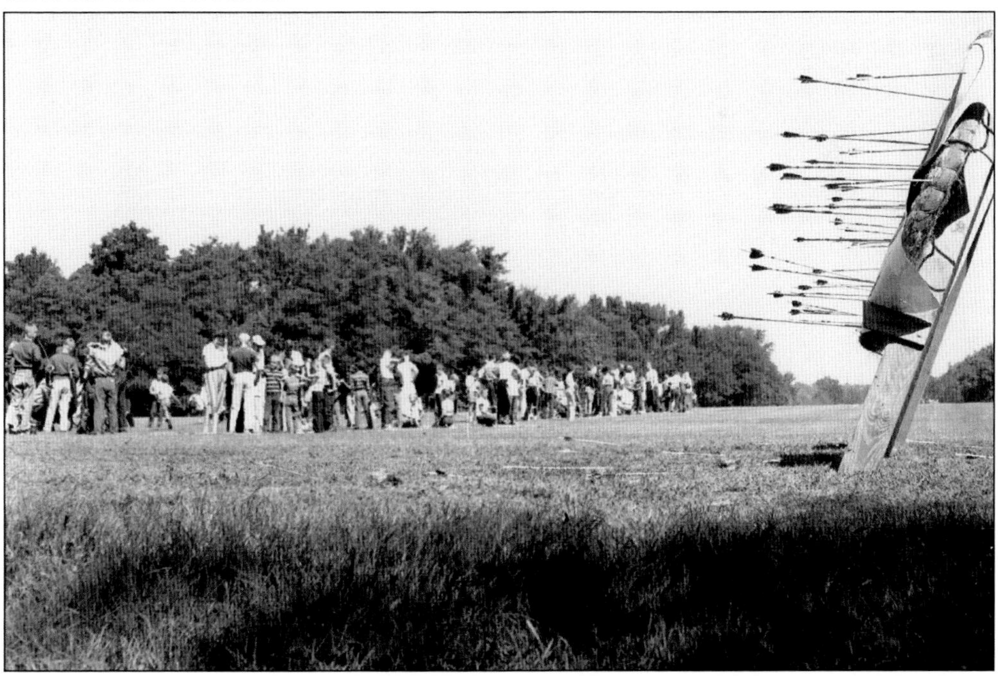

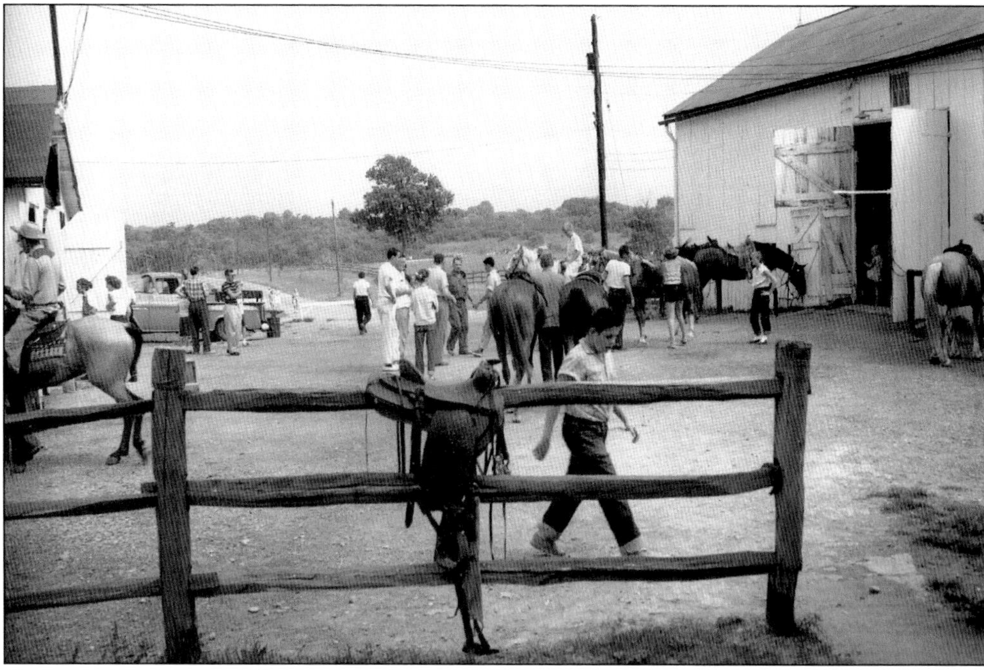

CALLING ALL RIDERS. Winton Woods opened an equestrian riding center in 1954. Park officials usually stabled 40 to 50 horses each year. However, on many occasions, there were more riders than available horses. The riding center offered lessons for riders of all ages, from circle pony trails to guided horse trails that ranged all over the park. About half the horses were stabled in the winter at Miami Whitewater Forest. Those horses that remained at Winton Woods were available for rental purposes for advanced riders, who were permitted to ride without staff supervision during the winter months.

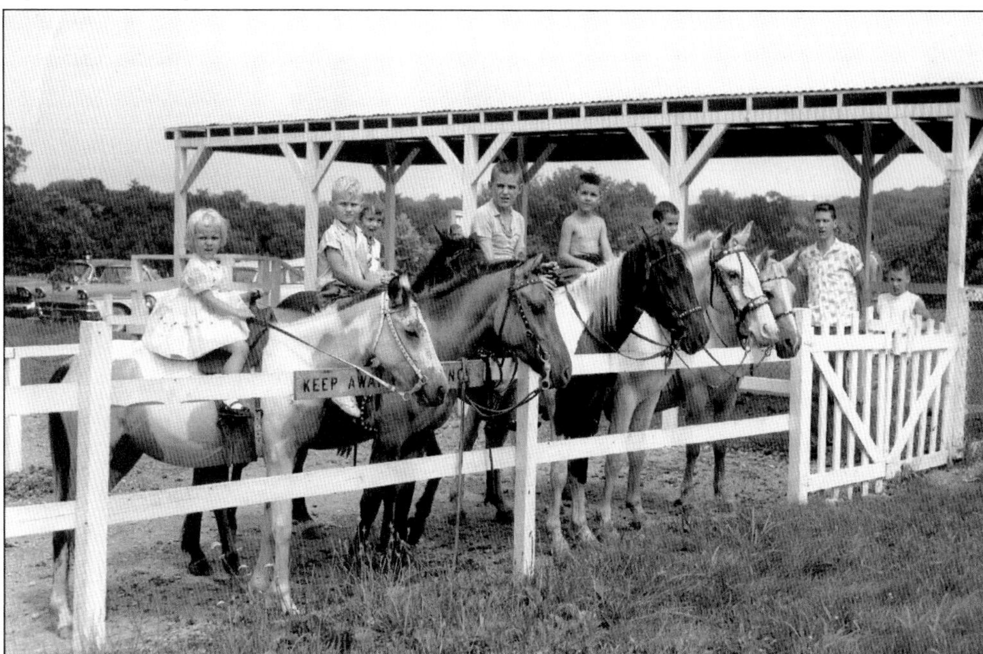

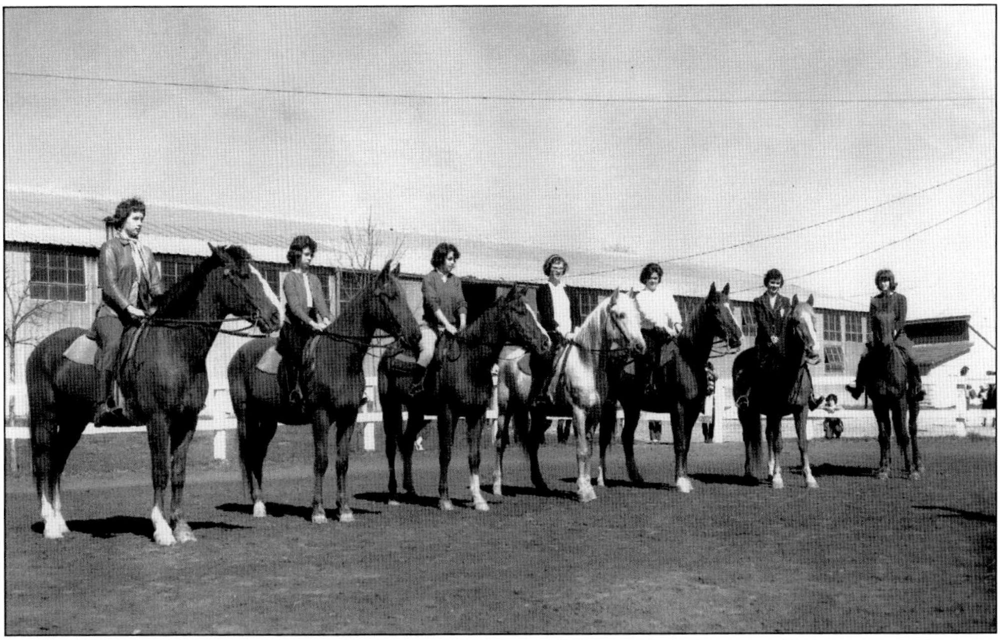

GIRLS AND HORSES. The affinity between girls and horses has been well documented, from classic movies such as *National Velvet* to toy lines such as My Little Pony. The riding center seemed to be no exception to this rule.

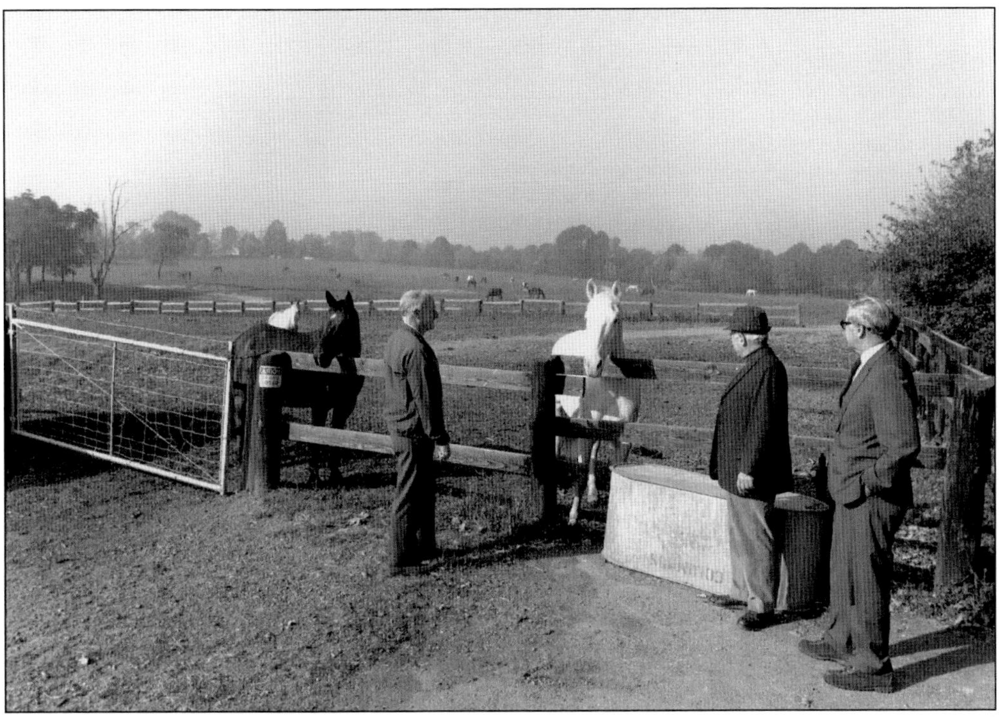

CLOSE ENCOUNTERS. Park commissioners, from left to right, Sam Benedict, Louis Nippert, and Justin Rollman inspect horses at the riding center. By the late 1950s, hayrides became another popular attraction at the riding center.

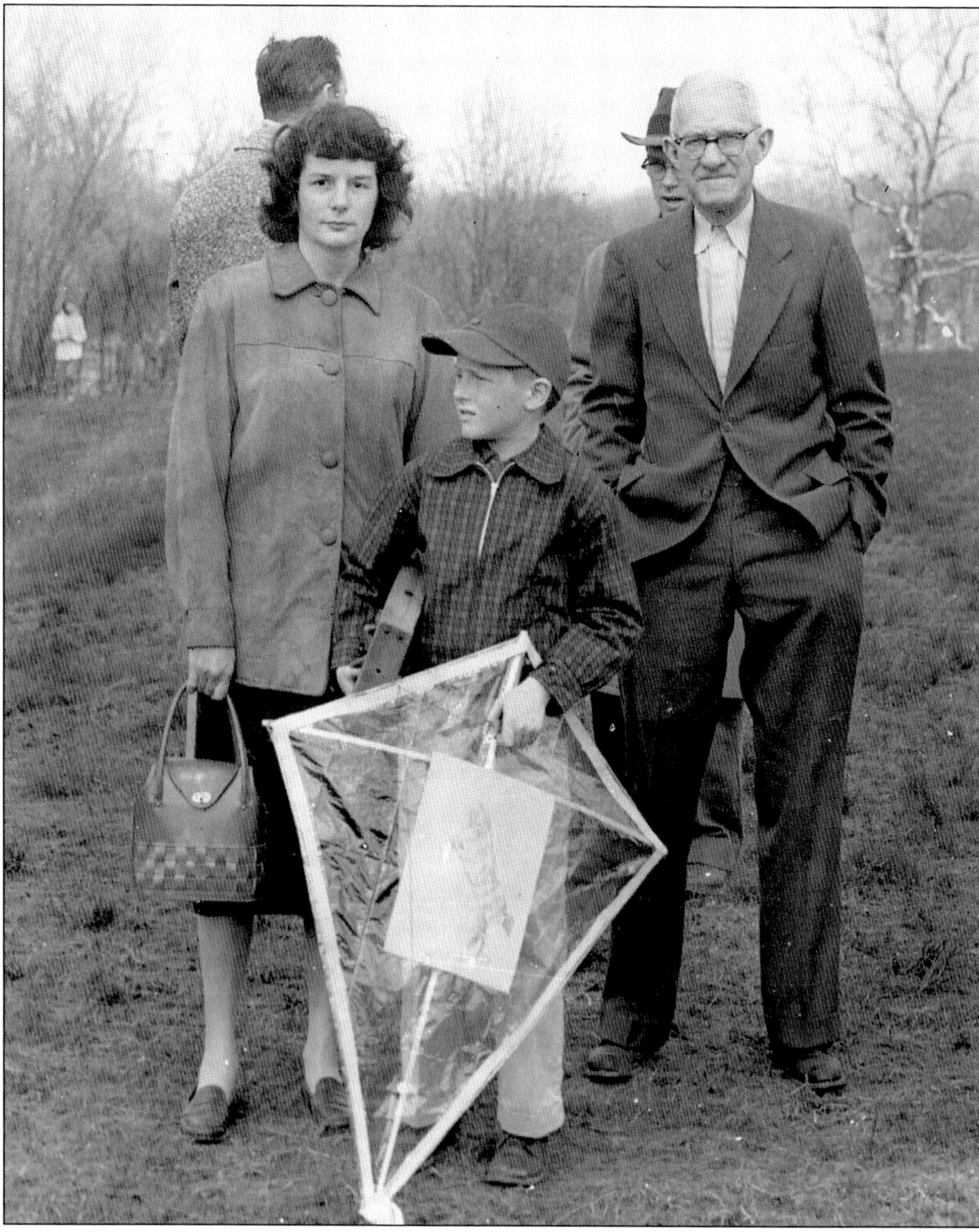

Let's Go Fly a Kite! Beginning in the mid-1950s, Sharon Woods began hosting an annual kite-flying contest each spring. Advertisements ran in local newspapers to generate interest among children. Awards were handed out for the largest and the smallest kite, the most creative design, and the highest-flying kite. Prizes were donated each year by St. Michael's Council of the Knights of Columbus, in Sharonville. Glenn Mason (center) won the prize for the largest kite in March 1957. His mother and great-grandfather William Tate accompanied the boy to the park.

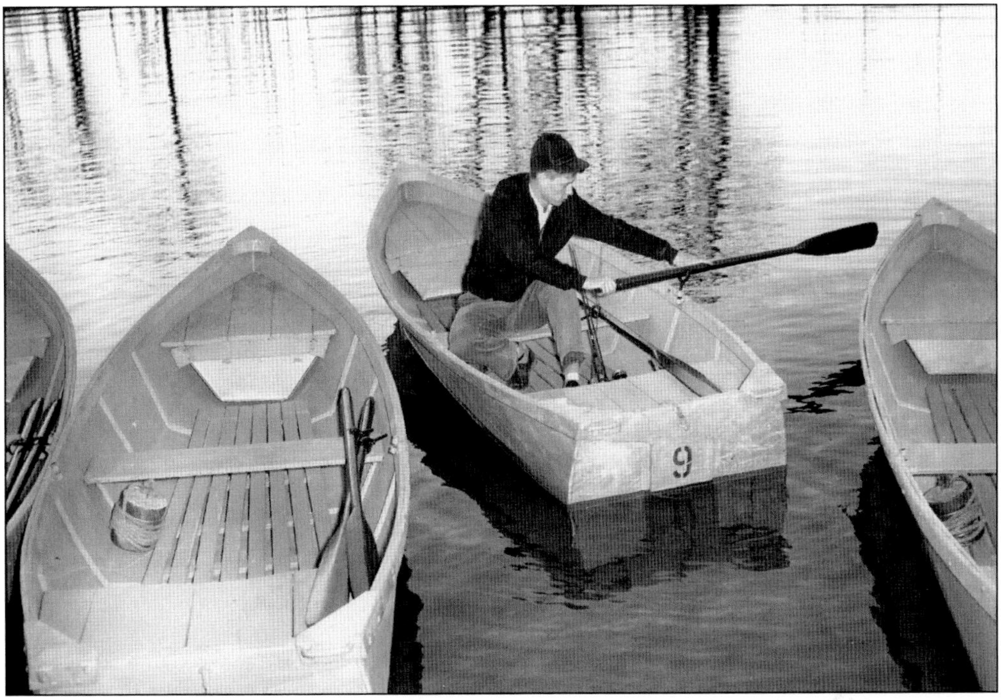

THE EARLY WORM GETS THE FISH. Harold W. Kamm, of Lockland, beats the crowds on opening day of the fishing season on March 17, 1957.

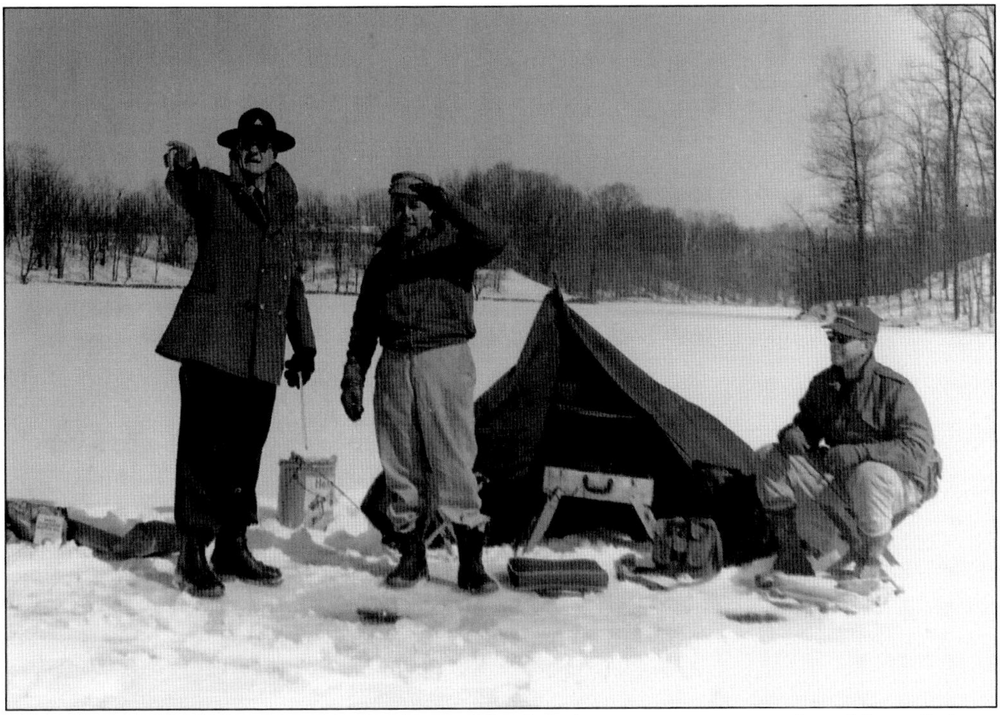

YEAR-ROUND FISHING. A ranger at Sharon Woods Lake assists two intrepid ice fishers. Fishing attracted more than 6,200 visitors to Sharon Woods in 1960.

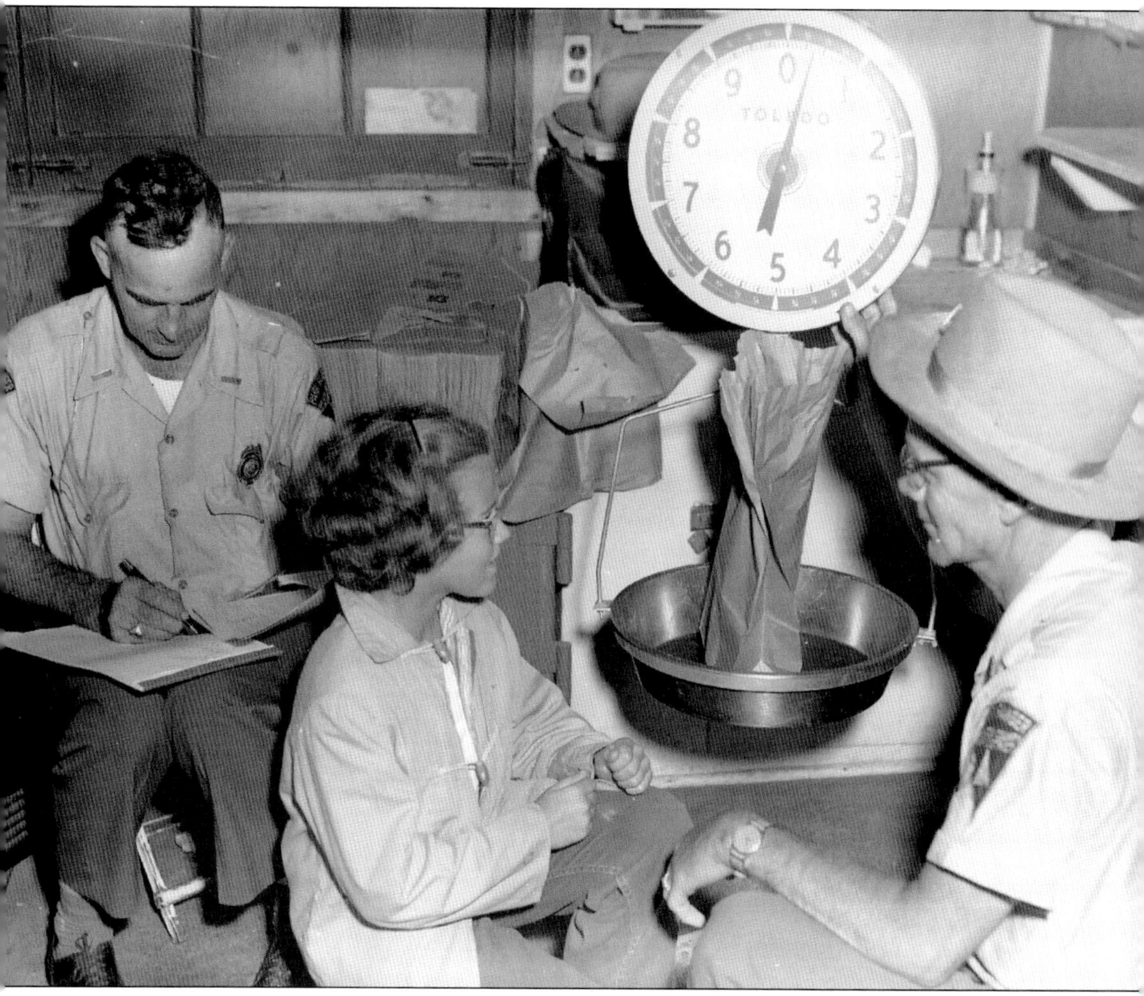

LEARNING EARLY. An old parable goes like this: "Give someone a fish, and they have food for a day. Teach them to fish, and they have food for a lifetime." Perhaps this was part of the reason why, in 1957, the Hamilton County Park District sponsored a fishing derby at its three parks. Learning any new sport or skill at an early age offers a sense of accomplishment and builds self-esteem. Park officials offered a series of free lessons in the weeks leading up to the competition. The final elimination round took place at Winton Woods Lake. Park commissioners were on hand to award prizes to the winners. Nancy Gentener (above) anxiously waits as park rangers prepare bait for the contest.

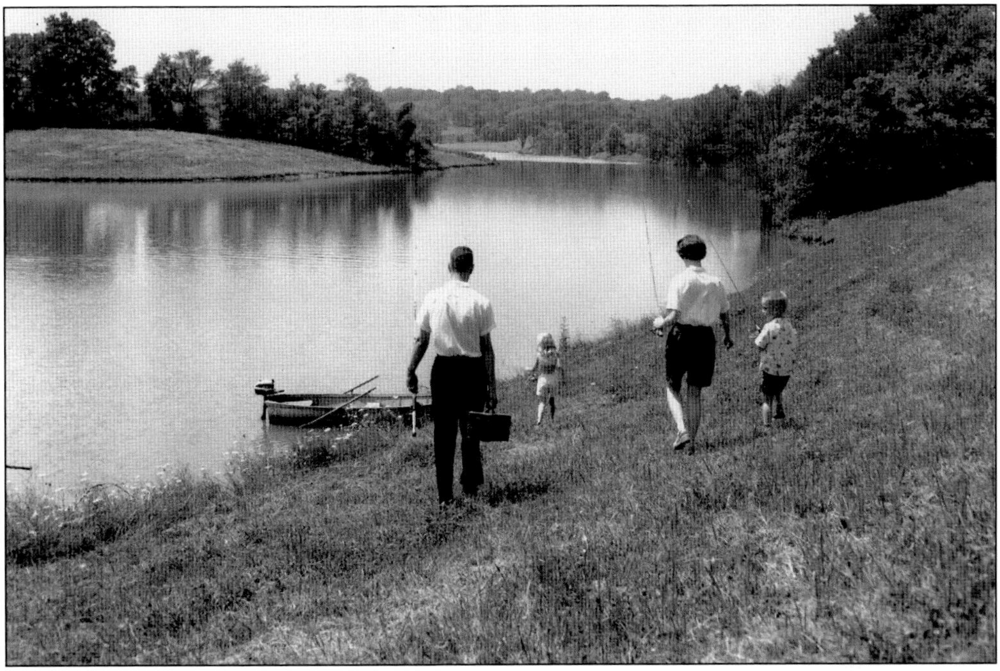

FAMILY FISHING. Winton Woods Lake attracted the most attention from area fishing enthusiasts. In 1960 alone, more than 11,000 people fished at the park. The larger lake and the new campground facilities made Winton Woods an attractive weekend getaway for families that enjoyed fishing.

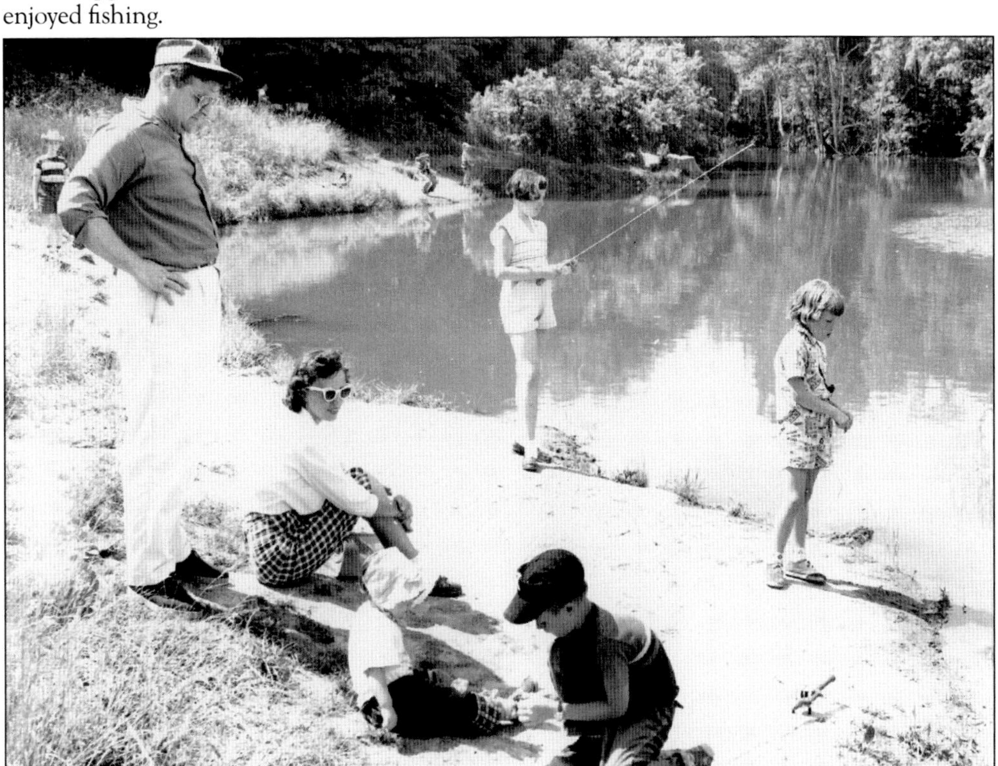

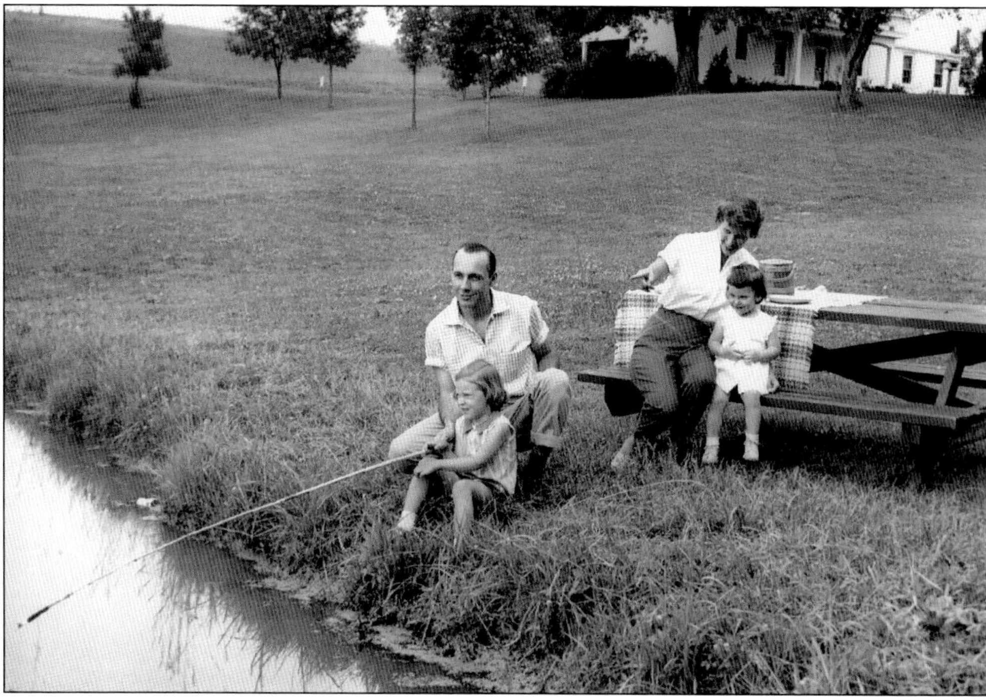

PATIENCE IS A VIRTUE. Greenhills residents Bill and Rita Galle offer pointers to their two young daughters as they engage in some family fun along the banks of Winton Woods Lake.

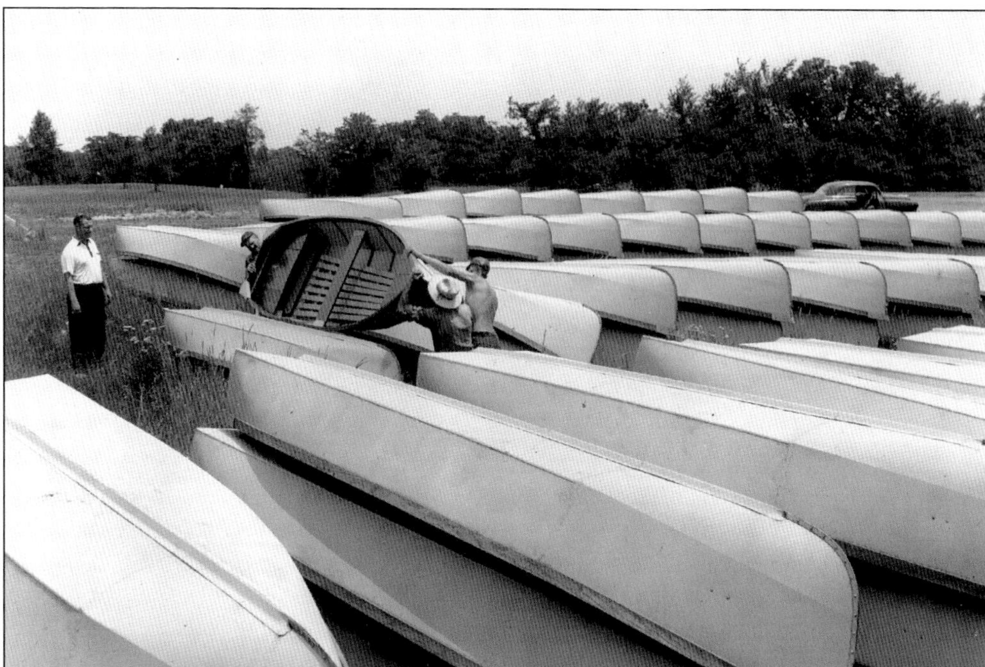

MAINTAINING THE FLEET. Each year thousands of rented boats made excursions at Sharon Woods Lake and Winton Woods Lake. Boats had to be maintained in observance of state water safety standards.

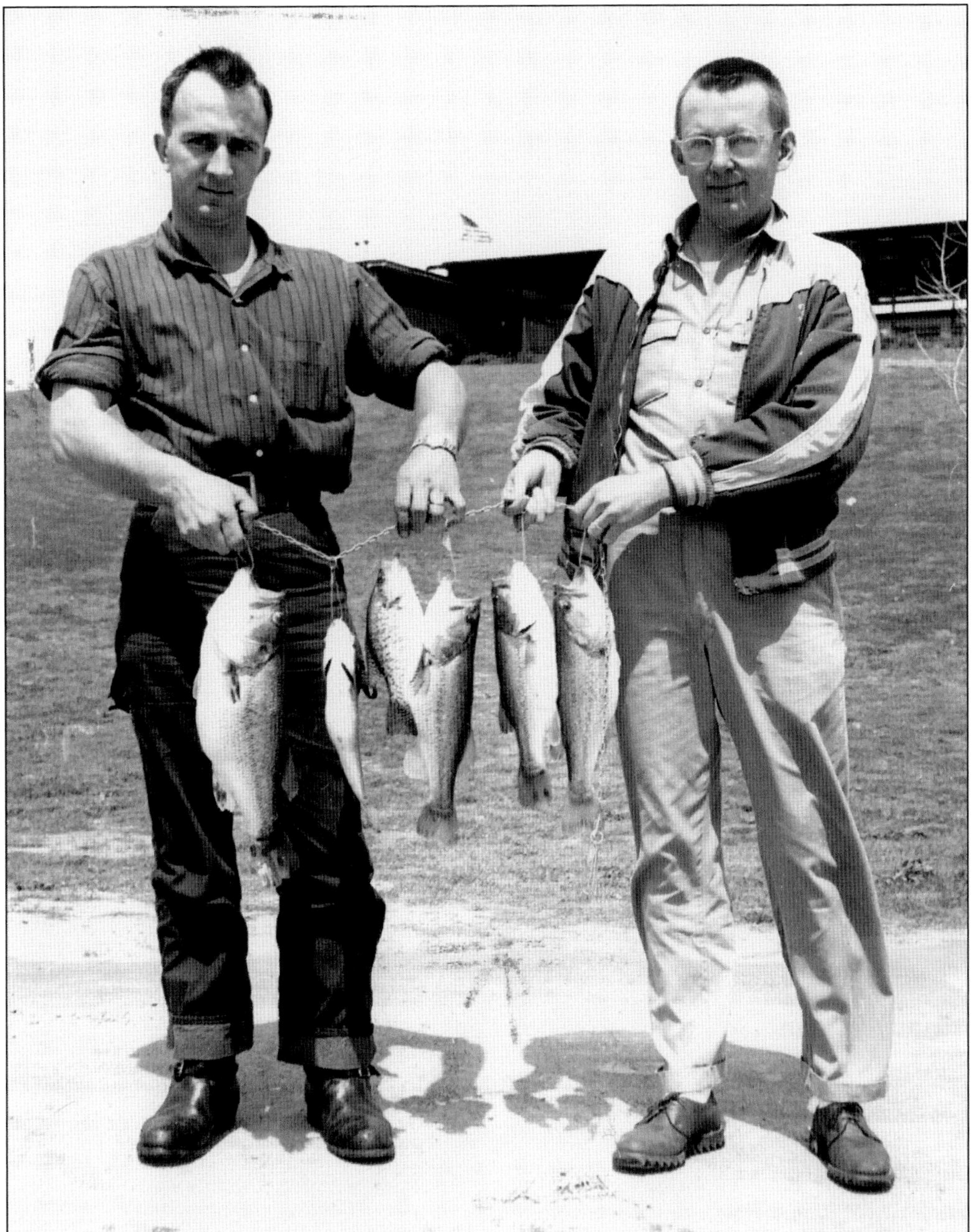

CATCH OF THE DAY. Two Green Township residents, Edward A. Clements (left) and Hubert Schultze, proudly display their fish caught at Winton Woods Lake. Park officials stocked Winton Woods and Sharon Woods with northern pike. Channel catfish enthusiasts had to travel to the Miami Whitewater Forest.

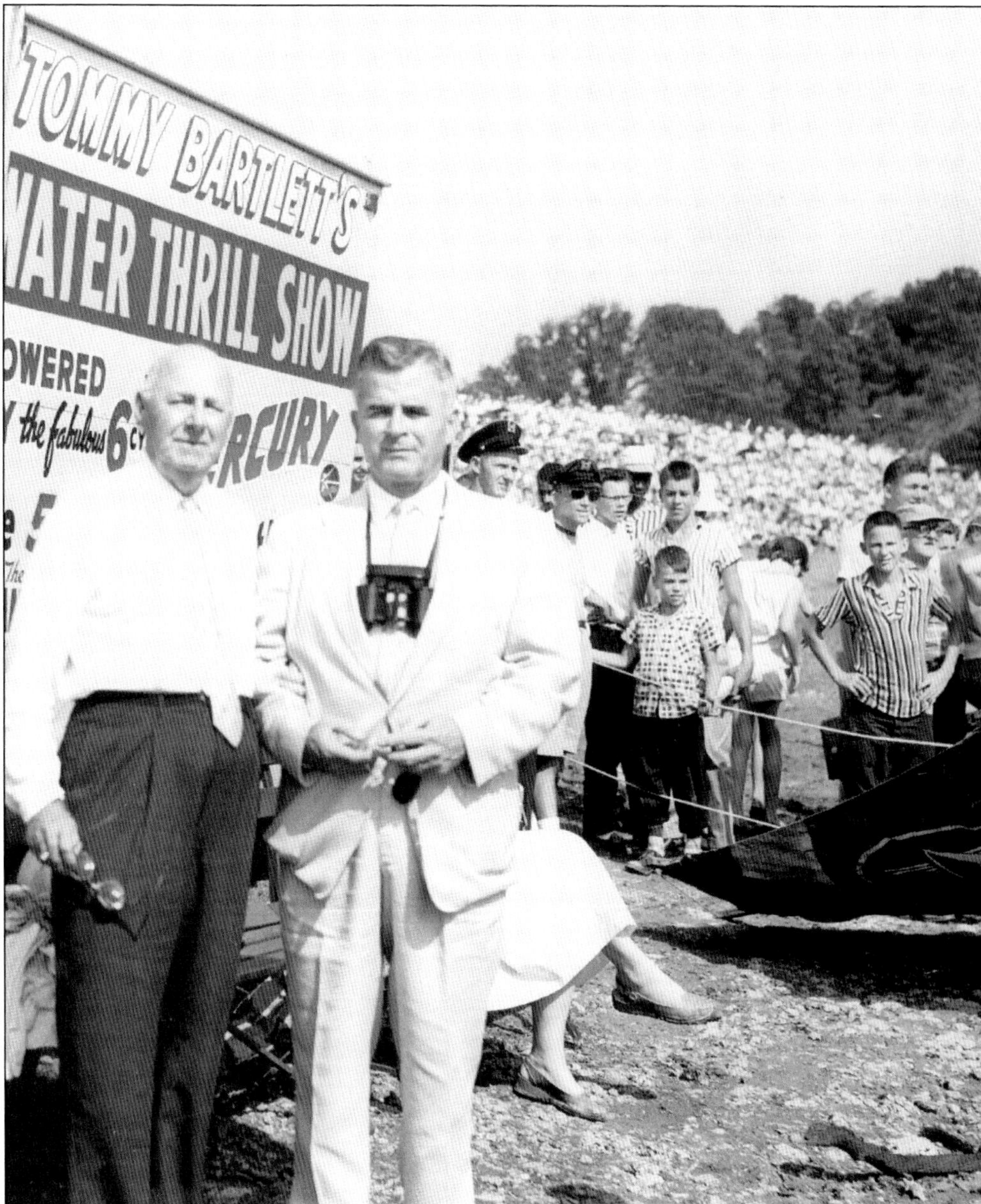

THE BIG DAY ARRIVES. Hamilton County park commissioner Sam Benedict (left) and Louis Nippert anxiously await the start of the Tommy Bartlett Water Thrill Show, which took place on August 3, 1958. The park district was eager to showcase all the recently developed areas in the park. An estimated 70,000–80,000 visitors streamed into Winton Woods that day to see the spectacle. Bartlett developed his shows at Cypress Gardens, Florida, and turned them into traveling roads shows. By the 1950s, four groups of performers toured simultaneously across the United States. Bartlett's shows even attracted the attention of the United States Service Organization. For two years, his performers entertained servicemen in such far-flung places as Guam, Okinawa, Burma, Japan, and South Korea.

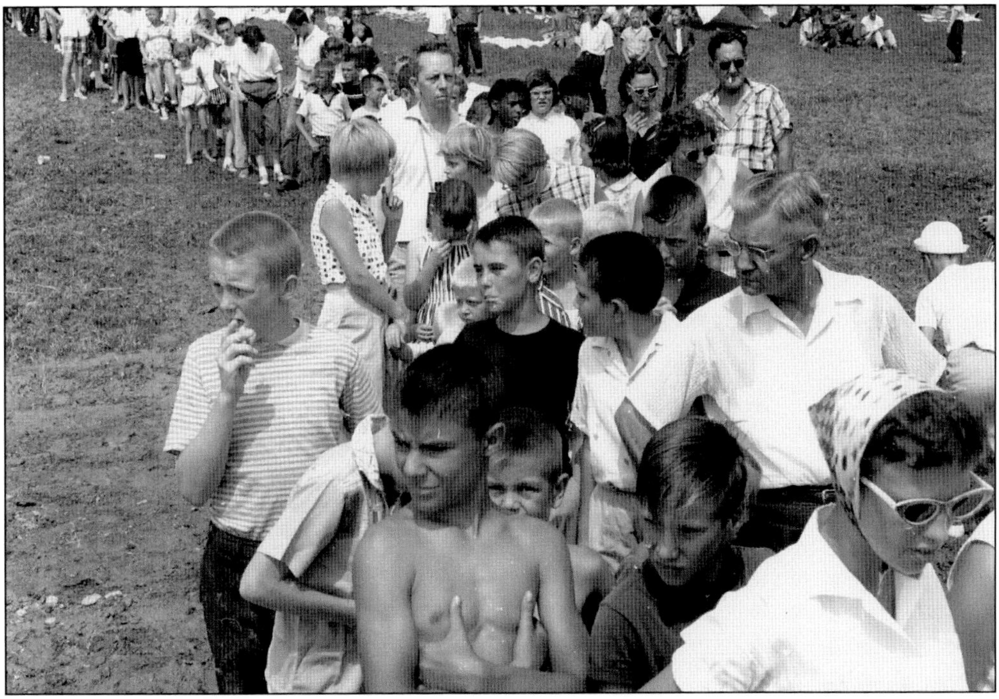

THRILLS AND SPILLS, BUT NO CHILLS. Eager onlookers arrived early to stake a small piece of turf. Some arrived hours prior to the event. Those who braved the sunshine were rewarded with a vantage point from the shores of the lake. Others sought out what little shade the young trees around the lake provided.

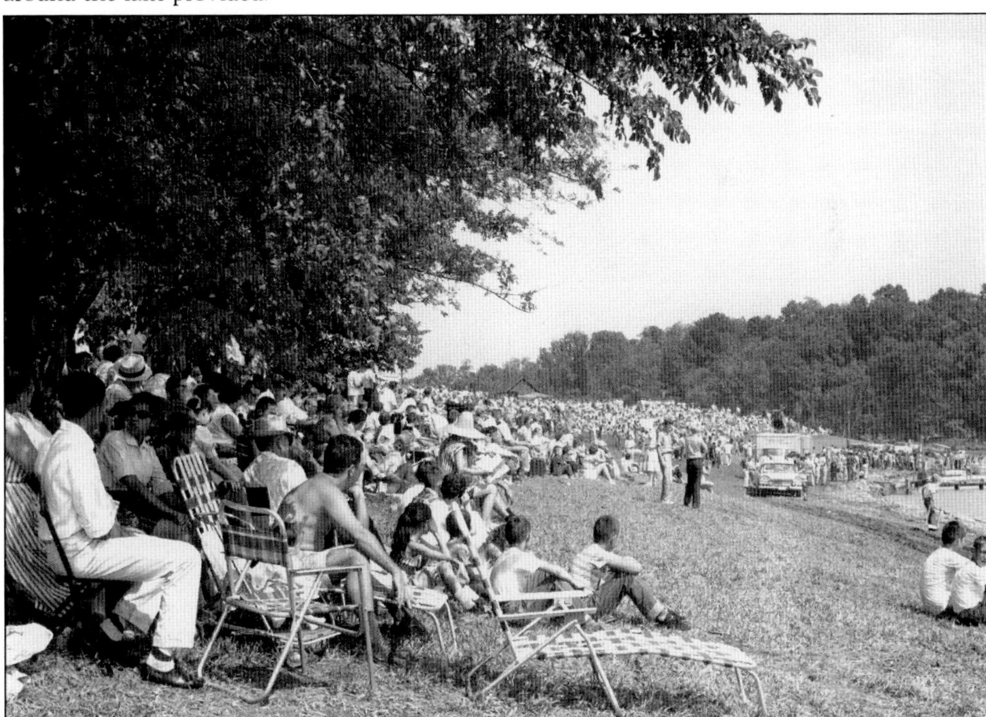

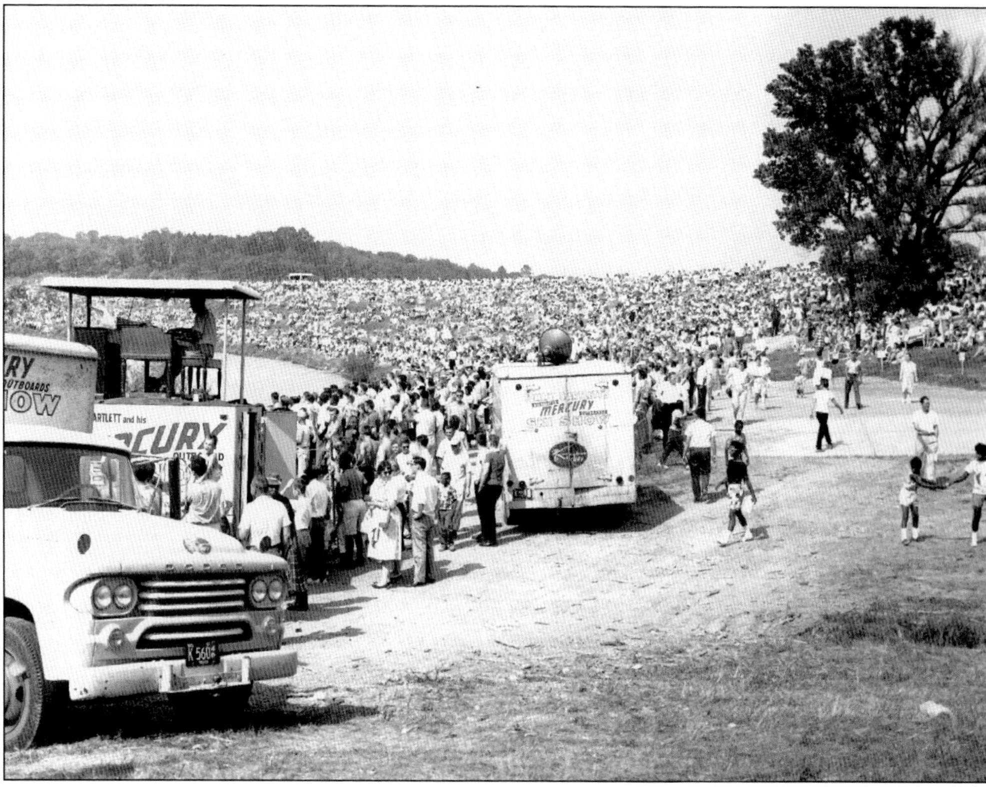

A MEMORABLE DAY. Motorboat rides were available to those guests who came early. Park officials were impressed with the massive turnout and the overall good behavior of the crowds.

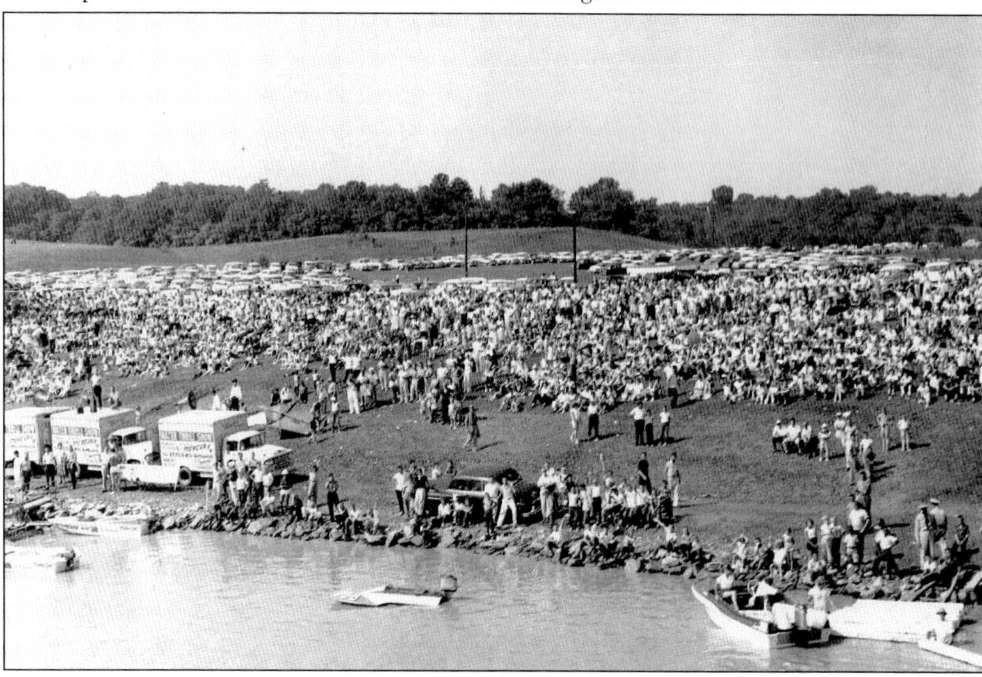

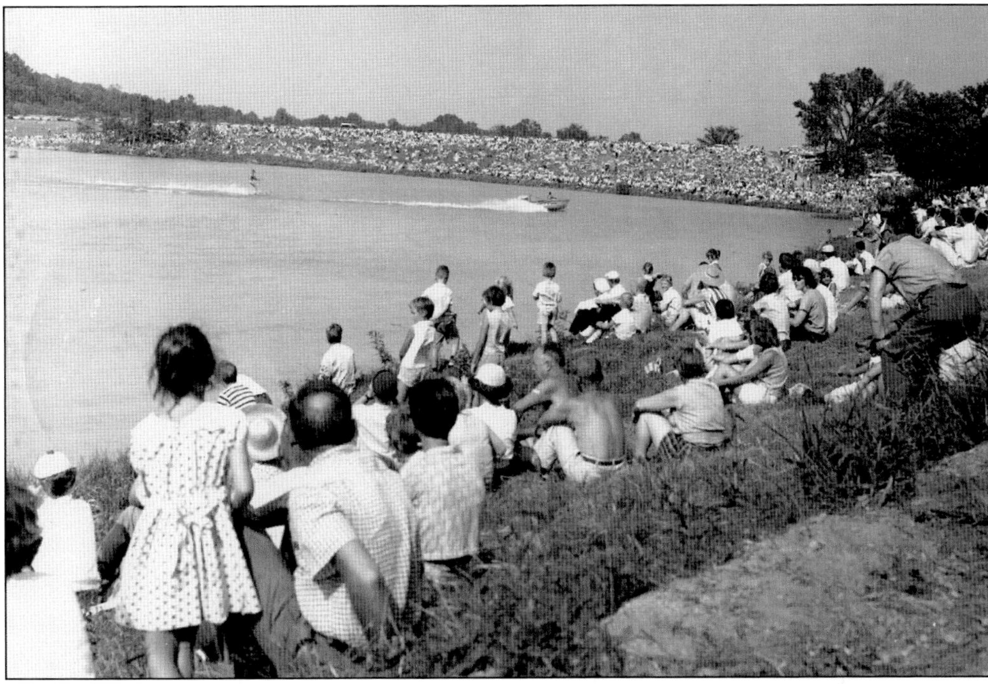

THANK YOU, TOMMY BARTLETT! An appreciative crowd delights at the acrobatic antics of the water-skiers (above). Park officials struggled to accommodate all the cars that arrived for the show. As crowded as the parking lot appeared, an estimated 20,000 people trying to attend the show found themselves stuck in traffic on roads leading into the park.

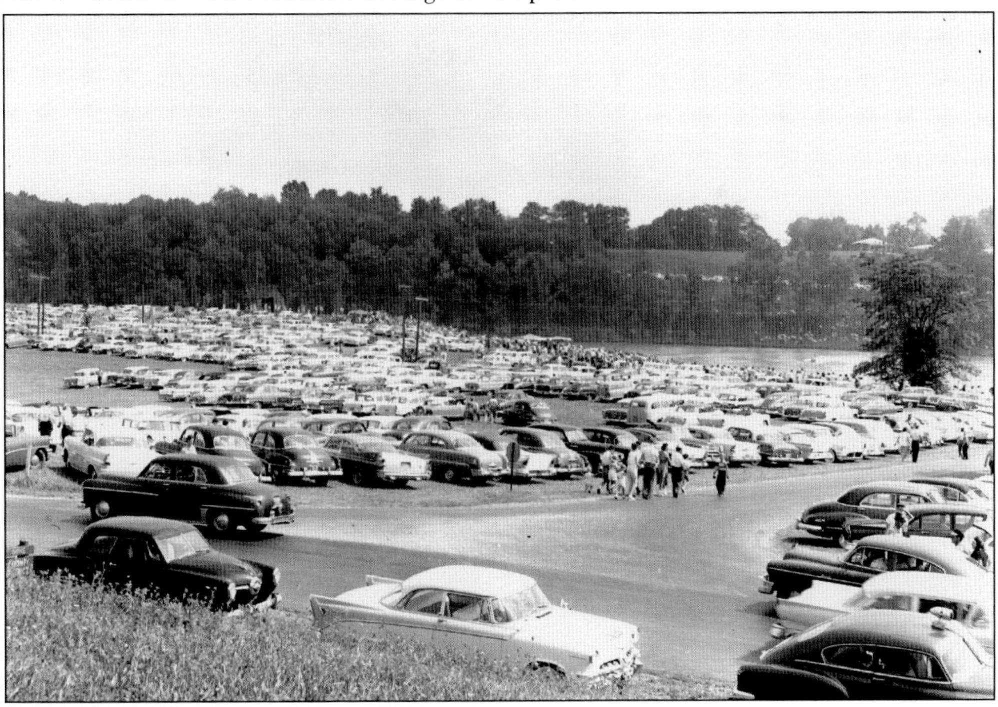

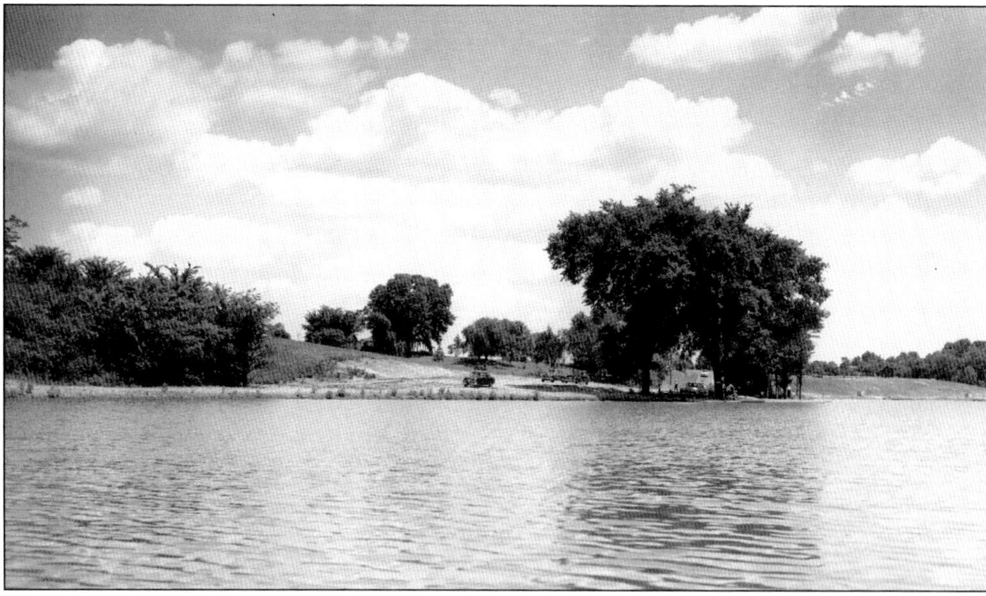

WINTON WOODS LAKE, IN GOOD TIMES AND BAD. Under normal conditions, picnickers enjoy the site on the shore on Winton Woods Lake (above). As previously stated, part of the rationale for creating Winton Woods Lake was to act as a flood-control reservoir. The Mill Creek rose to 62.2 feet during the Great Flood of 1937 and to an even more impressive height, 69.2 feet, in March 1945, when the Mill Creek Barrier Dam broke. Even the construction of the West Fork Dam did not protect the area completely. In January 1959, freakish weather conditions caused most of the state's smaller streams to flood their banks. Three to six inches of rain fell in a short period of time on snow-covered ground. The snowed melted and combined with the rain runoff to produce flood conditions in many parts of the state. During the 1959 flood, Harbor Point was nearly submerged (below).

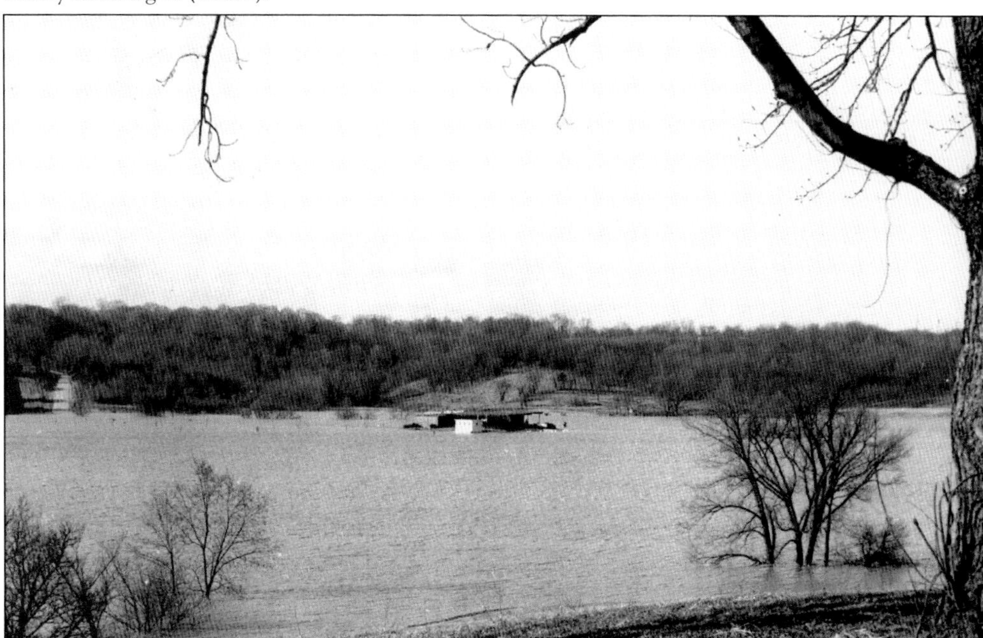

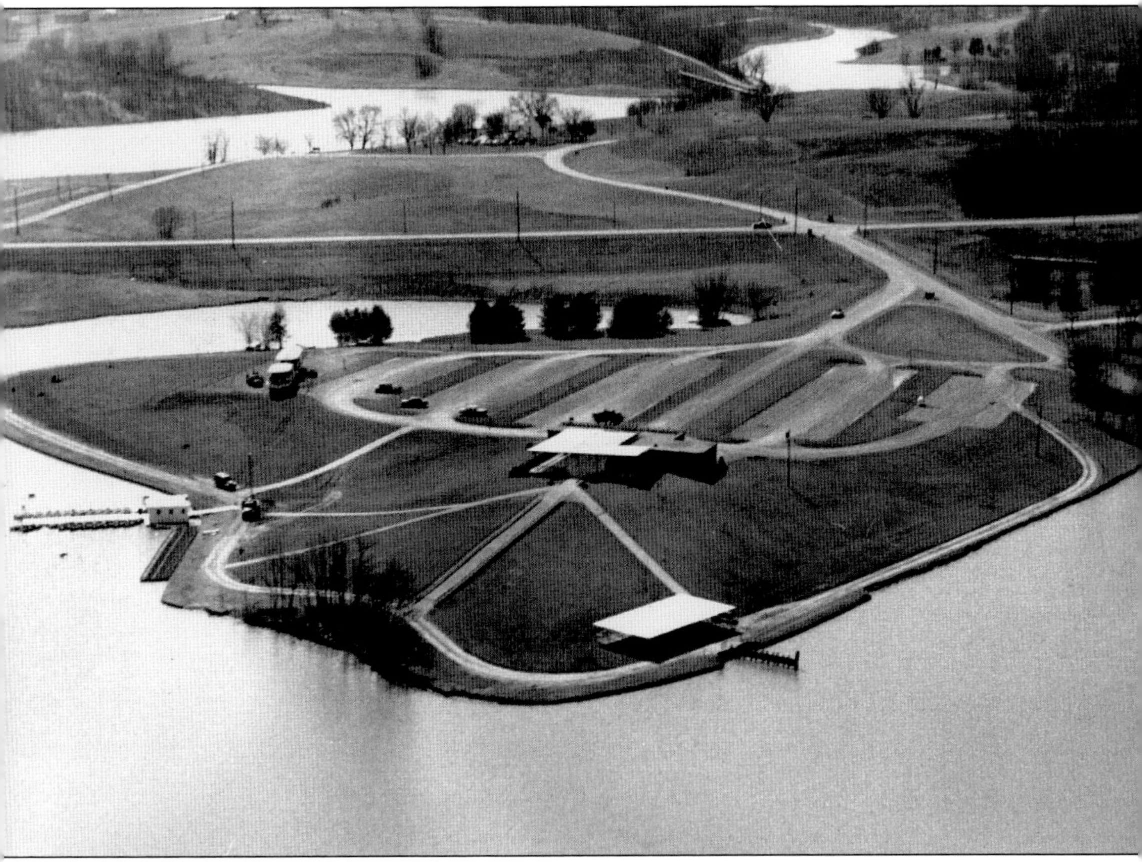

GOOD AS NEW. The aerial view of Harbor Point and Winton Woods Lake shows that by the summer of 1959, park workers cleared away all evidence of the floodwaters.

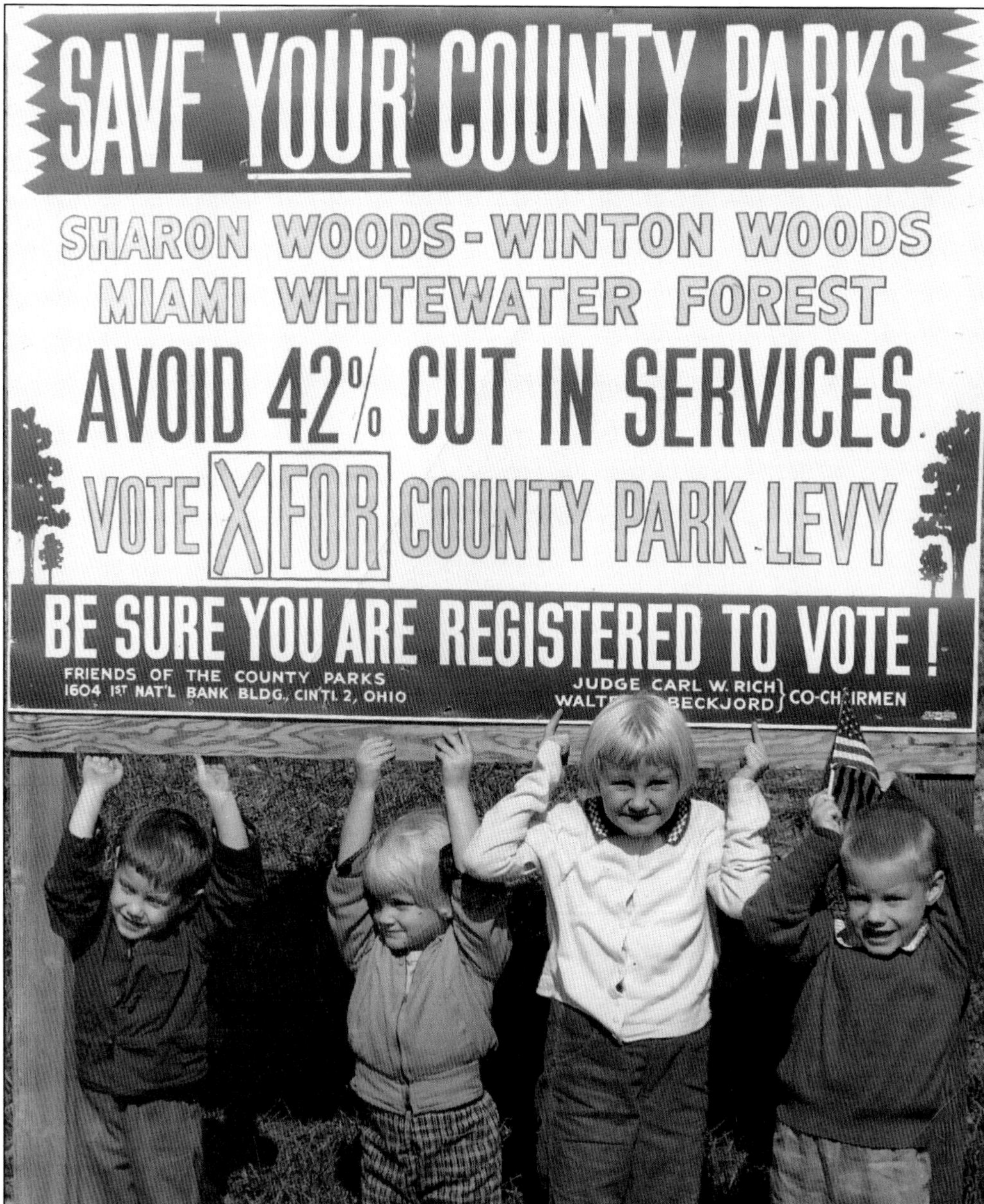

CALLING ALL VOTERS. Hamilton County park commissioners could point to many physical improvements and new services in the park district throughout the 1950s, especially at Winton Woods. In 1958, for the first time, annual attendance at the three county parks exceeded three million. Yet, throughout the decade, the park district mounted a series of tax levy campaigns, only to see them fall short of the necessary support. Levies were needed to help meet annual operating costs of the three parks. Commissioners also wanted to acquire new lands that could be developed into parks for future generations. During the 1960 election, Judge Carl W. Rich and Walter E. Beckjord served as cochairs of the Friends of the County Parks Committee to support the latest levy campaign. The committee issued a press release and photograph that featured four Greenhills children from the Croskey family: from left to right, John, 4; Jeri, 3; Jo Ann, 7; and Jimmy, 5, who appear with a sign that alerted voters of the upcoming levy.

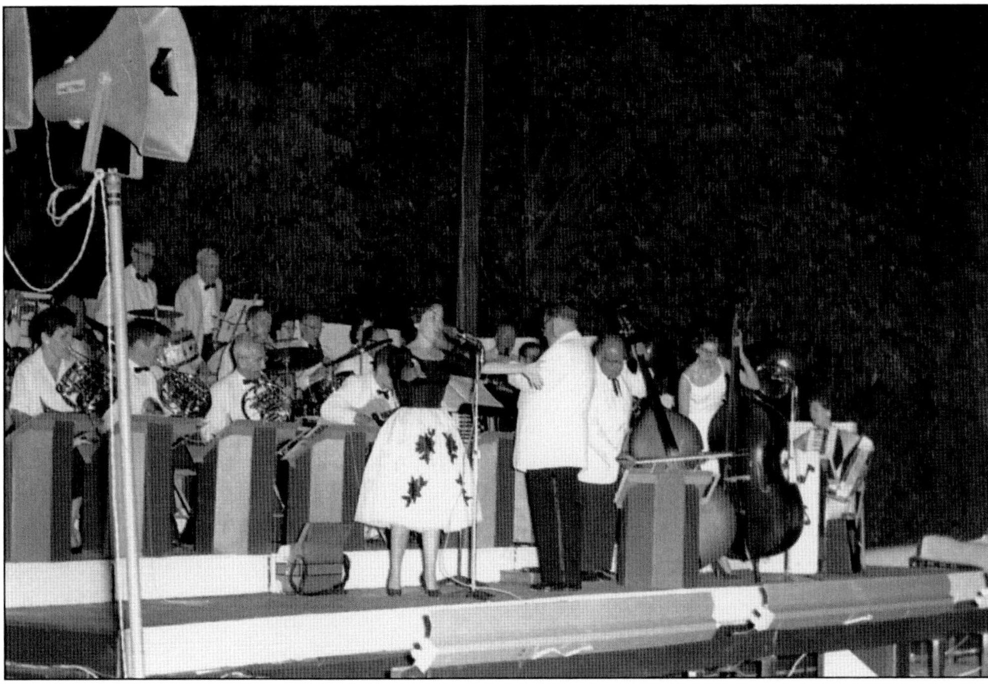

CONCERTS FOR A CAUSE. The idea of holding free outdoor concerts in Hamilton County parks dates back to the days of the New Deal in the 1930s. A WPA music group had petitioned the park commissioners for permission to organize a concert. The record is unclear if the concert ever transpired. Nearly two decades later, in 1958, the Cincinnati Musician's Association inaugurated an annual concert series. Musicians performed at Harbor Point in Winton Woods. During the 1960 season, concerts helped promote awareness for the upcoming levy.

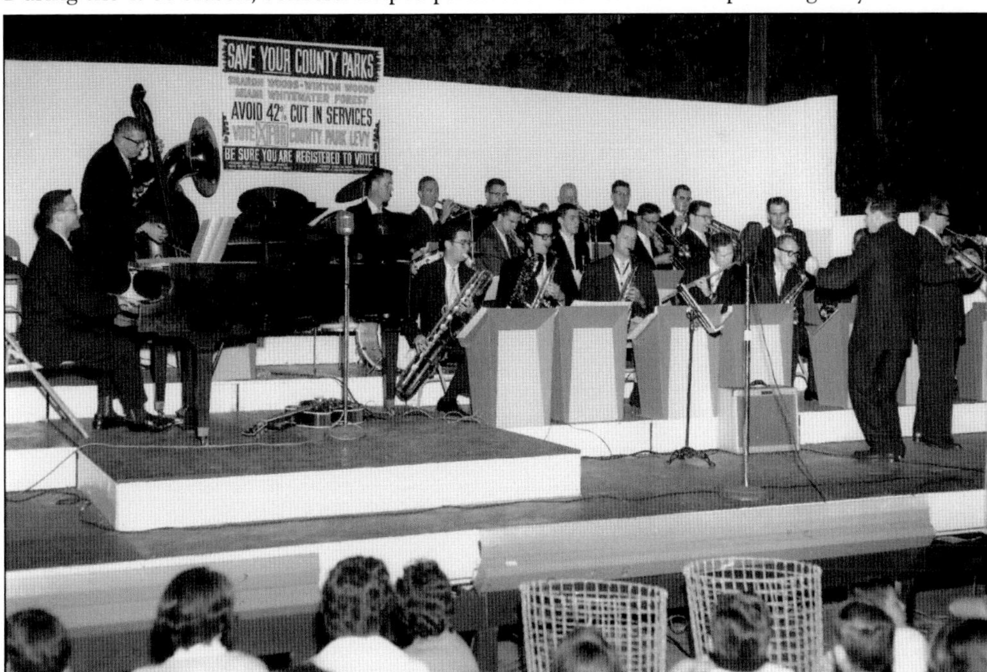

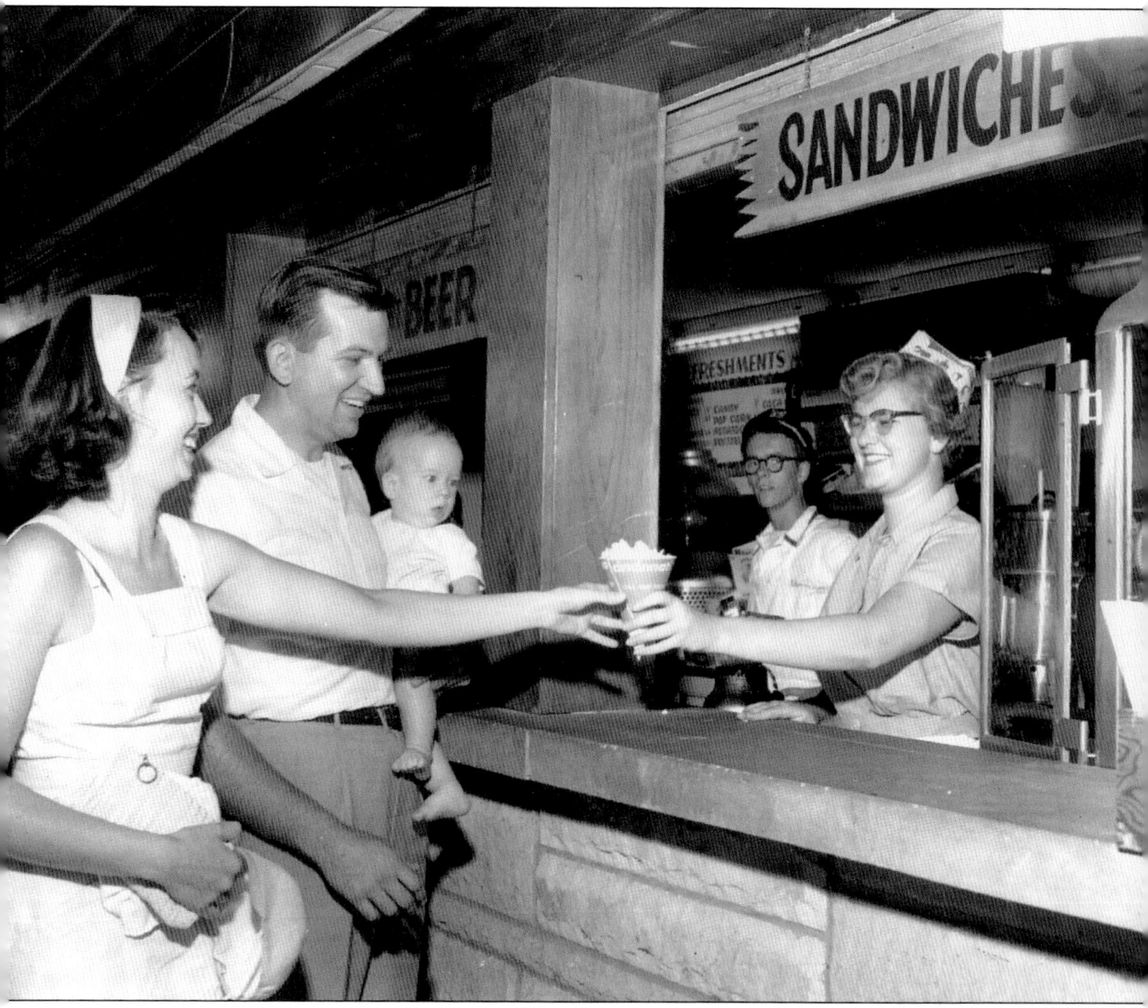

Showcasing the Parks. In the months leading up to the fall election, Hamilton County park commissioners drew attention to the best the parks had to offer their taxpayers. Guests enjoy refreshments at Winton Woods' Harbor Point concession stand on County Park Day in October 1960.

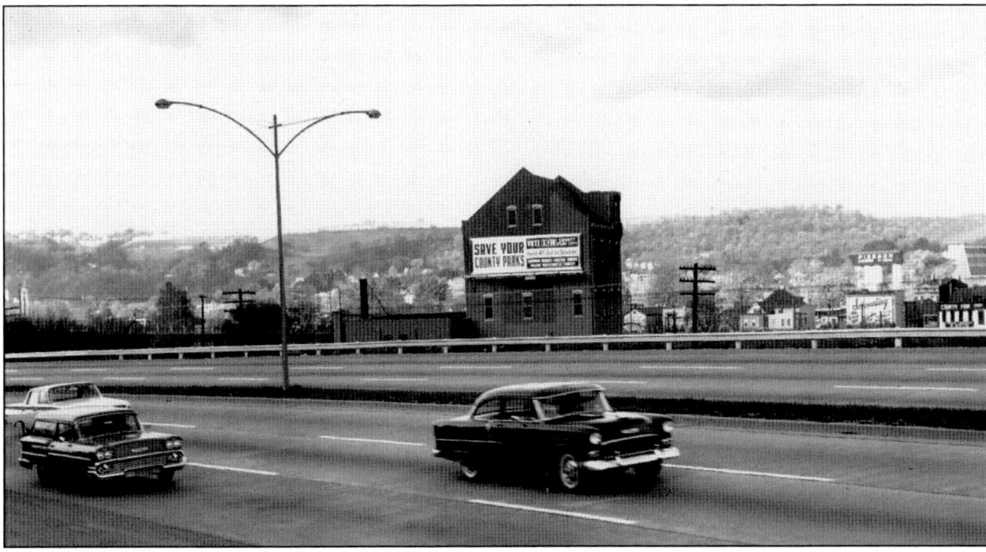

CREATIVE CAMPAIGNING. The Friends of County Parks Committee sponsored a billboard campaign in autumn 1960. Signs appeared on major commuter routes. It also assembled a telephone committee to place calls on the eve of election day to remind voters about the crucial levy. Two members of the telephone committee discuss campaign strategy with park commissioners Louis Nippert (second from right) and Sam Benedict (right).

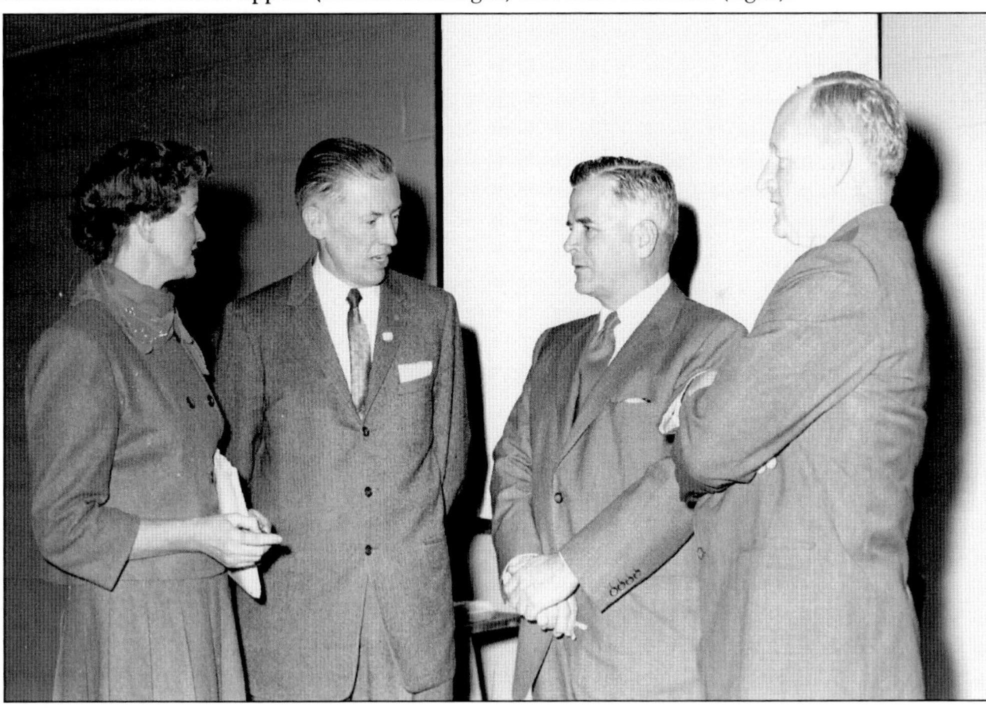

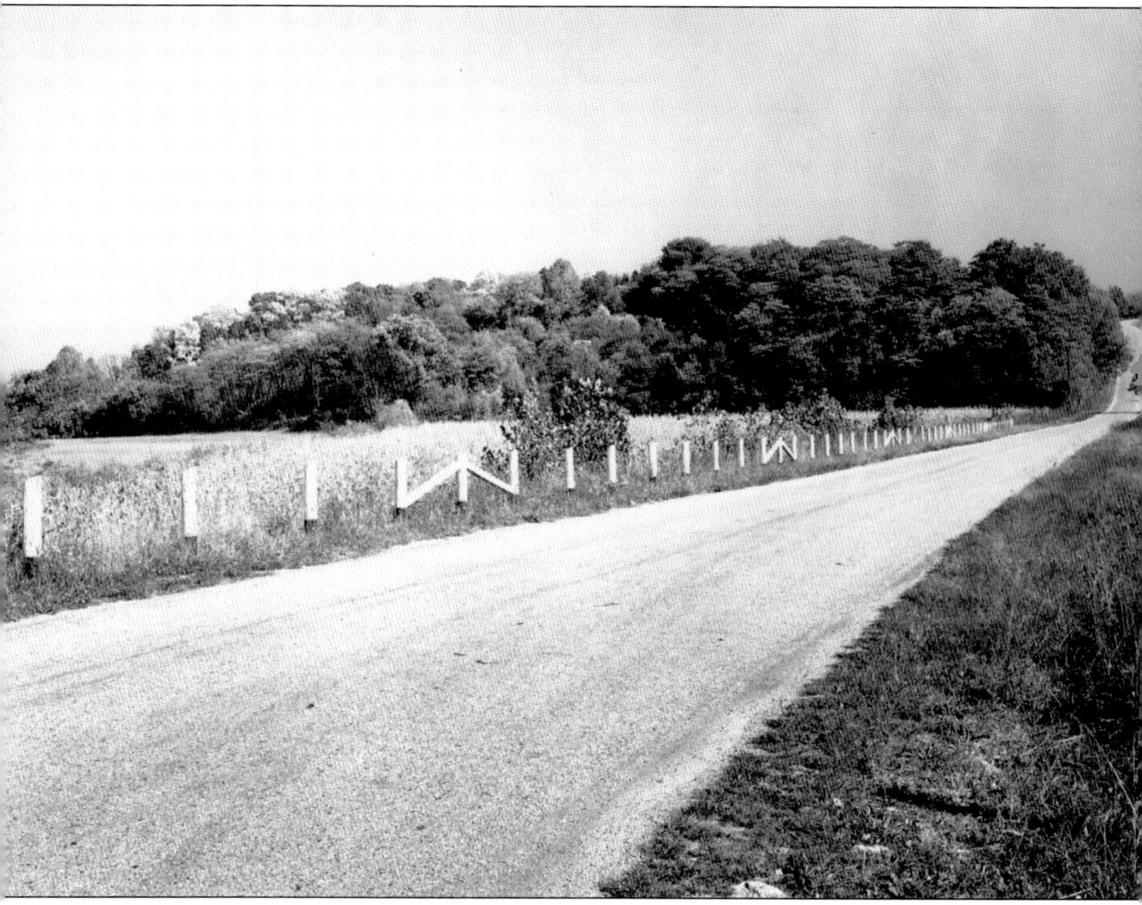

MUCH WORK TO BE DONE. In the end, however, efforts fell short and the levy failed. The voters' decision to turn down the levy raised many questions. Clearly Hamilton County residents voted with their feet each year; steady attendance at all the parks suggested a high level of support. The majority of voters, however, seemed content to endorse the status quo. They did not necessarily embrace the notion of paying higher taxes to enable the park district to expand. Moreover, the electorate's preoccupation with the presidential race may have overshadowed voters' awareness of local issues. One political commentator speculated that the televised debates between Democratic challenger John F. Kennedy and Vice Pres. Richard M. Nixon (which were the first of their kind) captured the attention of the nation. He concluded that the "television encounters between Nixon and Kennedy occupied so much of the political attention of the electorate that there was little left for local affairs." Consequences of the failed levy became clear. Some programs, such as archery, were disbanded. The park district adopted admission fees to the parks. Beginning in 1961, visitors were required to purchase either an annual sticker or a day pass for their vehicle. In addition, the schedule for improvements at Miami Whitewater Forest (above) would have to be deferred.

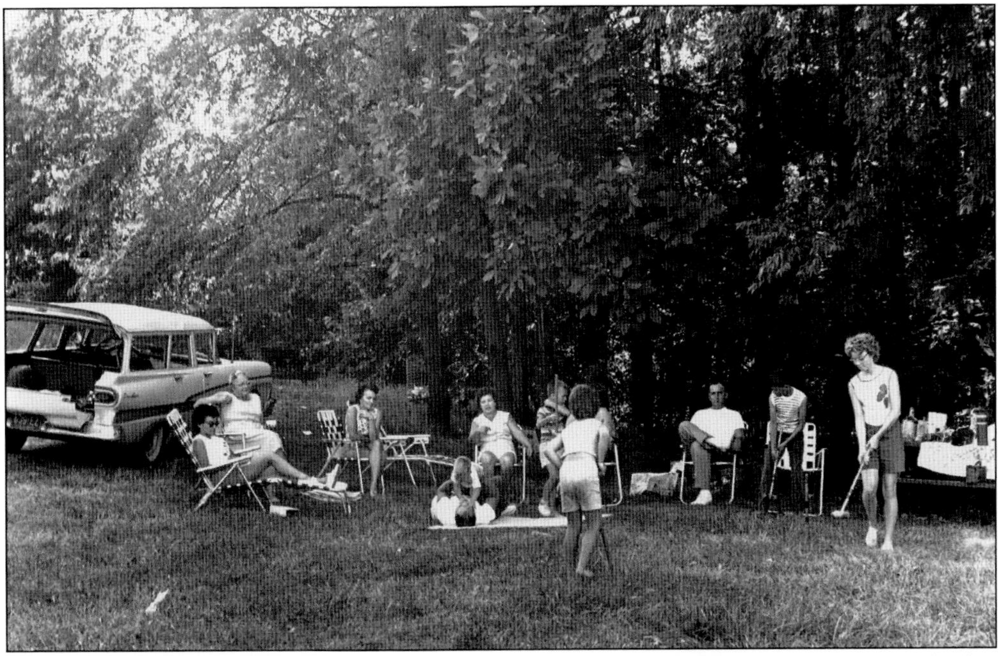

Biding Their Time. Meanwhile, visitors continued to make use of the picnic area and fished in the Timberlake region of the park.

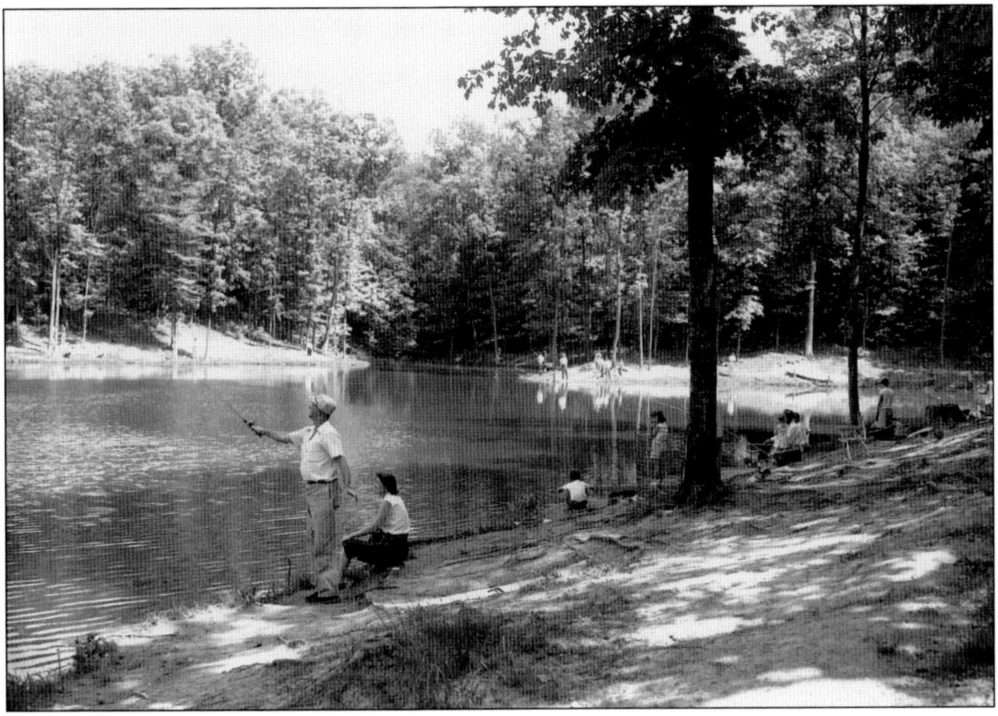

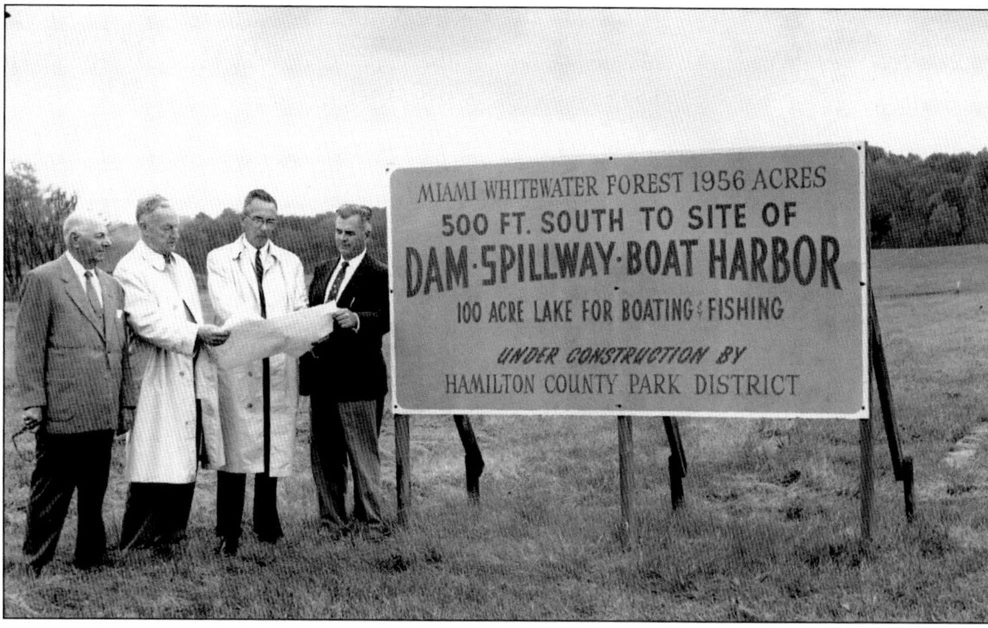

FORGING AHEAD. The Hamilton County park commissioners (above) look over blueprints for the excavation of the future lake and dam at Miami Whitewater Forest. Similar to the construction of Sharon Woods Lake in the 1930s, workers removed topsoil from the future lake site so it could be used to develop the sculpted areas of a golf course that was being designed.

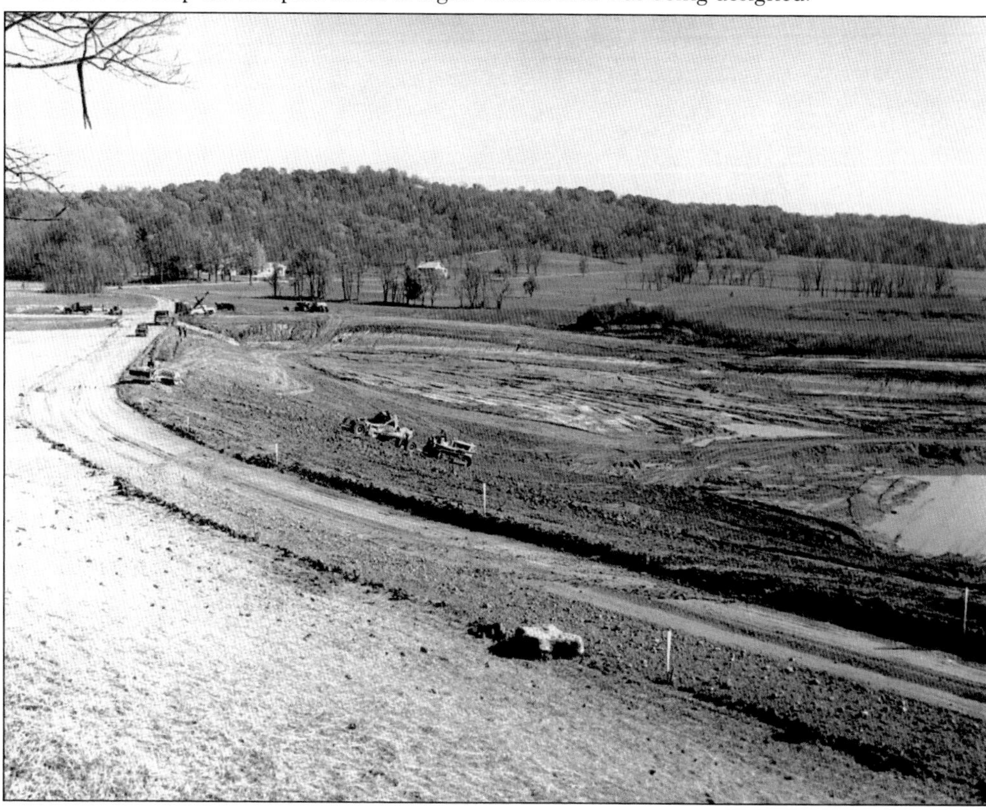

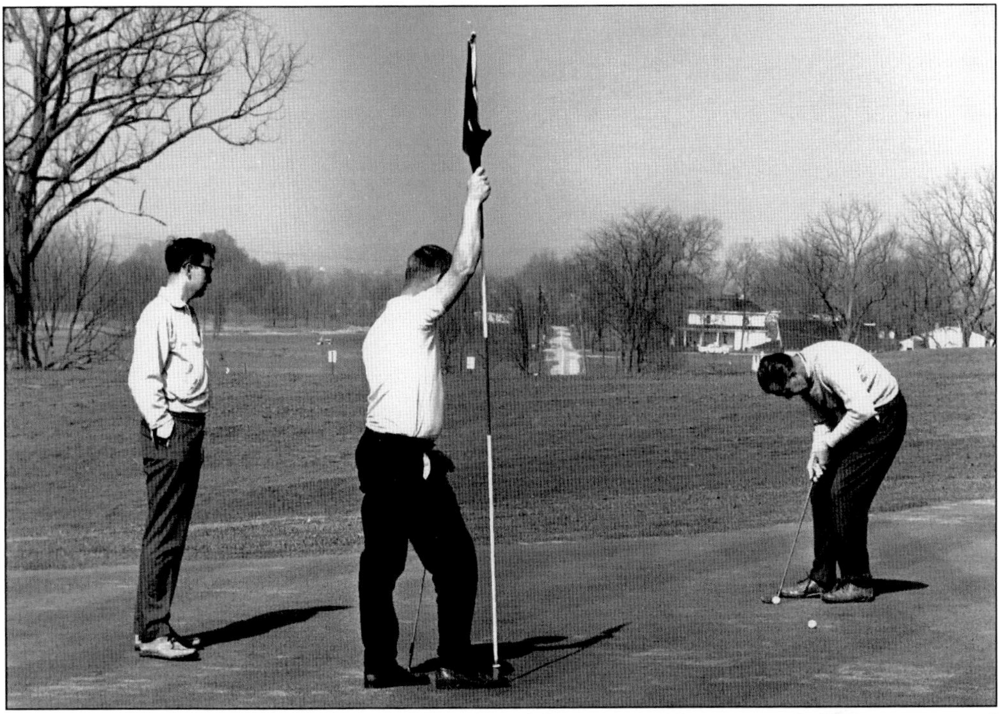

A THIRD GOLF COURSE. The front nine holes of the Miami Whitewater Golf Course opened for public play in May 1962. One year later, the back nine opened. The greens fee in 1962 was a mere $1.25. Golf manager Marty Kavanaugh organized an industrial golf league that included the Cincinnati Shaper Company, a machine tool company, and the National Lead Company, in Fernald, where uranium was processed for the nation's atomic and nuclear weapons during the cold war.

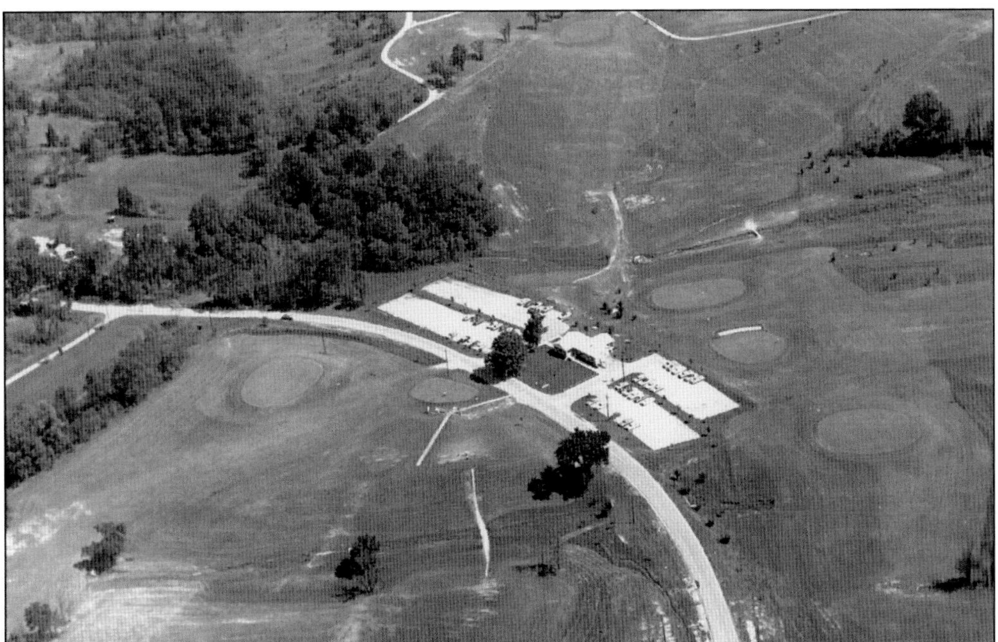

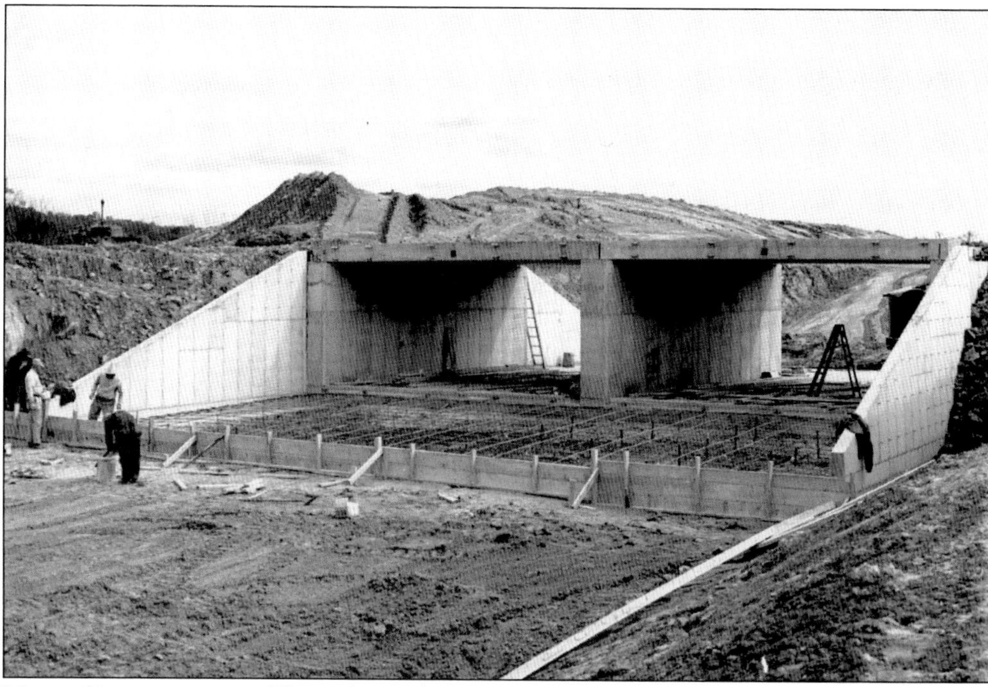

MORE CONSTRUCTION. Throughout the 1960s, workers were kept busy on a variety of construction projects at Miami Whitewater Forest. New roads were laid out and existing paths were paved. The lake excavation was finally completed in 1969. Three years later, the lake and a newly constructed boathouse were ready for visitors.

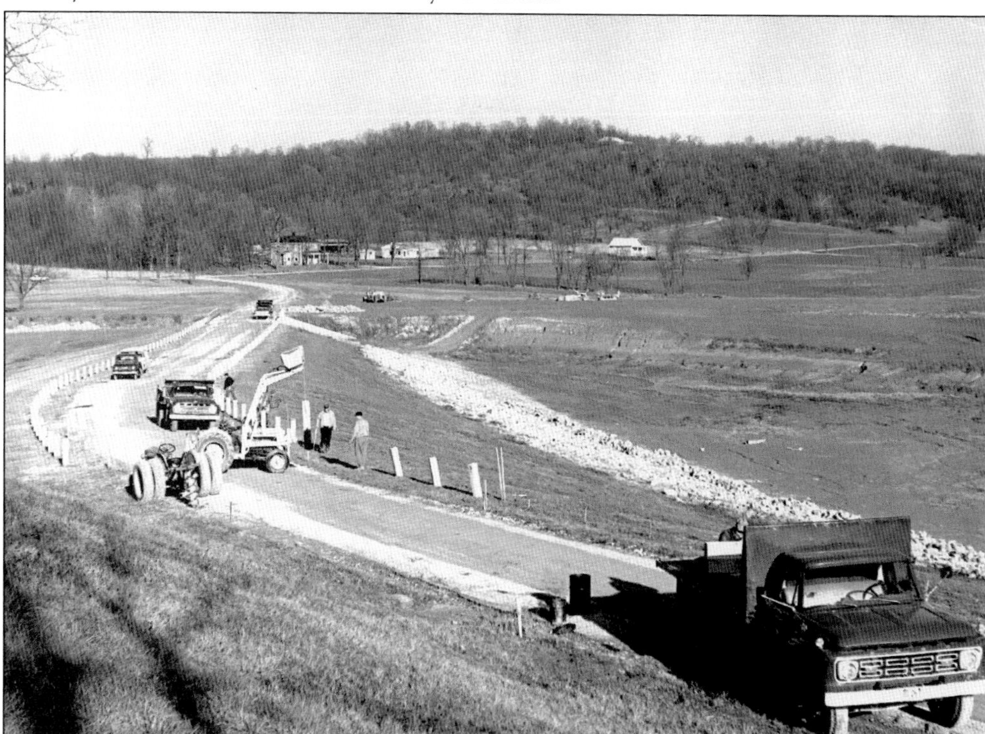

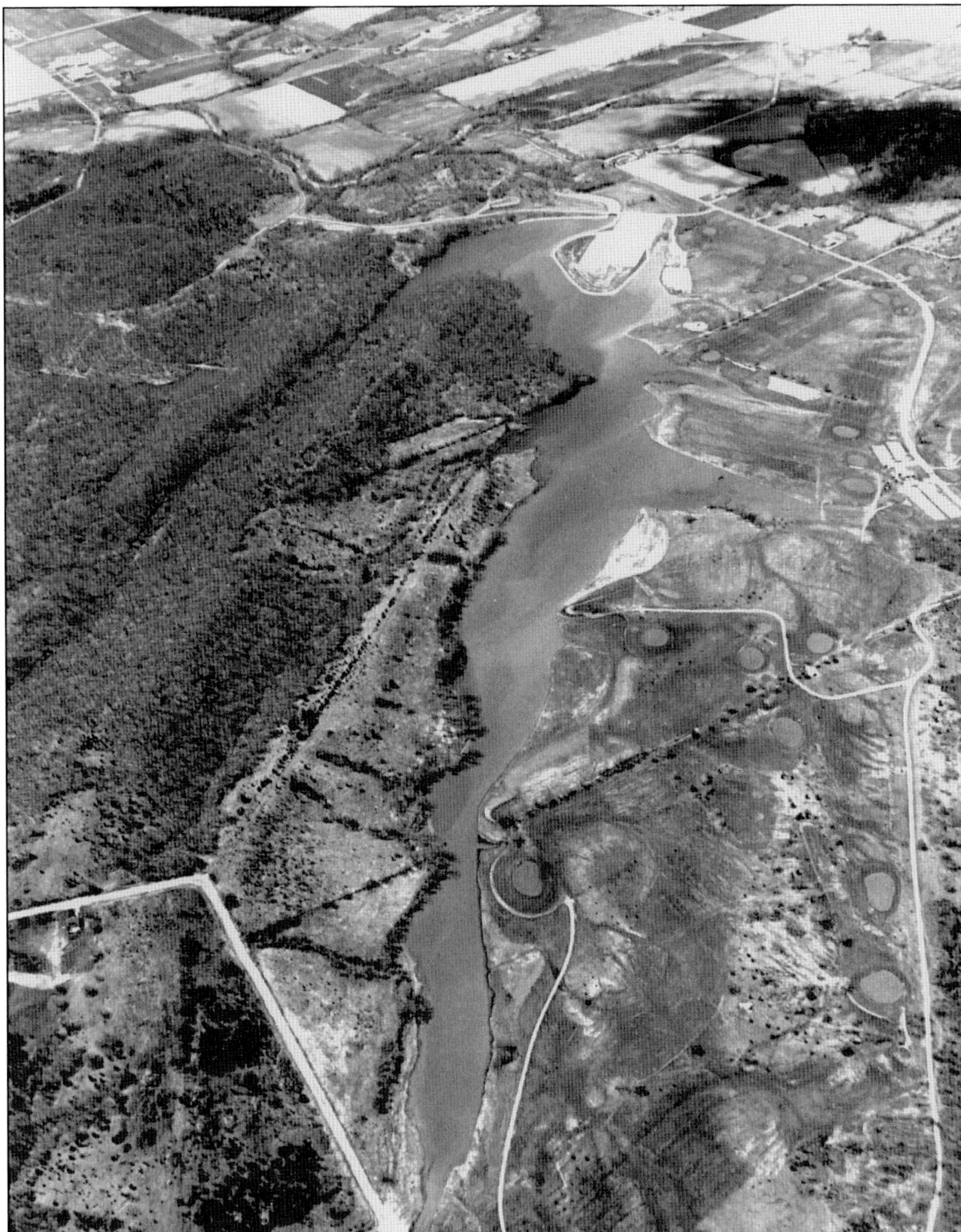

On Equal Footing. By the end of the 1960s, Miami Whitewater Forest had come into its own. Residents on the western side of Hamilton County could enjoy fishing and water recreational activities in the newly formed 85-acre lake or enjoy a round of golf. In 1969, park officials developed a unique braille trail for sightless visitors. The trail was the first of its kind in the state of Ohio.

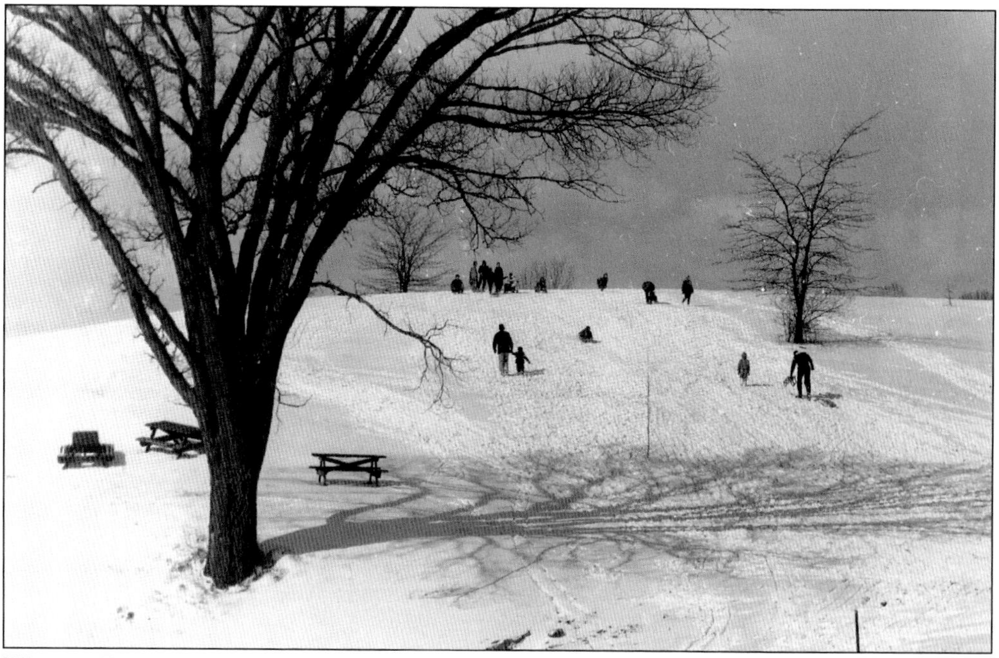

WINTER FUN AT WINTON WOODS. Hamilton County parks have provided opportunities for year-round outdoor recreation. Winton Woods Golf Course remained open for winter play. On occasion, after a good snowfall, groups of sled riders would take over the course temporarily. Others could be found ice-skating on Winton Woods Lake.

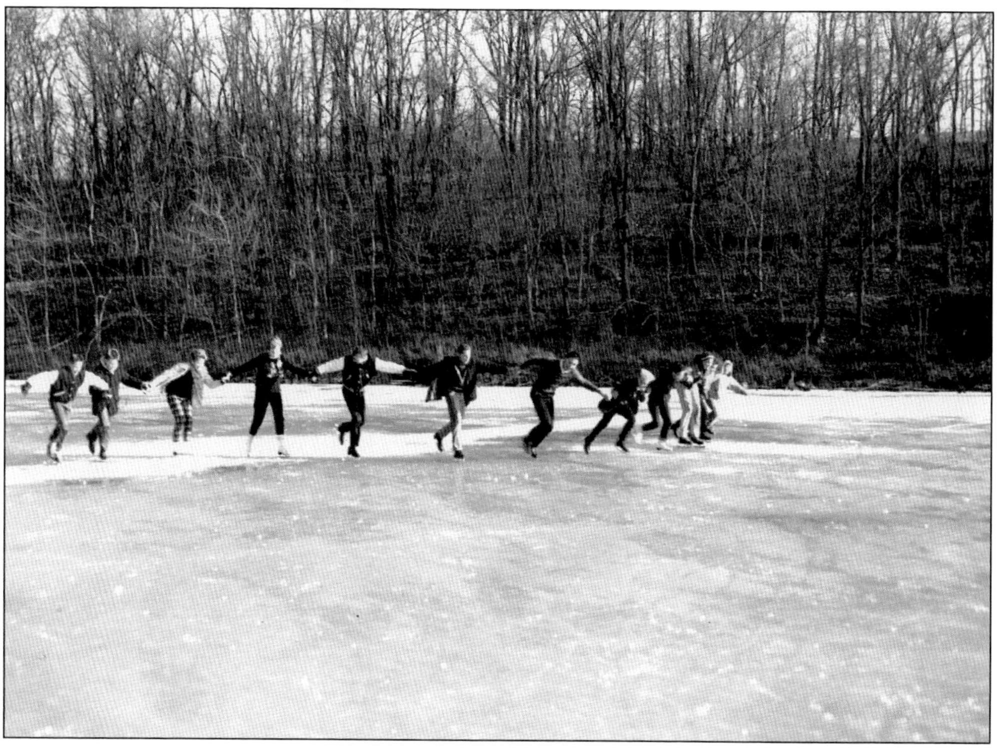

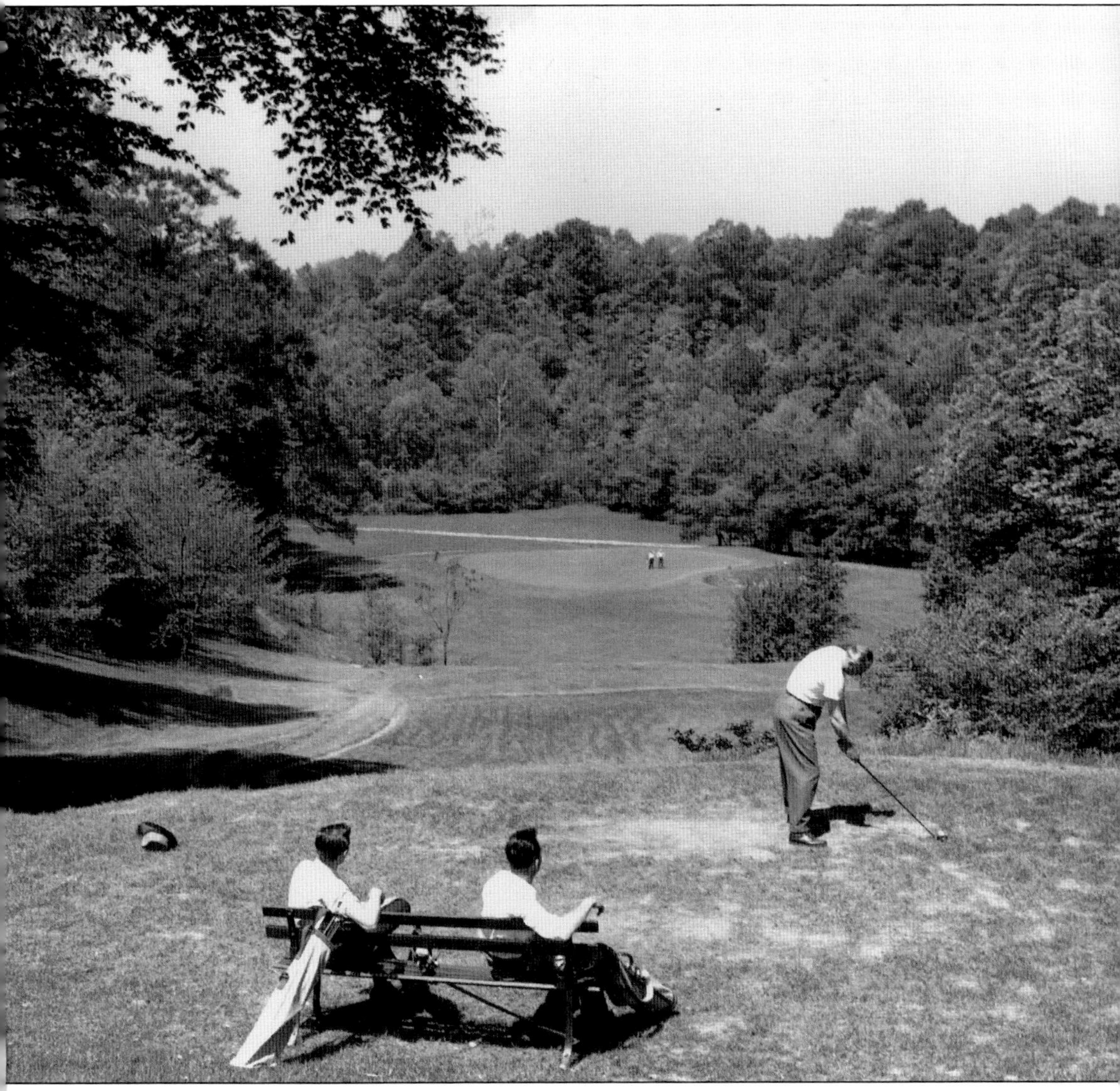

SHARON WOODS GOLF COURSE. It is easy to see how much the reforestation efforts at Sharon Woods paid off. Seedlings that were planted in the 1930s had grown into mature trees, offering many tree-lined fairways to challenge golfers. On a warm, sunny afternoon, two men watch as their friend hits his tee shot on the 185-yard par-three No. 8 hole. Or is it hole No. 17? The answer is—yes. The original design laid out this hole as No. 8. In the age before gas and electric golf carts, many golfers stopped playing after nine holes because of the steep climb up the No. 9 fairway to the clubhouse. The course was reconfigured to make the front nine holes flatter and less tiring. Old No. 8 became No. 17. In 1998, the course reverted back to its original design.

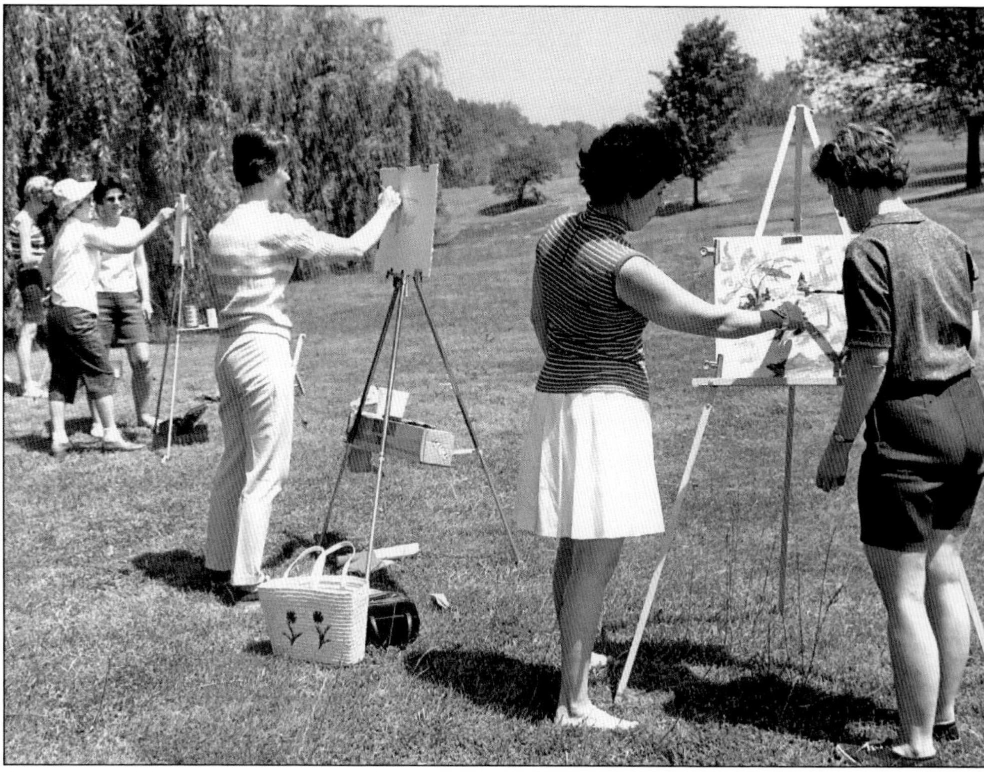

ART IN THE PARK. Aspiring artists learn new techniques in landscape painting over the course of several weeks in the summer of 1967 at Sharon Woods.

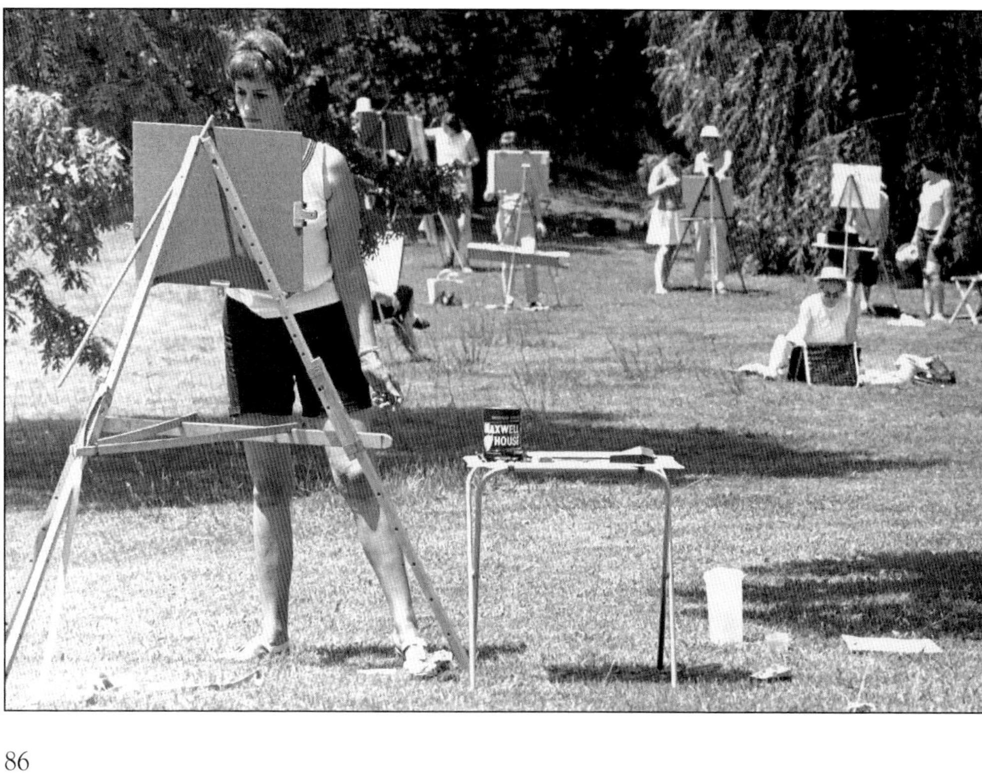

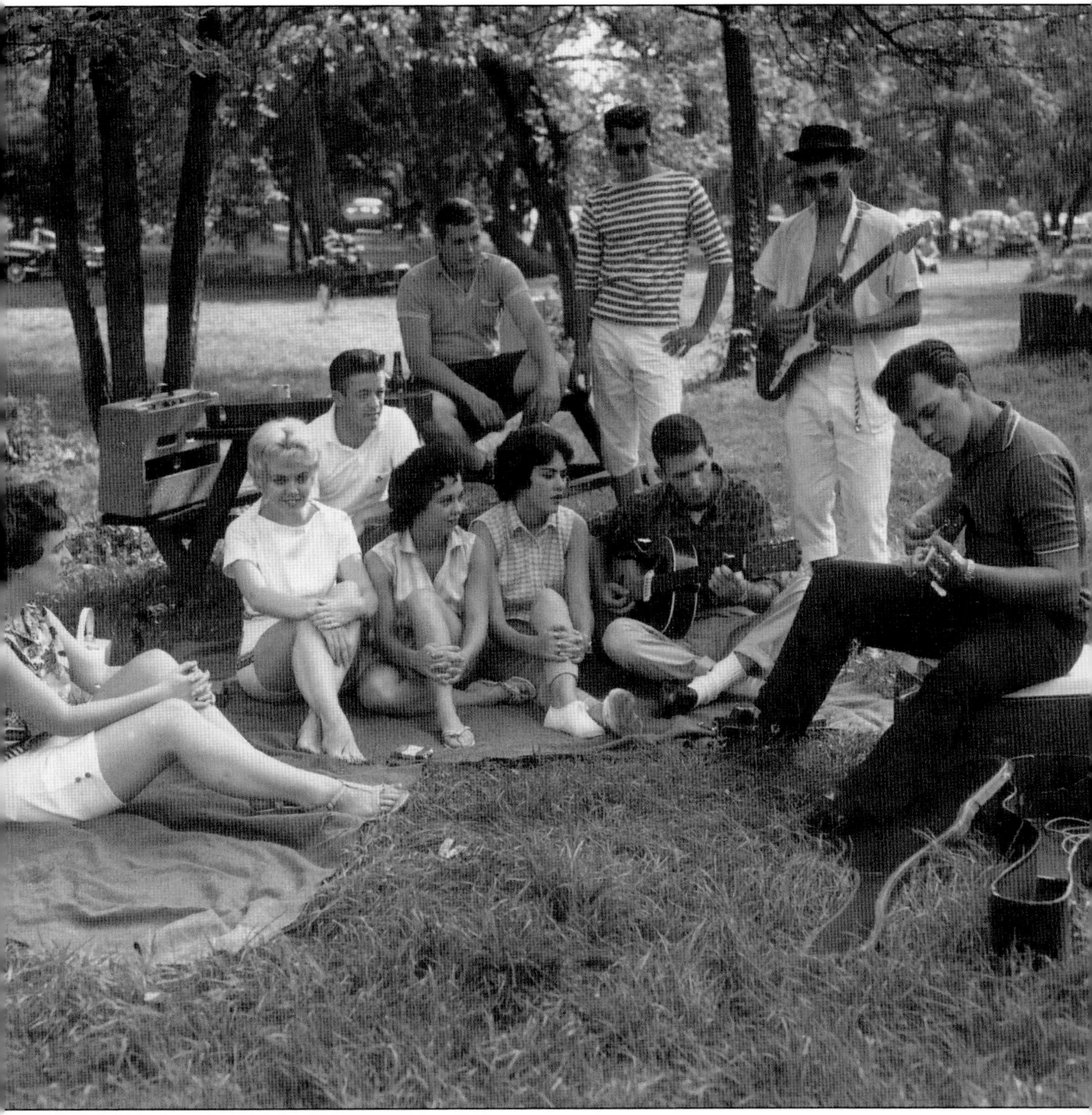

GROOVIN'. During the decade of the 1960s, rock and roll inspired a variety of emotional, exuberant, and often irrational responses on the part of America's teens. Adolescent girls sobbed joyful tears in 1964 when the Beatles invaded Crosley Field during their first United States concert tour. By 1967, some teens were "going to San Francisco" to join in the "summer of love." By decade's end, many young people from the Greater Cincinnati area journeyed to Max Yasgur's farm for the music event that defined the 1960s—Woodstock. So it seems logical that Sharon Woods acted as a magnet for young people, giving them an outdoor arena to practice, perform, and impress their friends.

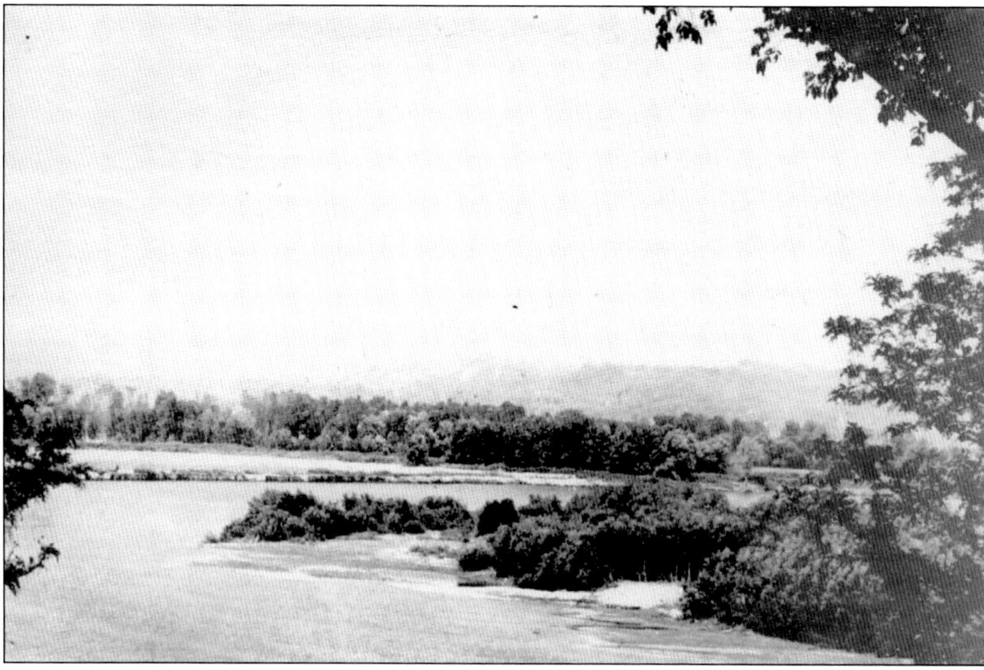

DOWN BY THE RIVERSIDE. In 1967, the Cincinnati Nature Conservancy deeded land in southwestern Hamilton County to the park district. Within the same year, park commissioners received contiguous lands that had been controlled by the Cincinnati Gas and Electric Company. The two land grants totaled about 1,010 acres of land. The area, which is situated at the junction of the Great Miami River and the Ohio River, would soon be developed into the county's fourth park. The park district was interested in creating a new park that would be convenient for residents of western Hamilton County. With the acquisition of this land, the total park acreage increased to an impressive 5,717 acres.

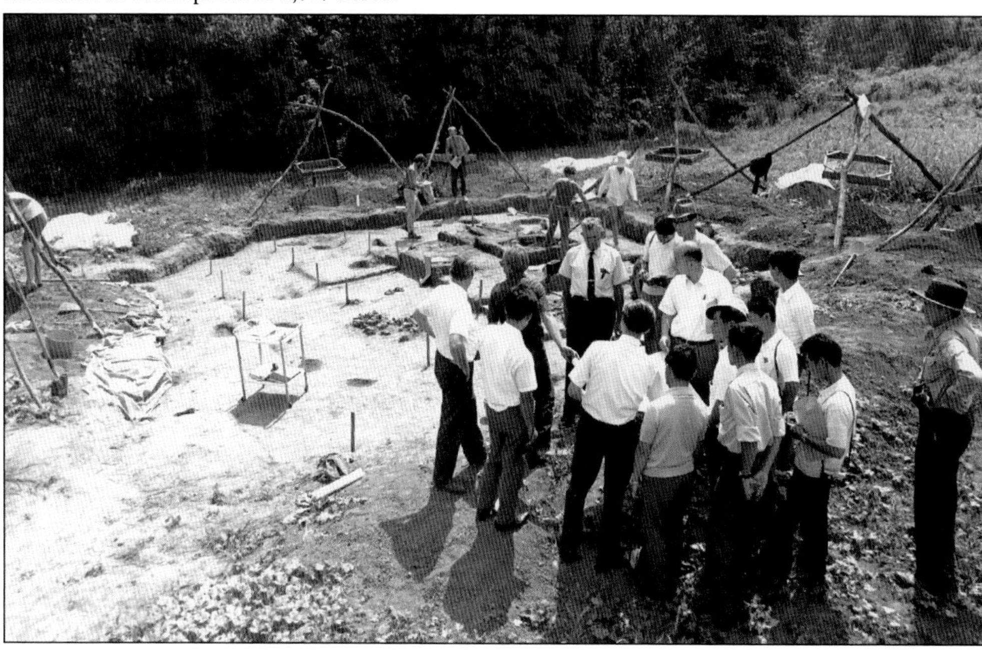

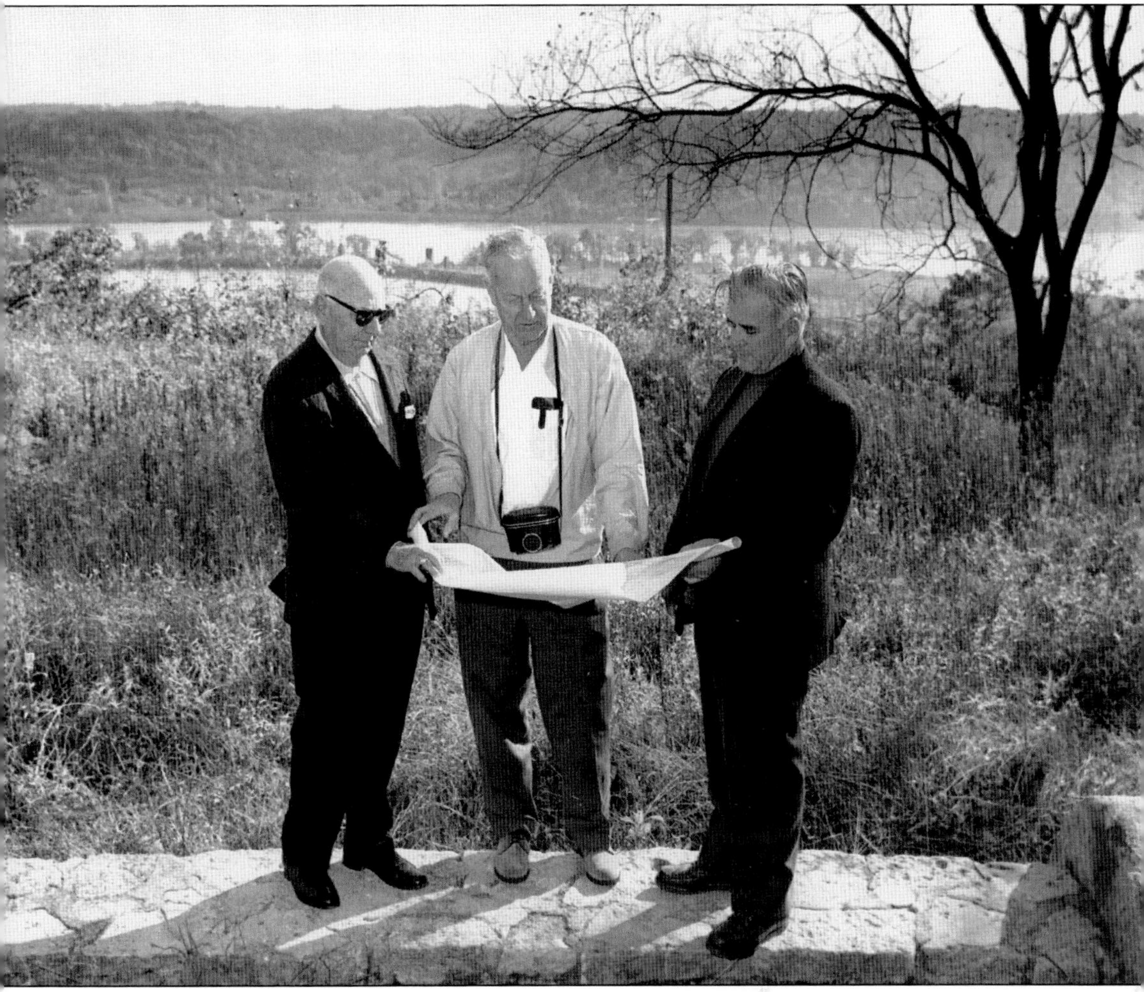

FORT MIAMI BECOMES SHAWNEE LOOKOUT. Park officials knew that the newly acquired land possessed enormous historic value. During the 1600s, the site had been occupied by Moundbuilders. A 19th-century archaeologist compared the Native American village at this site, known as Fort Miami, to Fort Ancient, located in nearby Warren County. Both Native American villages, it seems, were built as forts, on high ground that was highly defensible. Park officials decided to name the new park Shawnee Lookout after the Native Americans who inhabited the land in the 1700s. The Hamilton County Park District worked in conjunction with the University of Cincinnati to conduct an archaeological dig in the area. Once artifacts had been identified and preserved, the process of developing the county's fourth park began in earnest. In 1973, a group of concerned activists raised $9,000 to relocate and restore an old log cabin schoolhouse that was originally built in the late 1700s. By 1979, the park opened an 18-hole golf course.

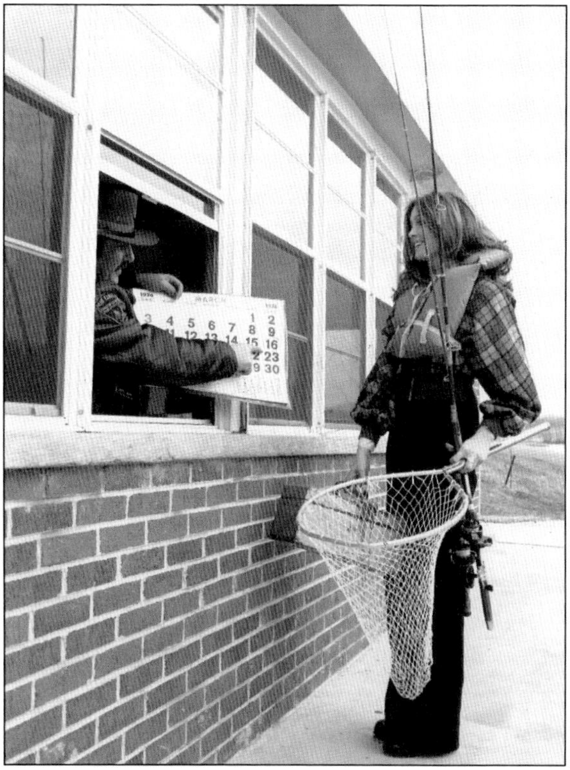

FISHING IS THE THING. Park officials wanted to remind fishing enthusiasts exactly when the season opened in March 1974. Sharon Walter poses for the shot on the left with park official Joe Carota. A group of unidentified teens (below) get some much-needed assistance from a helpful ranger.

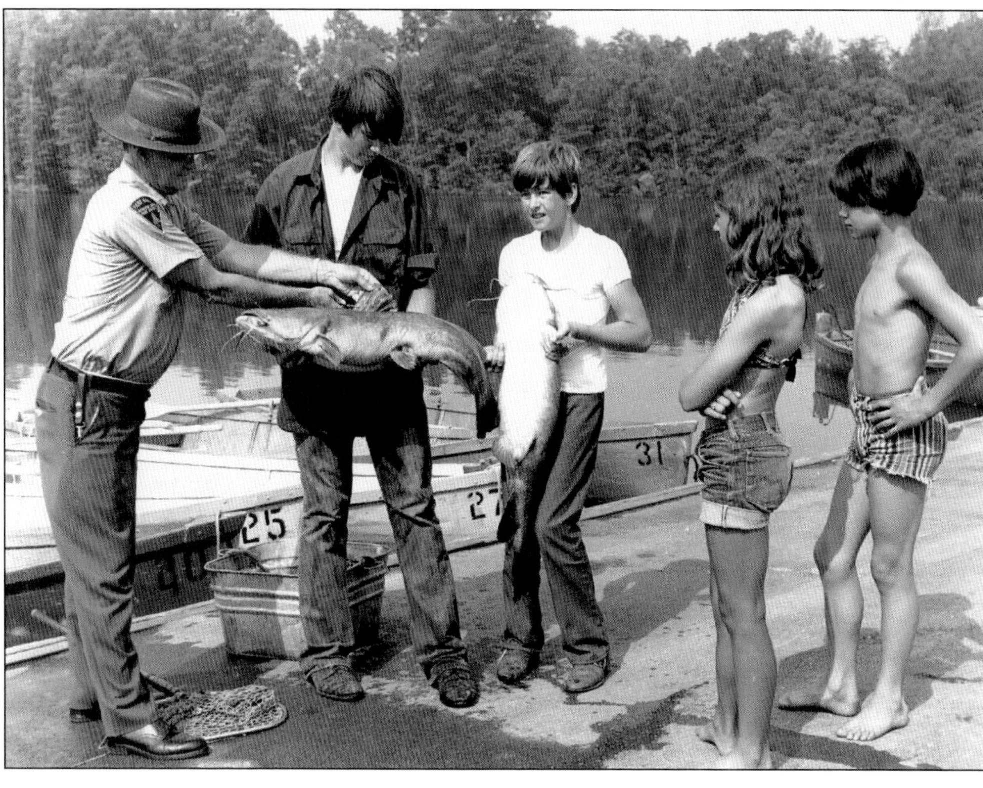

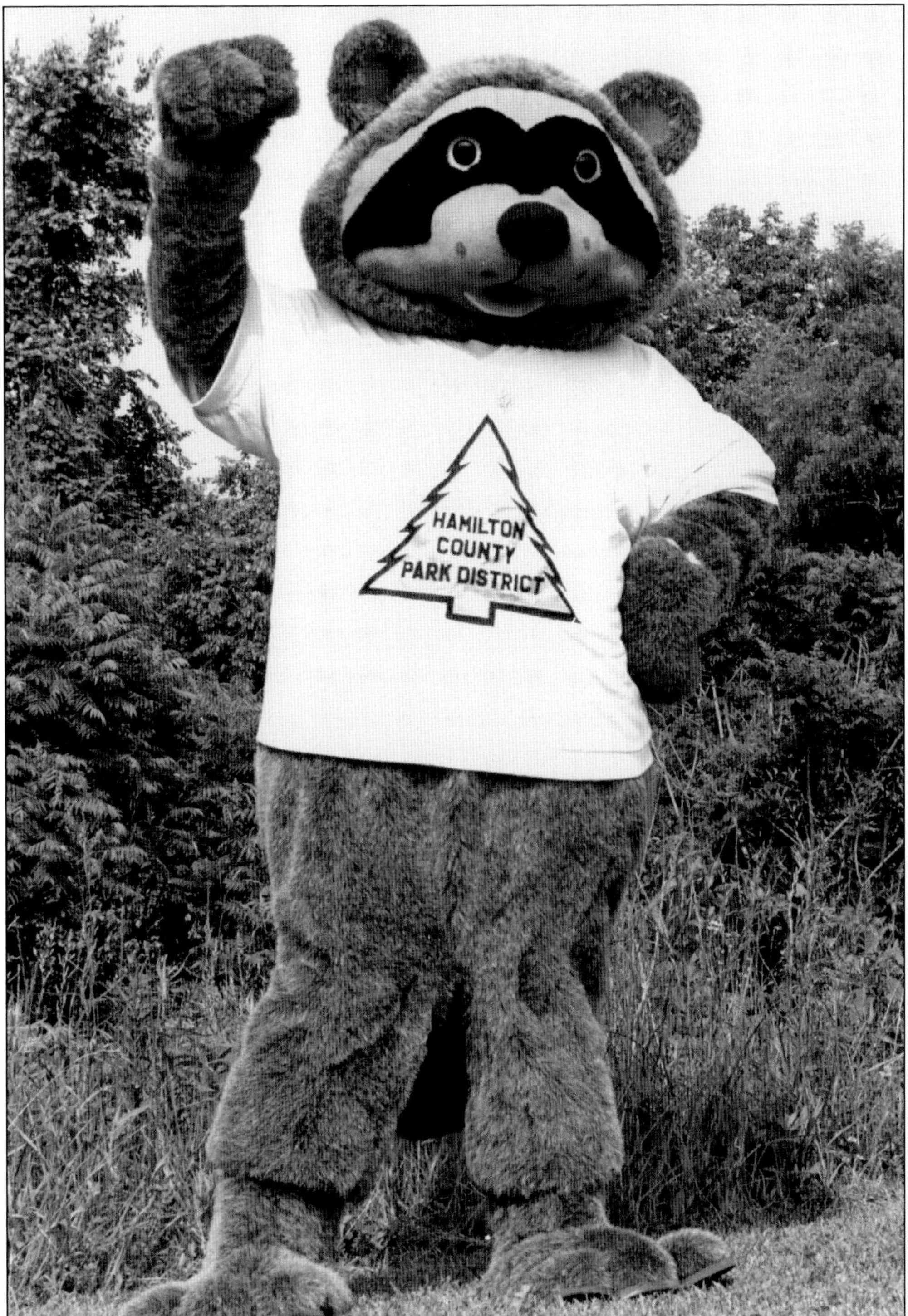

A New Mascot. In the early 1980s, Parky the Raccoon became the new face of the Hamilton County Park District. He became an identifiable presence in park publications such as *Evergreen*.

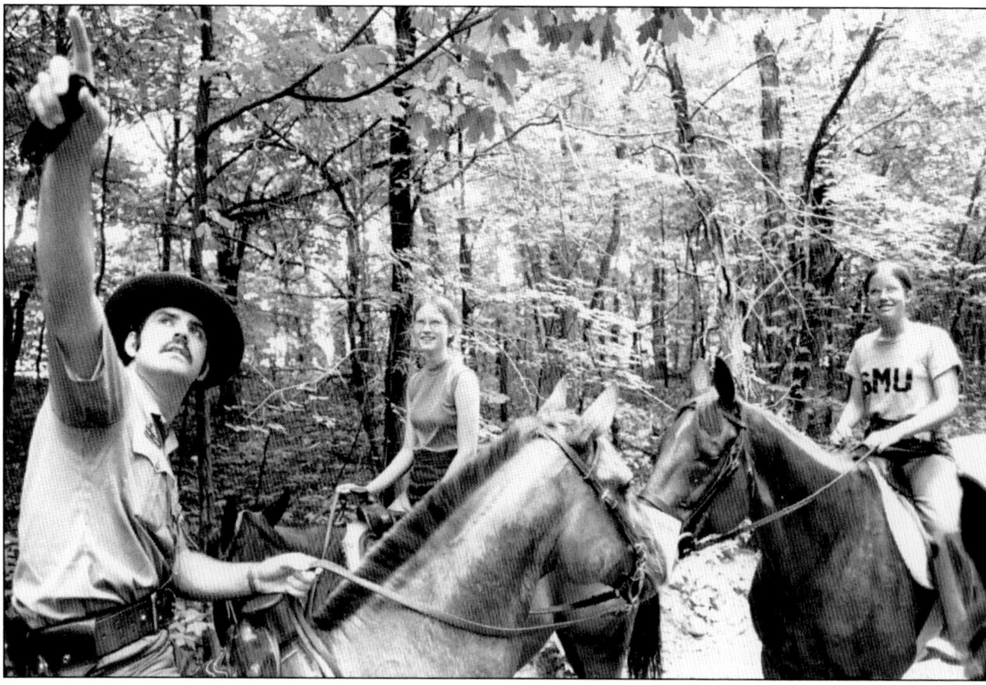

CONTINUED GROWTH IN THE 1970S. A mounted ranger (left) points out some natural wonders to two young riders in Winton Woods. As the park district entered into its fifth decade of service to Hamilton County, it could not have predicted how much more growth and expansion was in store. In 1973, voters approved a 10-year 5/10 mill tax levy for maintaining existing parks and acquiring new ones. Attendance was steady in the 1970s. The parks attracted millions of visitors on an annual basis. By the time the park district celebrated its 50th anniversary in June 1980, it had grown to 15 parks, including Woodland Mound on the eastern edge of Hamilton County.

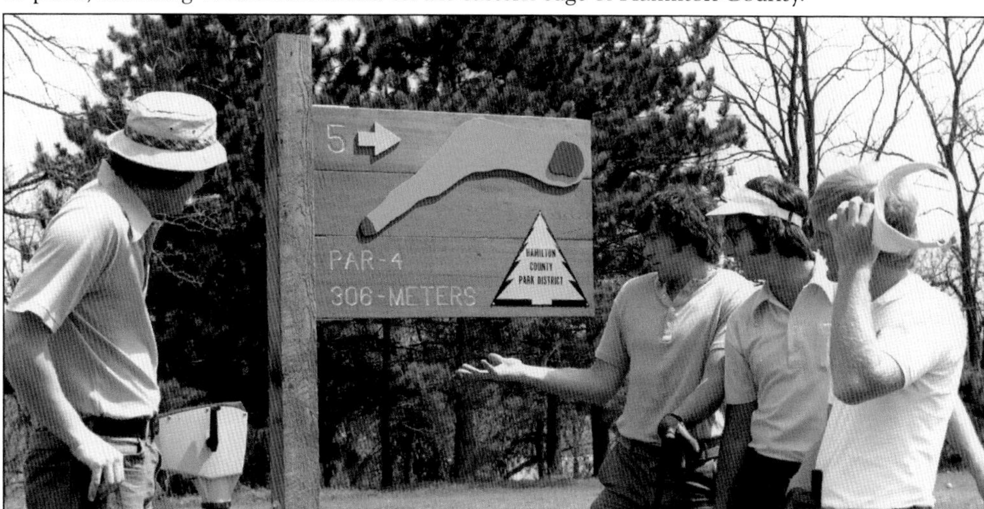

GOOFY GOLF. Pres. Franklin D. Roosevelt once said that he never expected to hit a home run every time he went to bat. It is fair to say that the decision in the 1970s to convert yardage markers on golf courses to meters left some park visitors wondering who was minding the store. The experiment was short-lived.

Three

Refining the Mission and the Message 1951–1980

In 1962, Rachel Carson, a quiet, unassuming career marine biologist and author, published her groundbreaking book *Silent Spring*. The book was an indictment of the unregulated use of pesticides. It traced the destructive impact such chemicals had on the environment. Carson was a pioneer in the field on environmental activism. Concern about pesticides led to concern over water and air pollution. Support for environmental awareness grew in the 1960s. Apollo 8 astronauts transmitted the first photographed images of Earth from outer space. Those images underscored to many the fragility of the planet.

On April 22, 1970, the first-ever Earth Day was observed. An estimated 250 million Americans participated in mass gatherings on village greens, college campuses, and parks to discuss their mutual concerns about the environment. The United States Congress adjourned for the day so that lawmakers could return to their districts and hear from their constituents. Within a few months, in December 1970, Congress passed legislation that led to the creation of the Environmental Protection Agency.

An apocryphal quote often attributed to Mark Twain goes something like this: "If the end of the world was coming, I should like to be in Cincinnati, as it is always twenty years behind the times." In many matters of politics, culture, and style, this expression usually rings true. In the area of forward-thinking environmentalism, however, the Hamilton County Park District seemed to be ahead of the curve. The park district hired its first part-time naturalist in 1949. A full-time naturalist was placed on staff three years later. Park staff provided a myriad of opportunities to engage visitors of all ages in some form of nature education. Day camps reached out to schools and Scout troops. Nature hikes, camera outings, and more formal lectures and classes appealed to adults. Parks could and should be places for outdoor recreation. But they were also safe havens, areas where pristine conditions could be preserved and protected. Sharing that vision with the public became the mission of park rangers and naturalists.

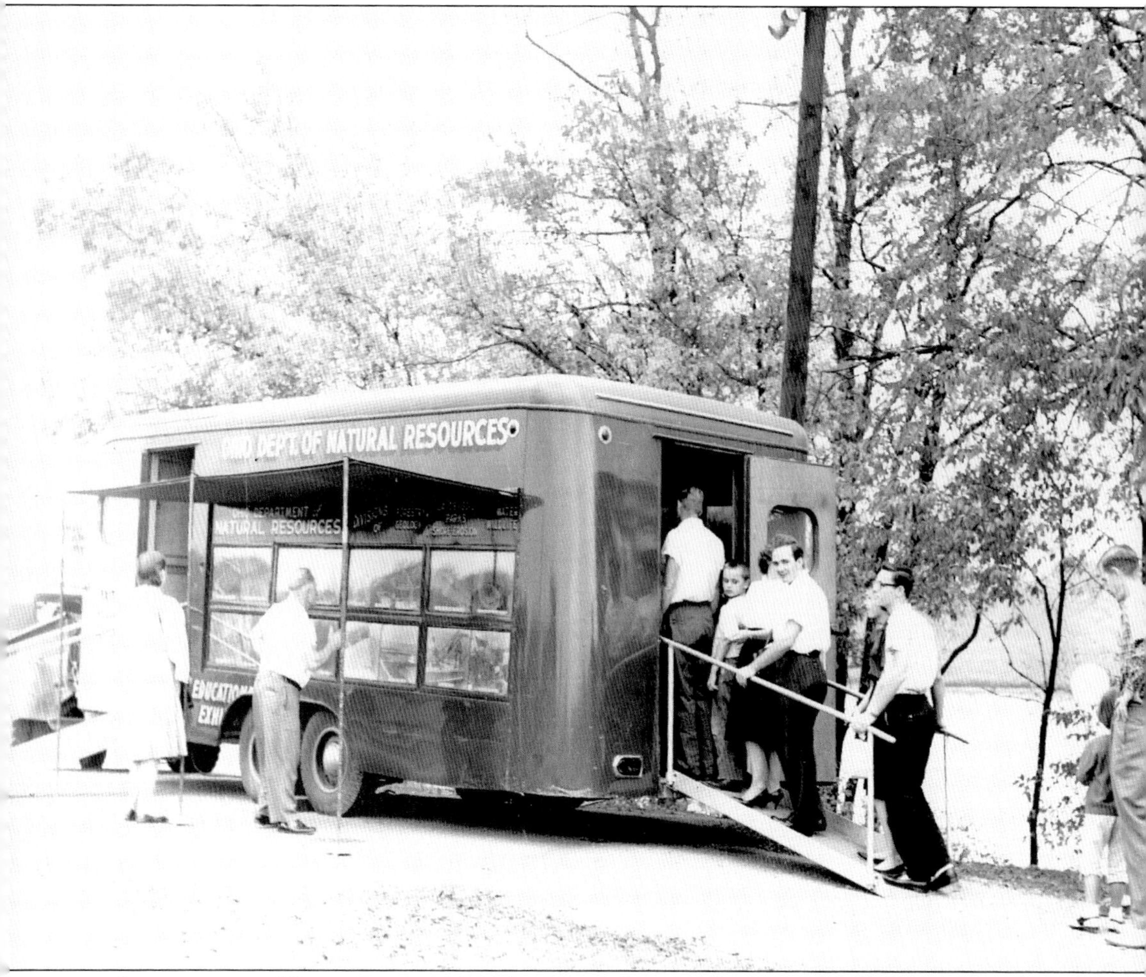

GETTING THE WORD OUT. In October 1960, the Hamilton County Park District borrowed trailers from the Ohio Department of Natural Resources during its observance of County Park Day. The trailers were mobile units used around the state that promoted a better understanding of the state's limited natural resources.

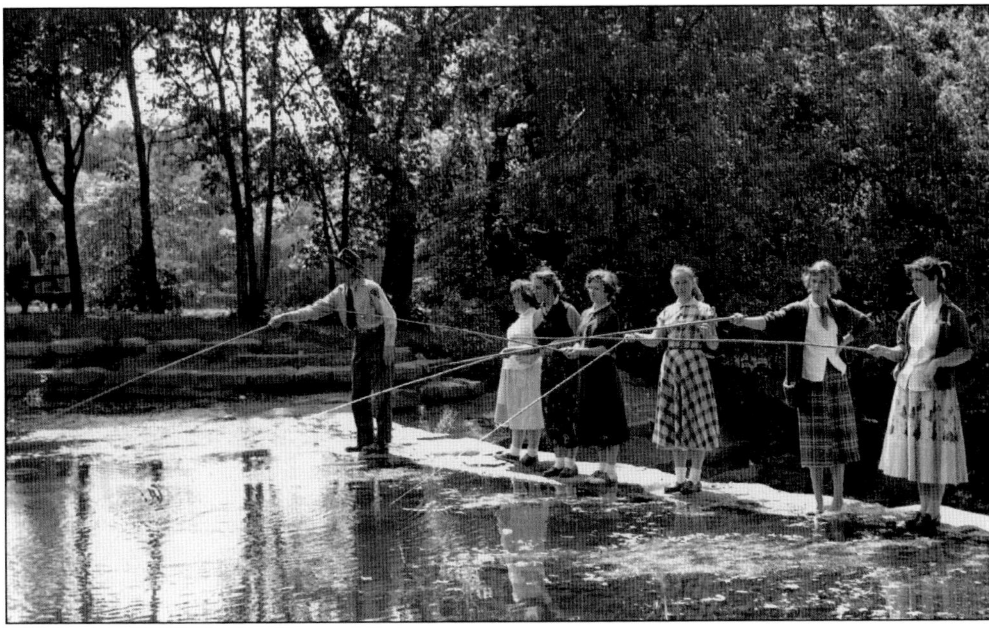

DAY CAMP DAYS. A ranger at a Sharon Woods day camp (above) teaches young girls how to cast and reel. A group of children enrolled in a 1957 day camp at Winton Woods (below) get an opportunity to fish. Day camps usually lasted for a week. Park rangers and naturalists organized nature walks, presented informal talks on wildlife and natural habitats for animals, and, of course, planned opportunities for outdoor fun.

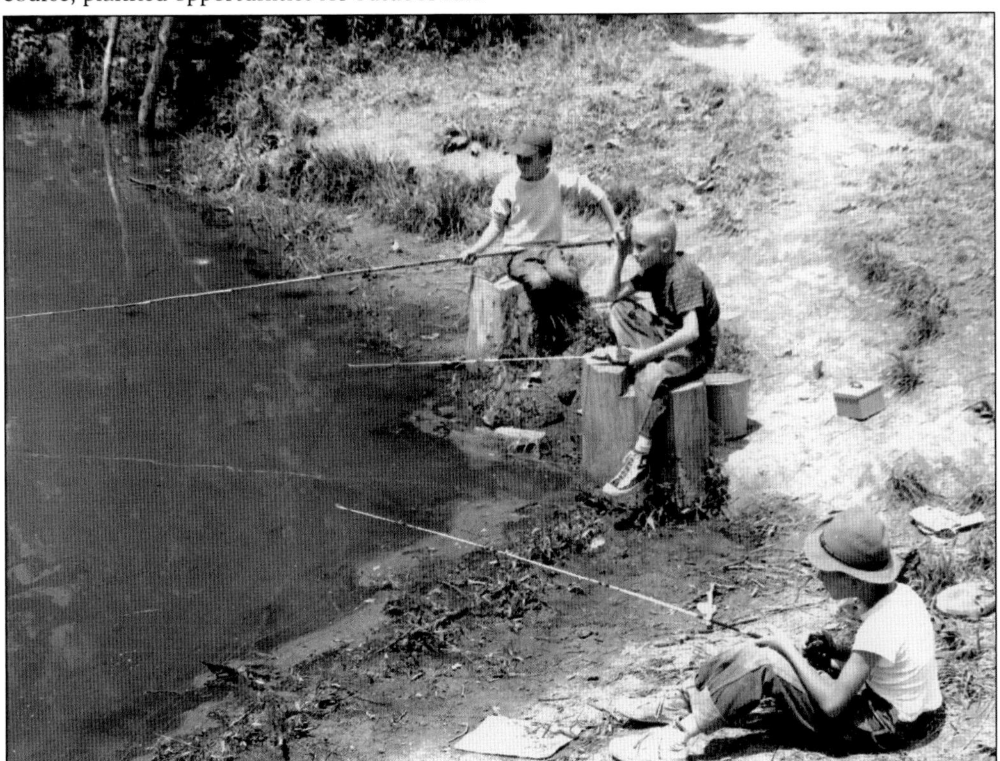

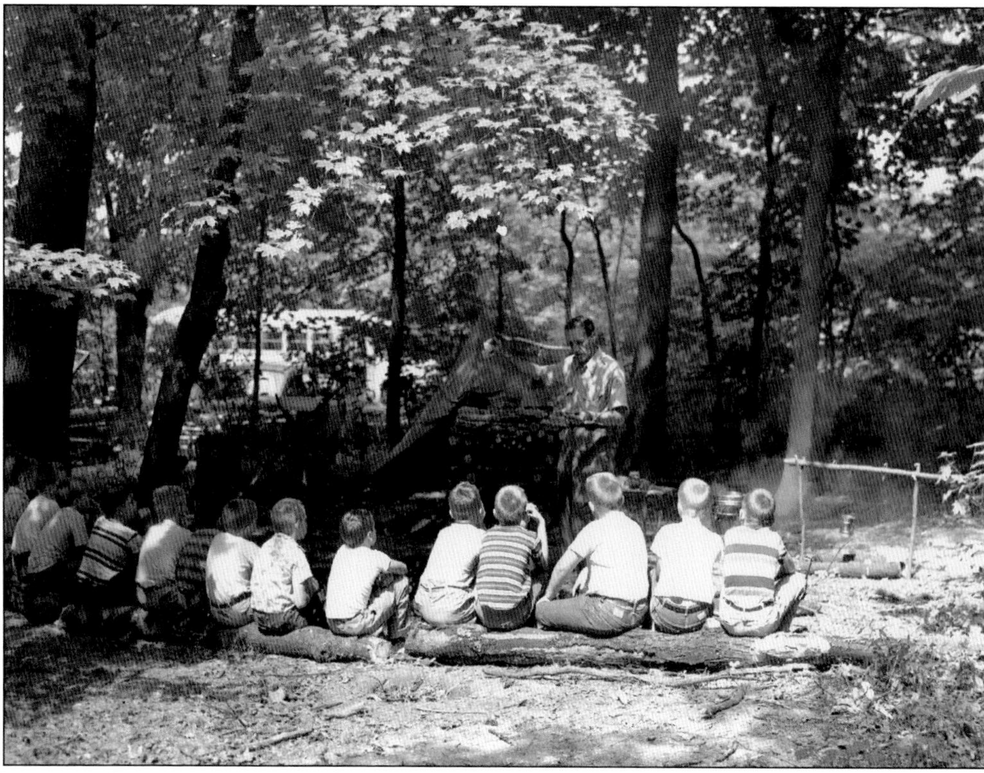

LOADS OF FUN. Some attentive boys learn outdoor cooking skills from park ranger Mike Weber (above). Day campers turn out en masse for some guided activities in a Sharon Woods meadow (below). An estimated 12,000 children attended summer camps at Sharon Woods and Winton Woods in the late 1950s.

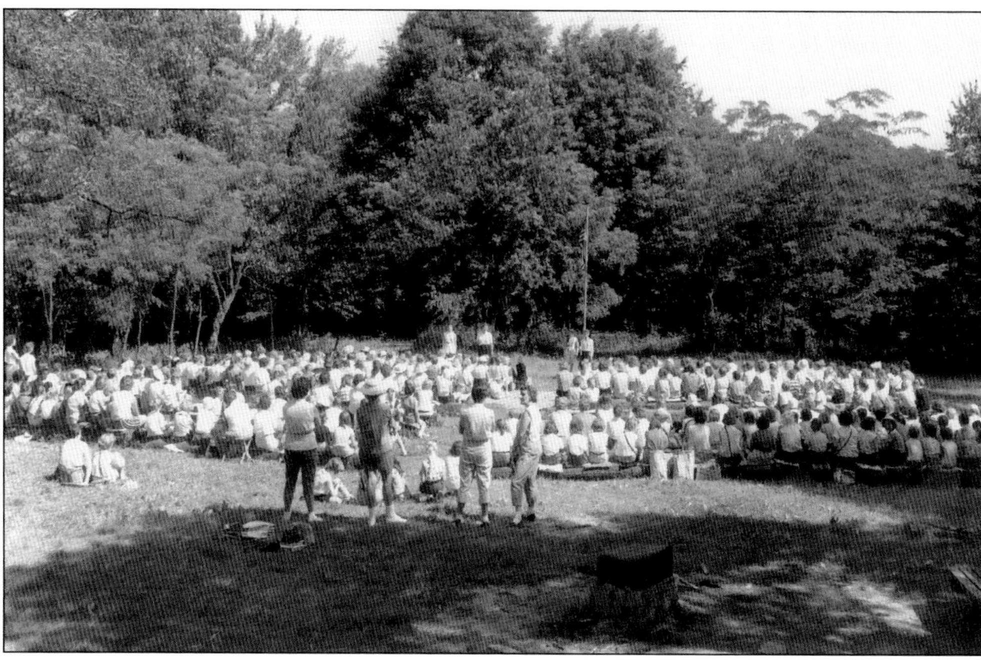

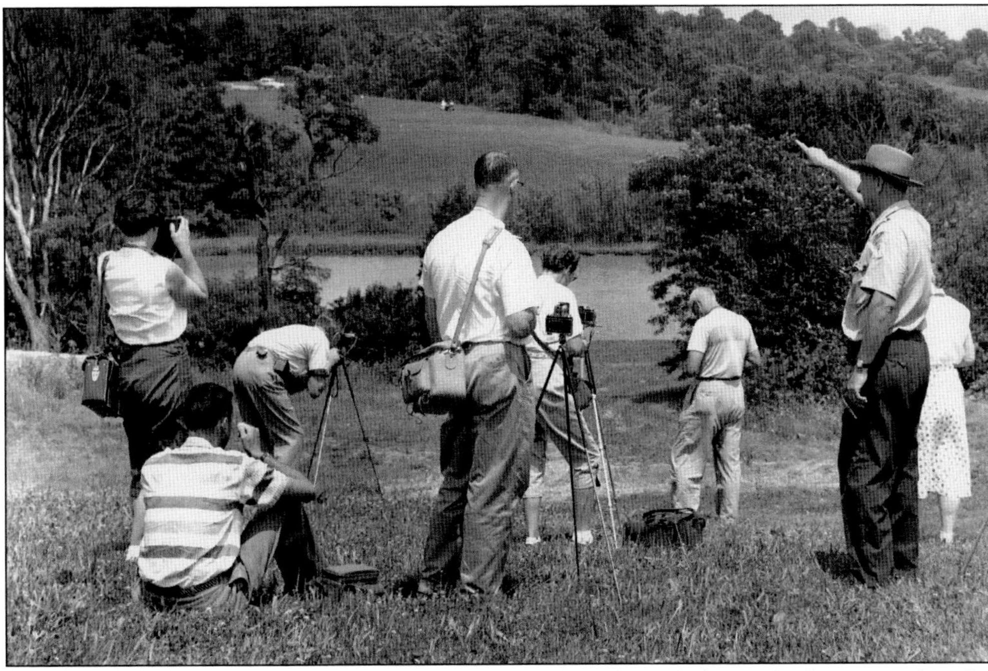

NATURE AND SHUTTERBUGS. Starting in the late 1940s, the park district had sponsored guided camera walks and photograph contests. Park ranger J. Herbert (Herb) Heger (above, right) informs this group of camera enthusiasts about this impressive Winton Woods vista. Mr. and Mrs. Wes Faller Jr. (below), of Mount Healthy, participate in the 1958 photograph contest at Winton Woods.

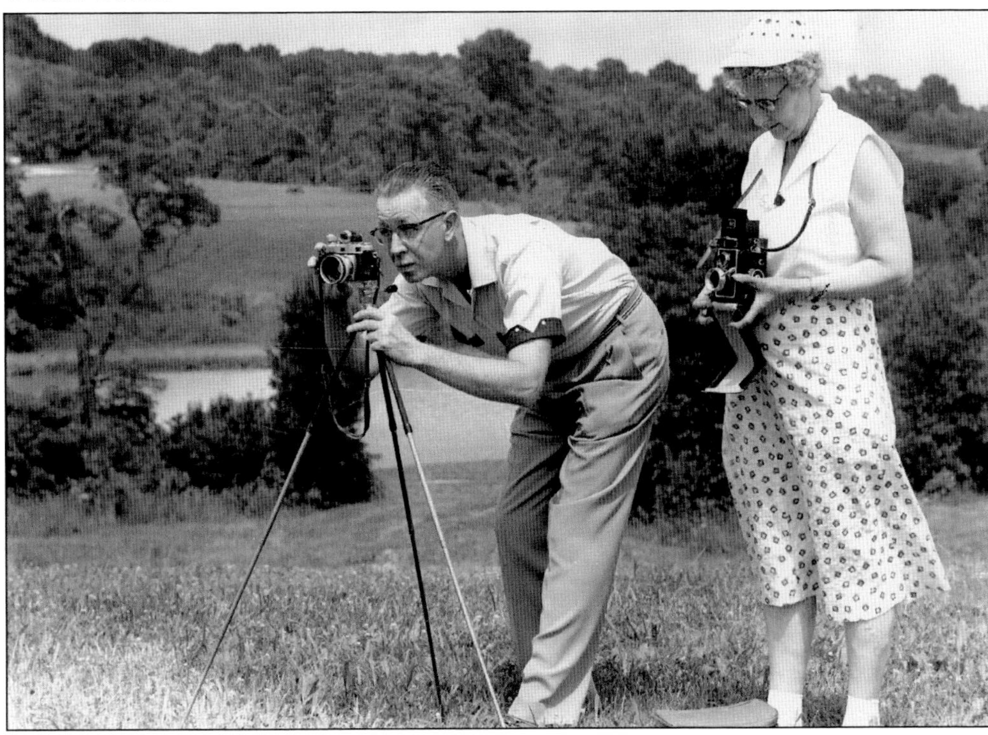

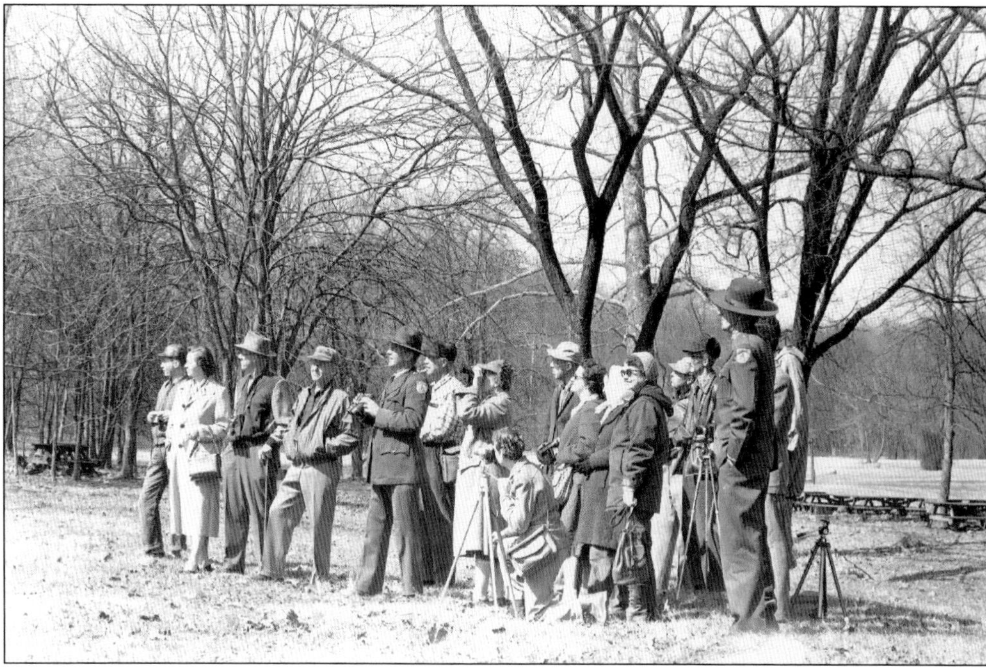

VIEWING NATURE THROUGH A DIFFERENT LENS. Park ranger and naturalist Warren Wells (far right) points out bird activity for a group on a March 1957 camera walk at Sharon Woods. George McKay (below) and his family scoot in for a close-up shot of the destroying angel fungus at Miami Whitewater Forest.

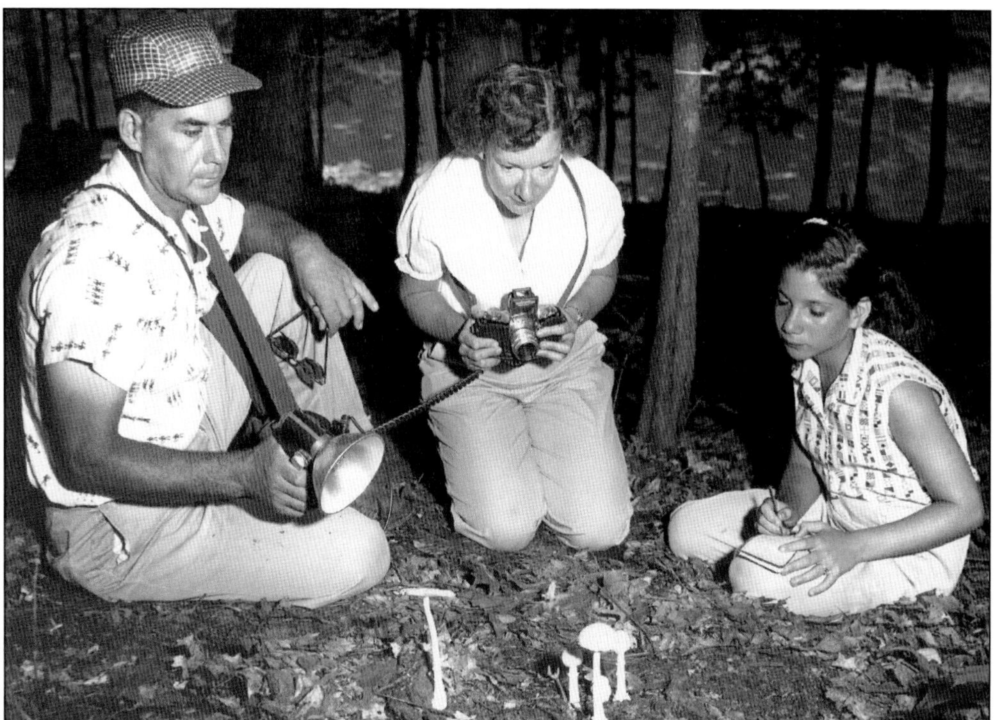

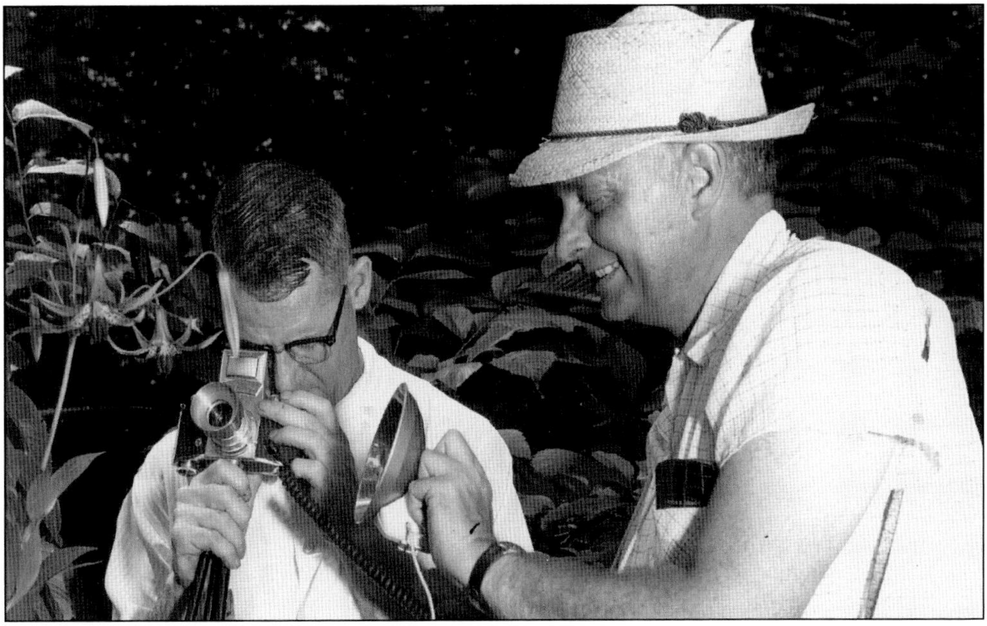

EXPERIENTIAL LEARNING. Naturalists hoped camera walks would instill a new and lasting appreciation of the natural wonders housed in the county parks. John Kuhn (above, left) and A. Pfetzing (above, right) assist each another in close-up work on a rare Canadian lily. Herb Heger (below, right) helps Jean Mosier (below, far left) and Ed Roberts on a Winton Woods camera walk.

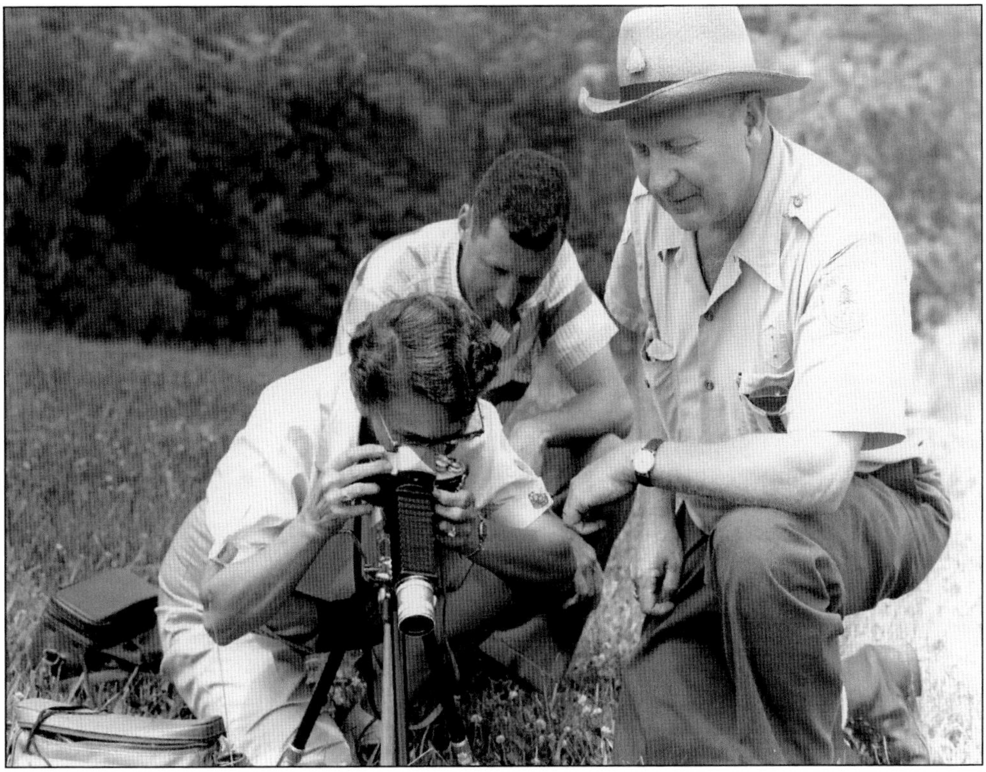

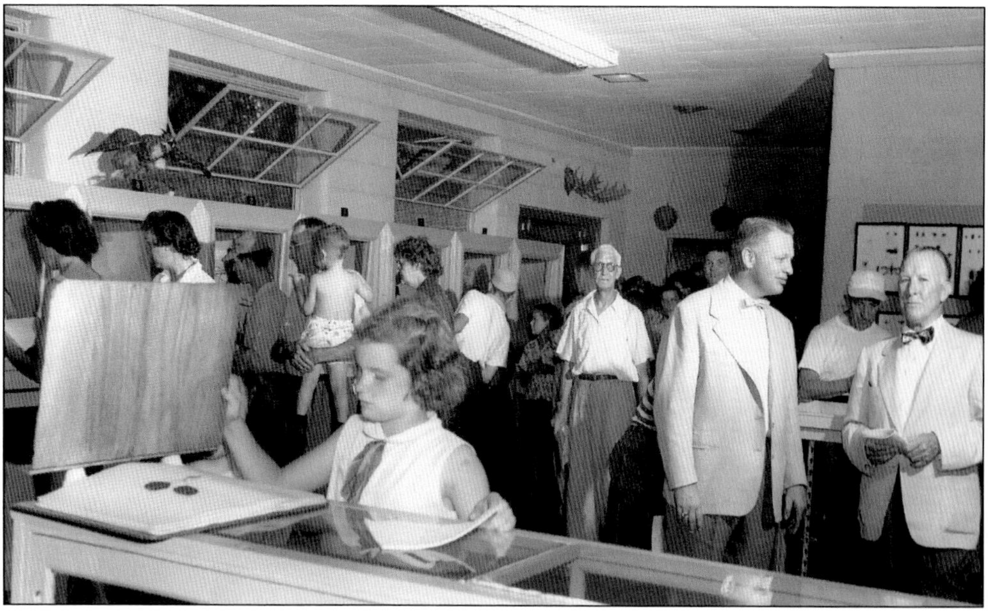

HONORING A LEGEND. Beginning in the early 1950s, park rangers used the ranger station at Sharon Woods for demonstrations in nature education. Park naturalists had assembled displays of stuffed animals, reptiles, birds, and insects. The makeshift museum attracted about 30,000 visitors each year. By 1953, plans for a permanent nature center at Sharon Woods were nearly complete. That May, Hamilton County park commissioner Alfred K. Nippert informed the board that he would resign his position due to declining health. He had served the park district since his appointment in 1936. A few weeks later, when the new nature center opened, it was dedicated to the outgoing commissioner. In 1960, then commissioner Louis Nippert (below, right), who succeeded his father in 1953, is seen chatting with Alfred M. Husted, who had retired in 1959, after 29 years of service as director of the park district board.

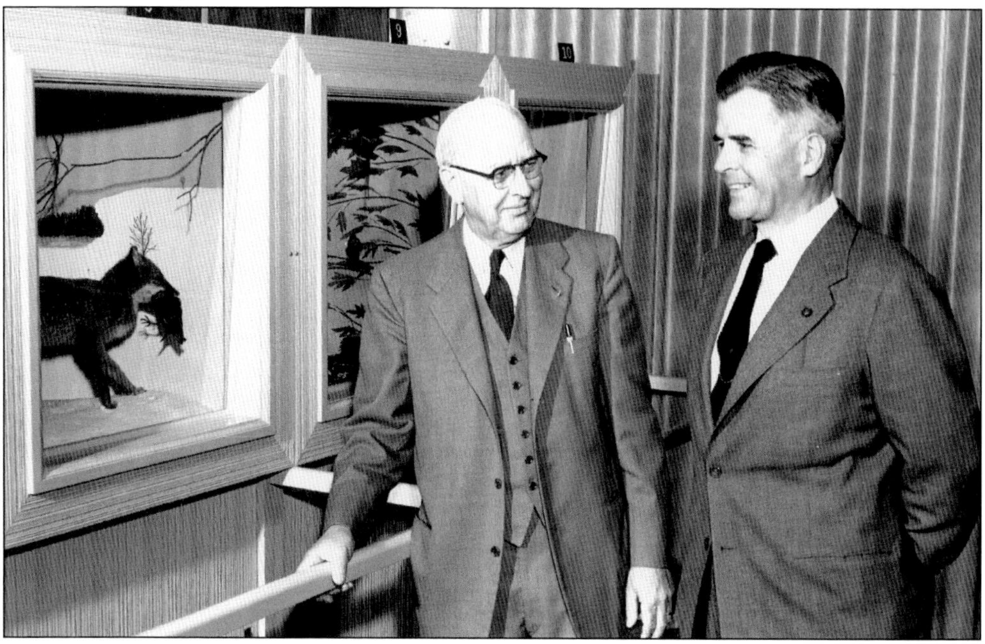

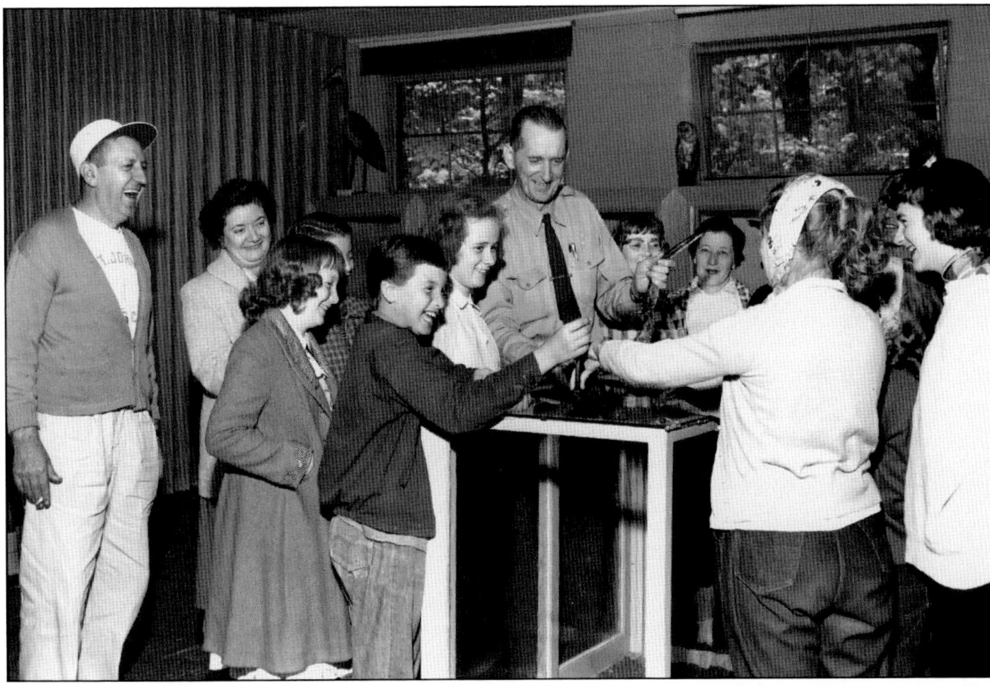

WORKING THE ROOM. Park ranger Capt. Chester Pickering shows off the collection of stuffed animals at the Nippert Nature Center to appreciative onlookers. Pickering obviously took great pleasure giving these presentations to young people.

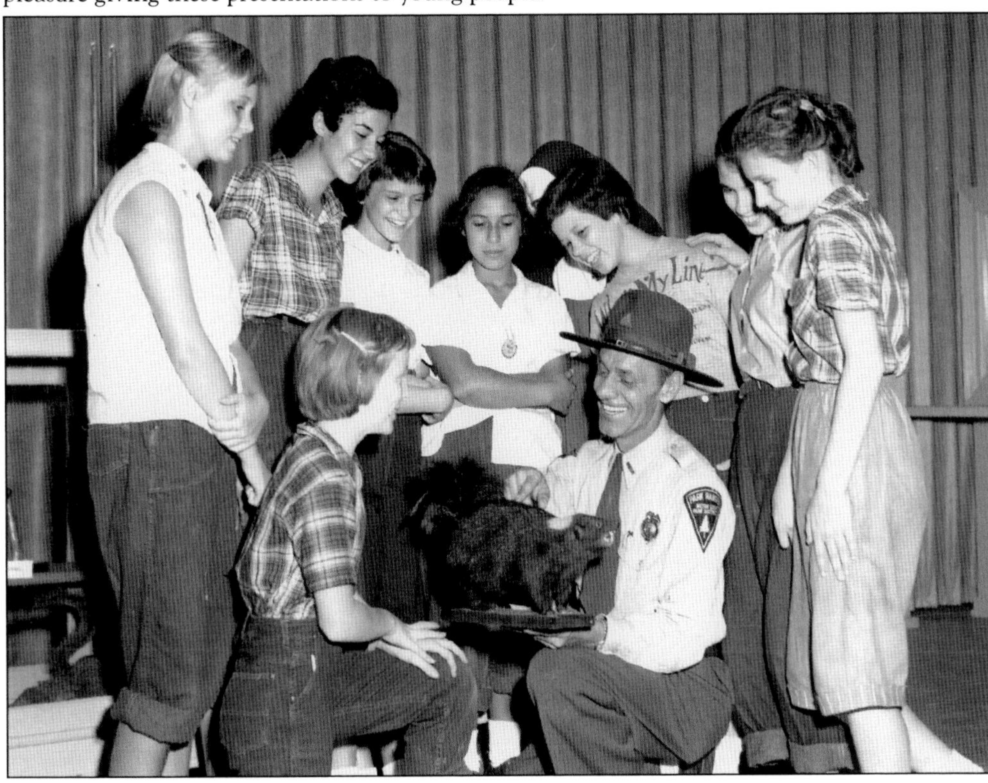

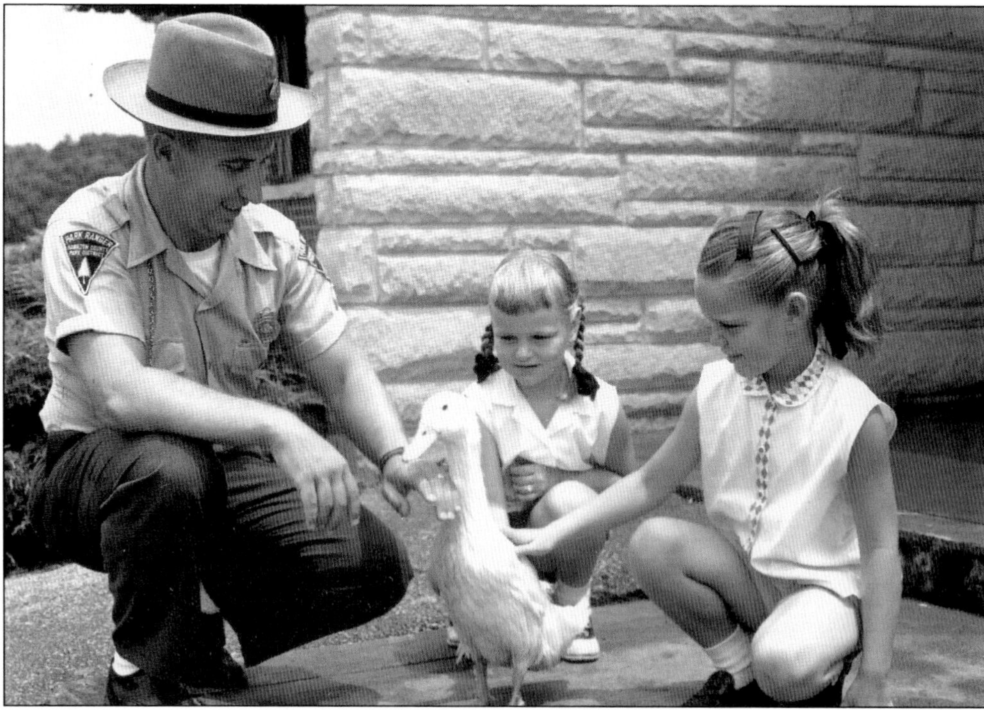

WATERFOWL FUN. A Sharon Woods park ranger allows two young girls to get some hands-on learning. The duck does not seem to mind.

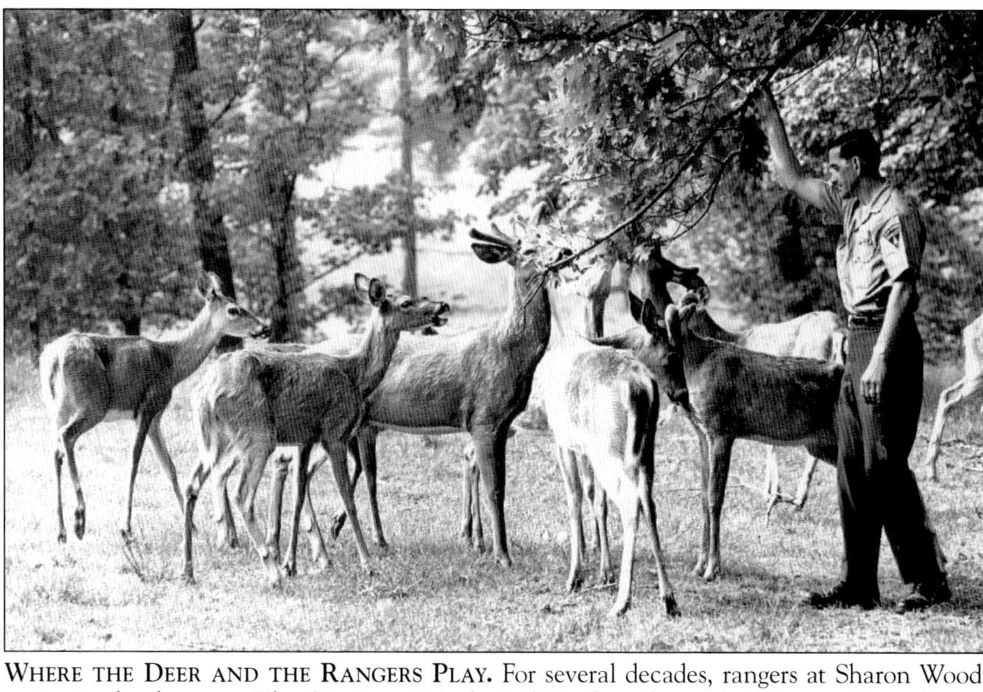

WHERE THE DEER AND THE RANGERS PLAY. For several decades, rangers at Sharon Woods maintained a deer pen. The Cincinnati Zoological Gardens donated six brown fallow deer to the park district. Several other whitetail deer were donated by the state Division of Wildlife. Rangers maintained the pen for many years.

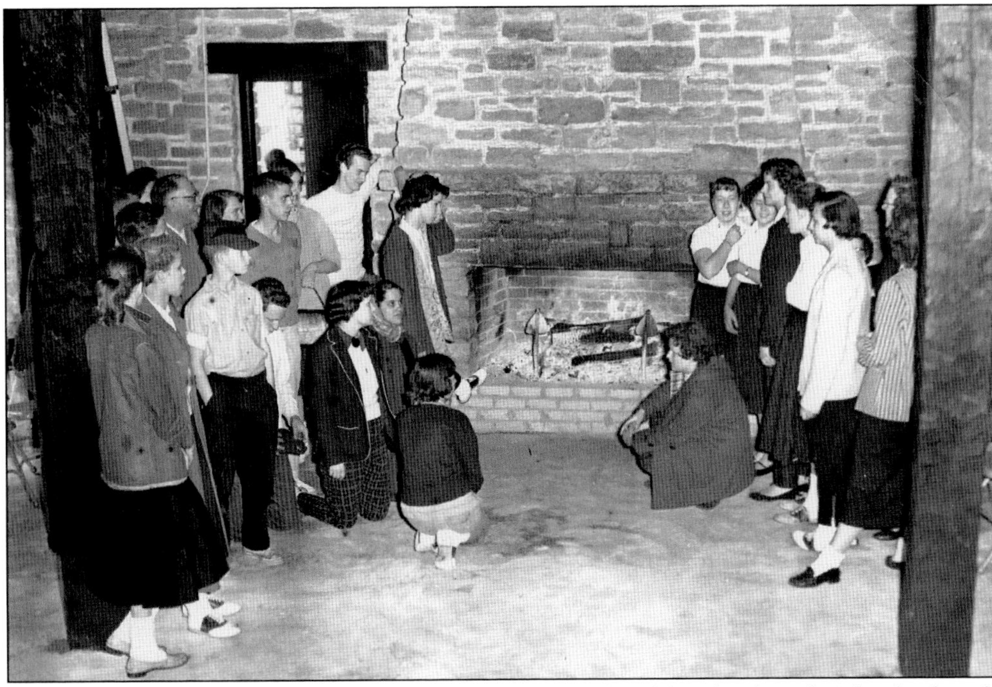

BACK TO NATURE. Members of the Salvation Army Cadets (above) take refuge by the fireside of a lodge at Sharon Woods. Senior Girl Scouts (below) clear fallen trees from a section of Winton Woods.

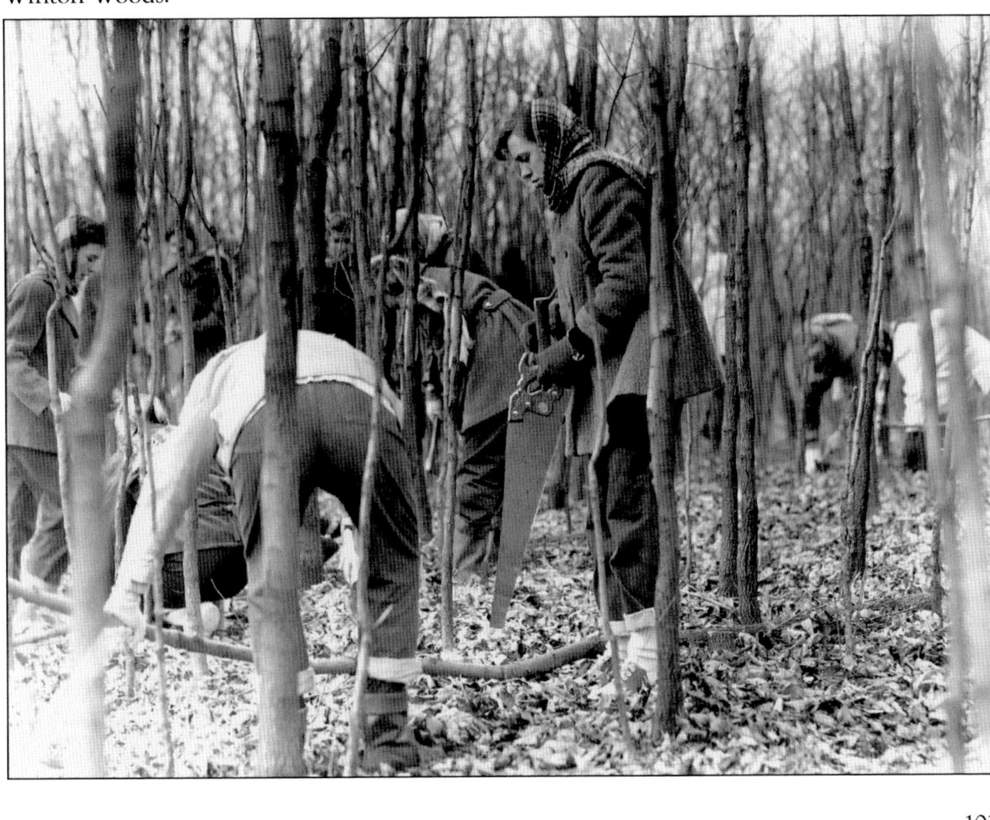

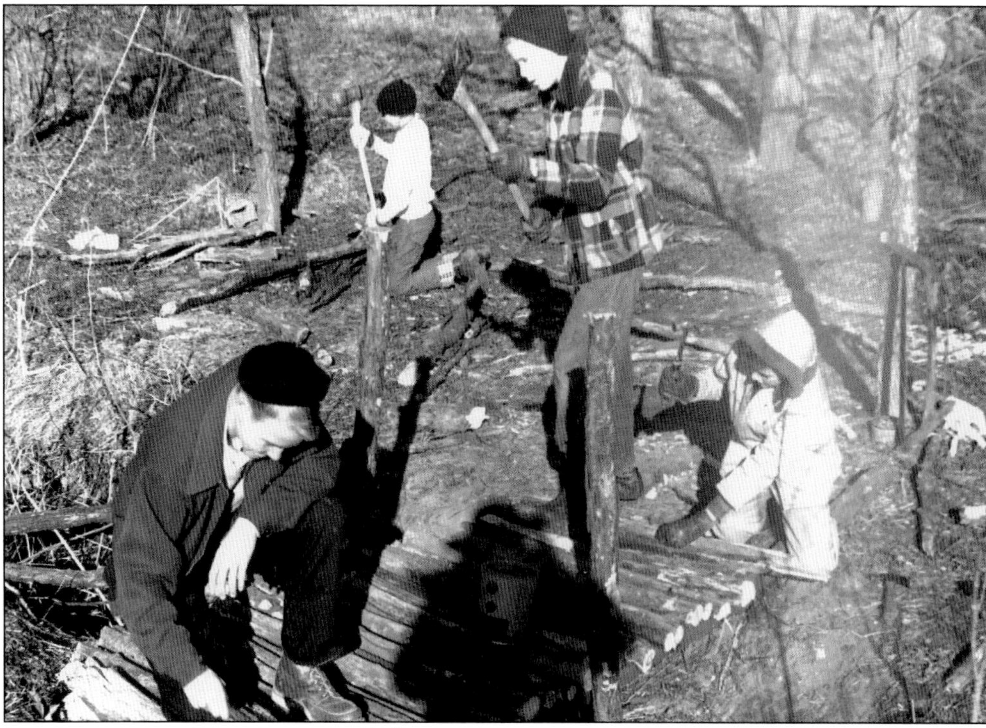

SERVICE TO THE PARKS. A Greenhills Boy Scout troop devotes time and energy to building bridges and blazing hiking trails at Winton Woods. The Boy Scouts combined community service and outdoor activities into most of the requirements for badges and advancement.

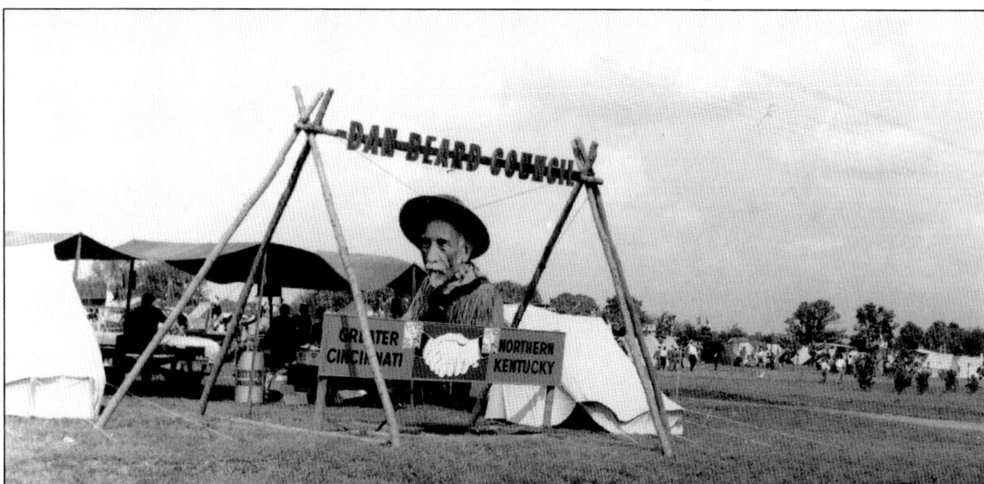

YOUNG OUTDOORSMEN. Daniel Carter Beard, a Cincinnati-born illustrator and naturalist, helped found the Boy Scouts of America in 1910. For the next 31 years, he served as the organization's national commissioner. His legacy lived on through the activities of area Boy Scouts in the Dan Beard Council, which comprised counties in southwestern Ohio and northern Kentucky. During the 1960s, the Dan Beard Council invited area troops to participate in a weekend-long jamboree at Winton Woods. While park officials said that approximately 8,000 groups used the parks for overnight campouts, the jamborees usually accounted for about two-thirds of the total.

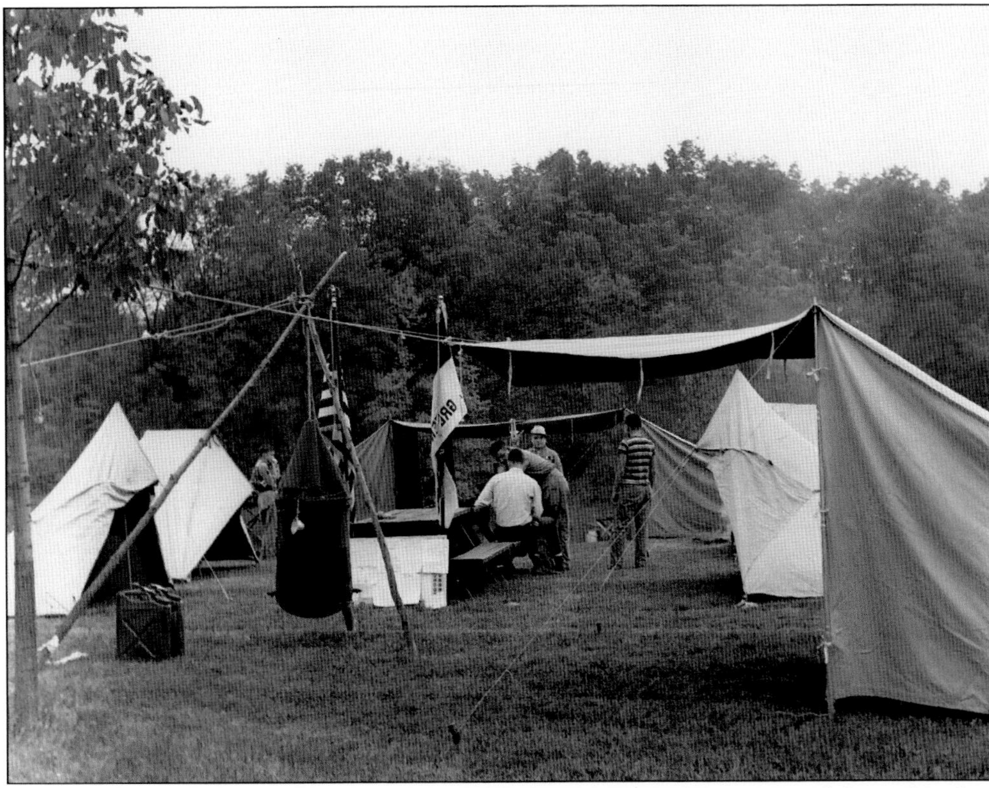

TENT CITY. Local Boy Scout troops converged on Winton Woods campground for weekends of wholesome fun.

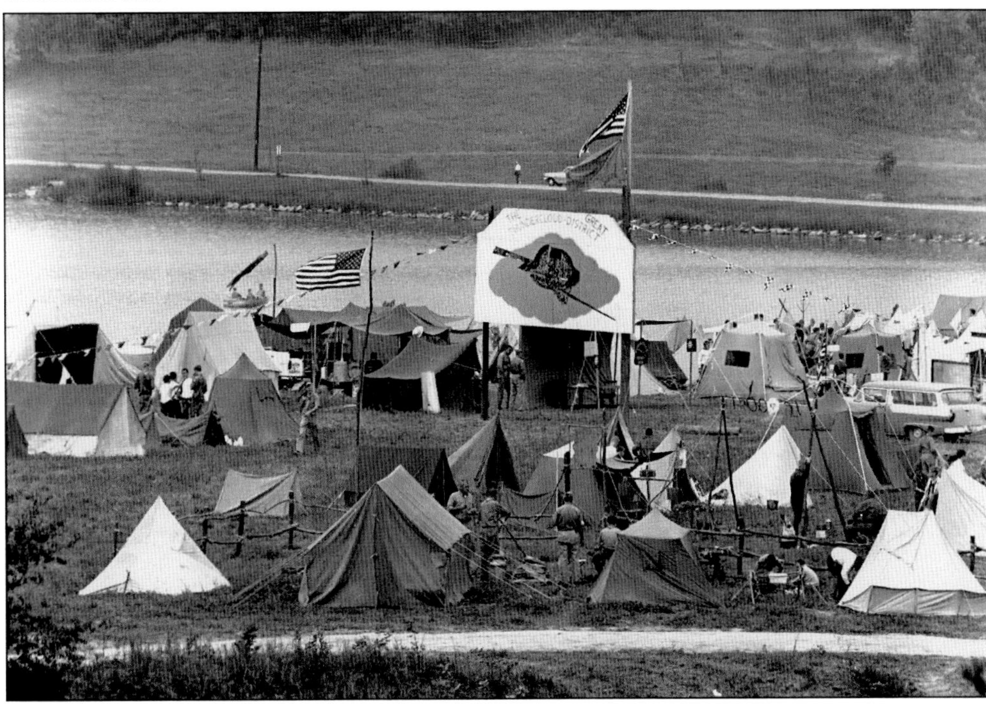

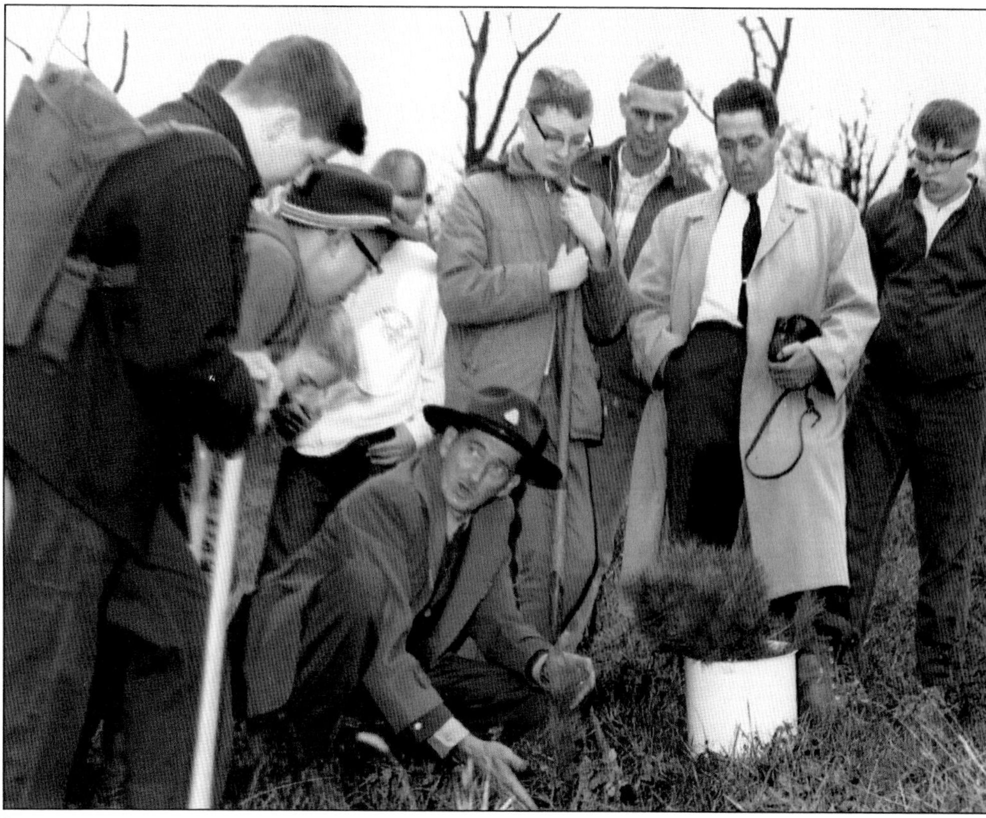

LEARNING FROM THE BEST. Park naturalist Warren Wells (above, center) instructs Scouts who had volunteered to assist in a park reforestation project. Wells counsels the boys on the appropriate depth for planting trees. Wells began his service to the park district in 1955 and was a longtime presence in nature education initiatives. In 1971, Wells received the Ohio Conservation Achievement Award for his work in promoting ecology and conservation. Wells had guided more than 18,000 adults and children of various field trips around the parks.

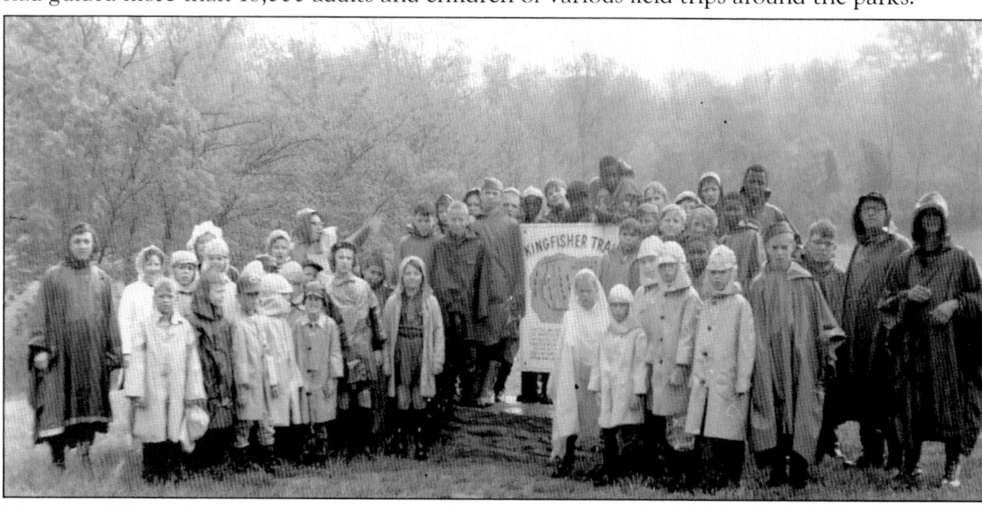

NATURE WALK. This Scout group poses for a picture as it completes a nature walk on the Kingfisher Trail at Winton Woods.

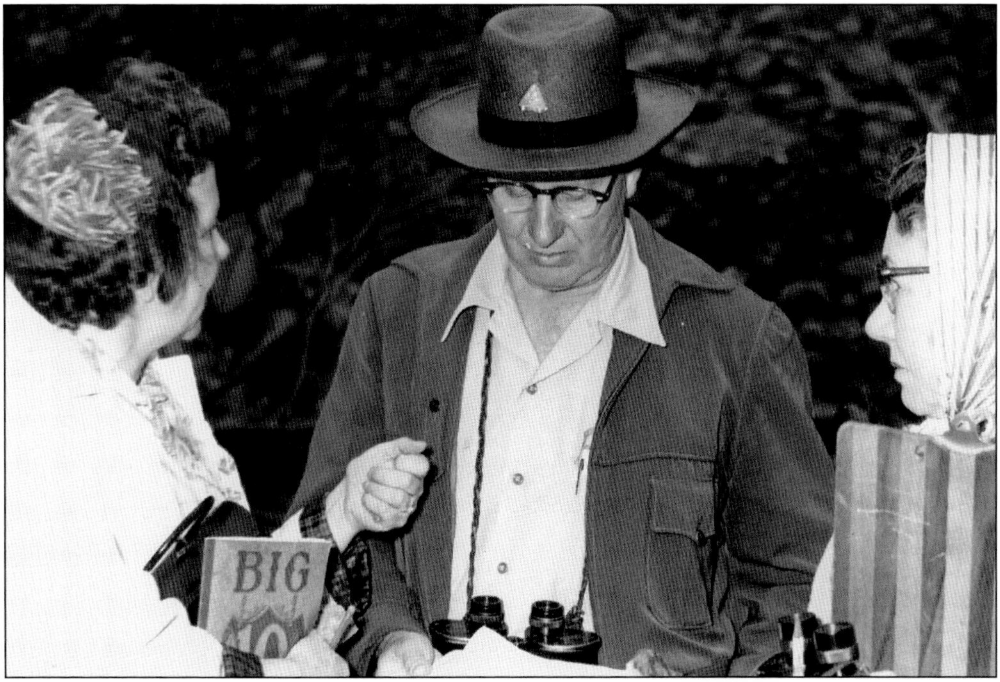

ADULT EDUCATION. Beginning in 1957, the Hamilton County Park District partnered with the Department of Geology at the University of Cincinnati to offer a graduate-level course entitled Field Studies in Natural History. For nine consecutive Saturday mornings, students met at one of the three parks. University of Cincinnati faculty and park naturalists taught sessions on plant and animal life, geological formations, and fossils. Park naturalist Herb Heger (above, center), who served as the program's codirector, answers questions from his 1959 class. Below, students examine a wide array of specimens that were found in the parks.

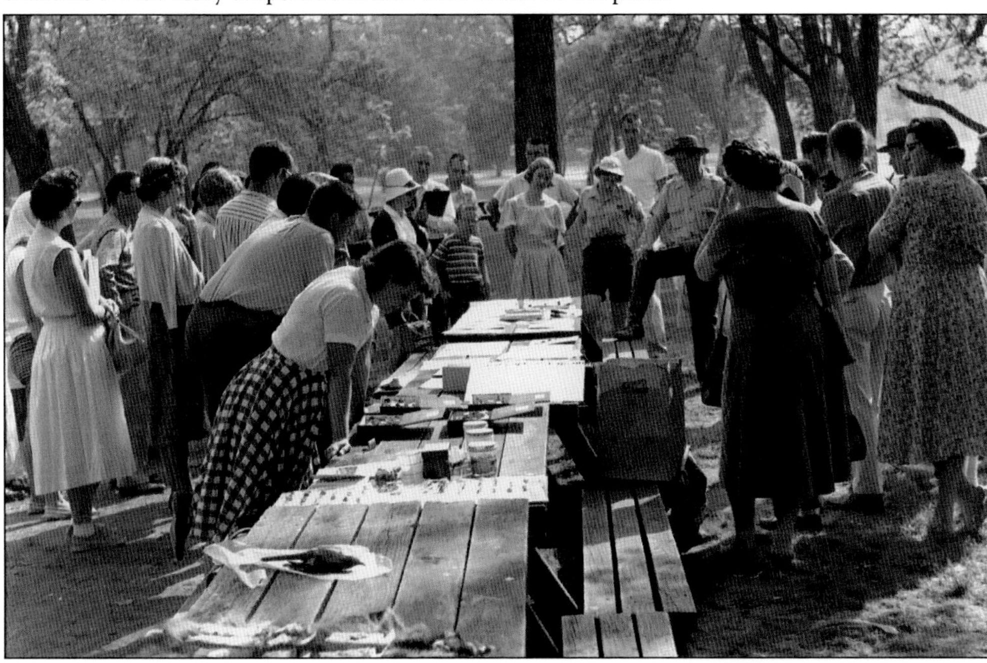

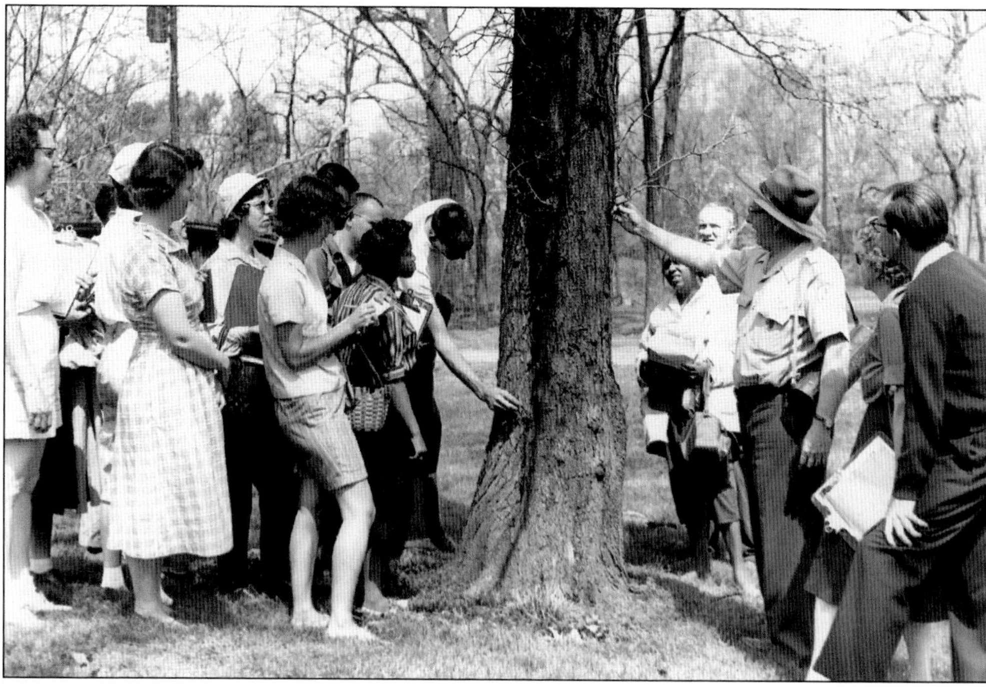

LEARNING ABOUT NATURE, FROM NATURE. Herb Heger (above) leads this 1960 class in tree identification at Sharon Woods. Dr. Jack Gottschang (below, center) prepares a snakeskin at his session. By 1960, enrollments in the field studies course had doubled since the program started.

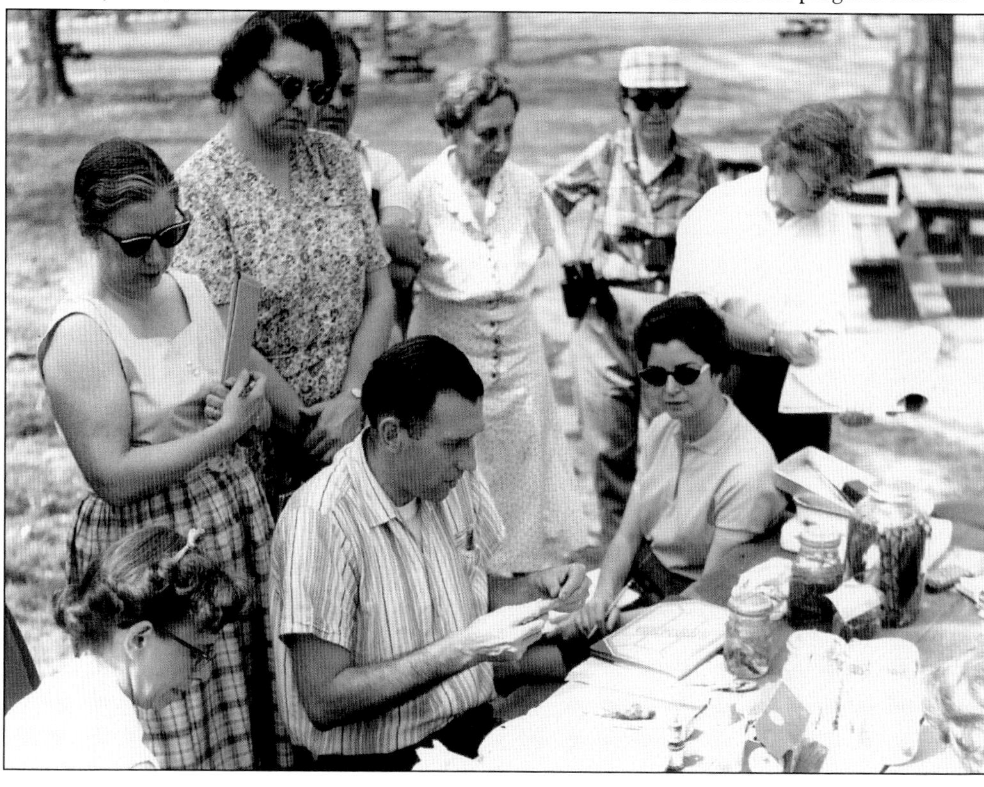

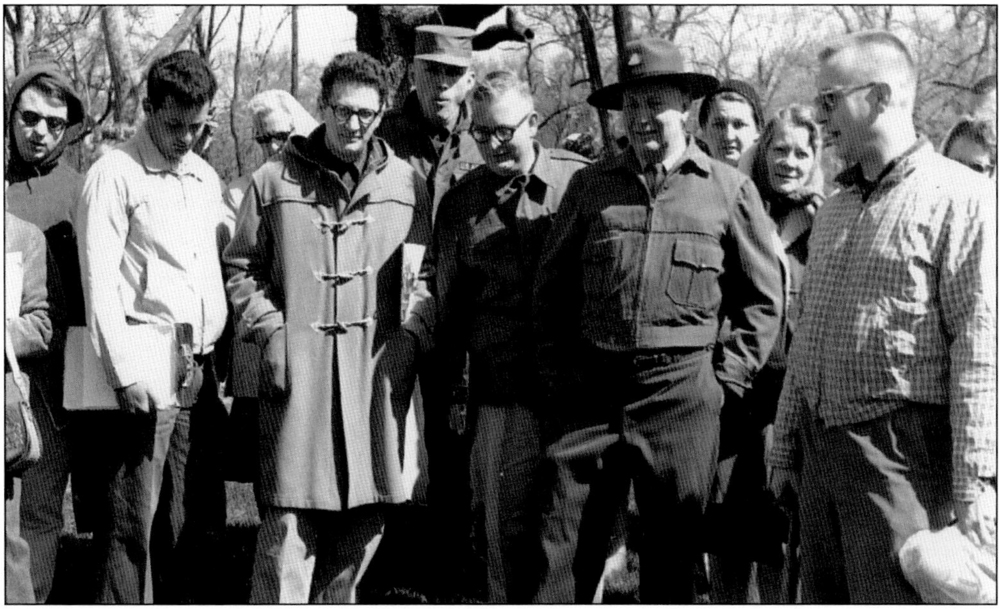

OHIO'S PREHISTORIC RECORD. The Sharon Woods Gorge represented the ideal site for studying the region's fossil record. During the Ordovician period, some 450 million years ago, trilobites and other marine life were the dominant species. In more recent geological times, glaciers reshaped the contours of three-forths of the state, cutting river valleys, creating hills and moraines, and establishing new lakes. Herb Heger (above, center) and Dr. Frank Koucky (above, right), an assistant professor of biology, discuss the boulder that was deposited by a glacier in Sharon Woods. Students (below) study under Koucky's supervision.

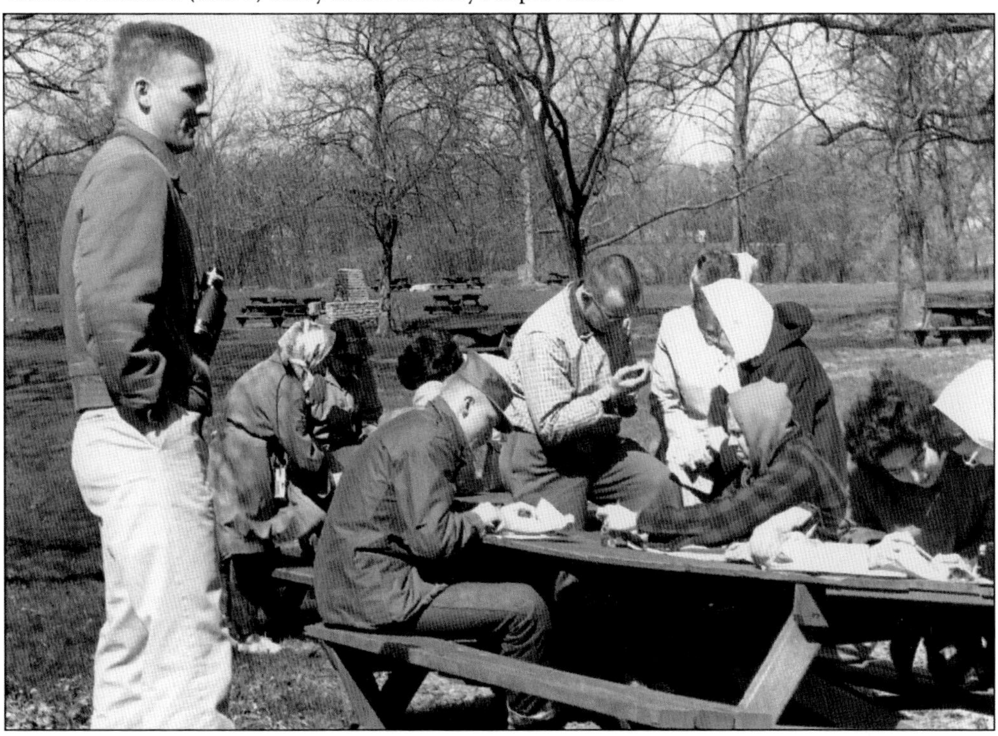

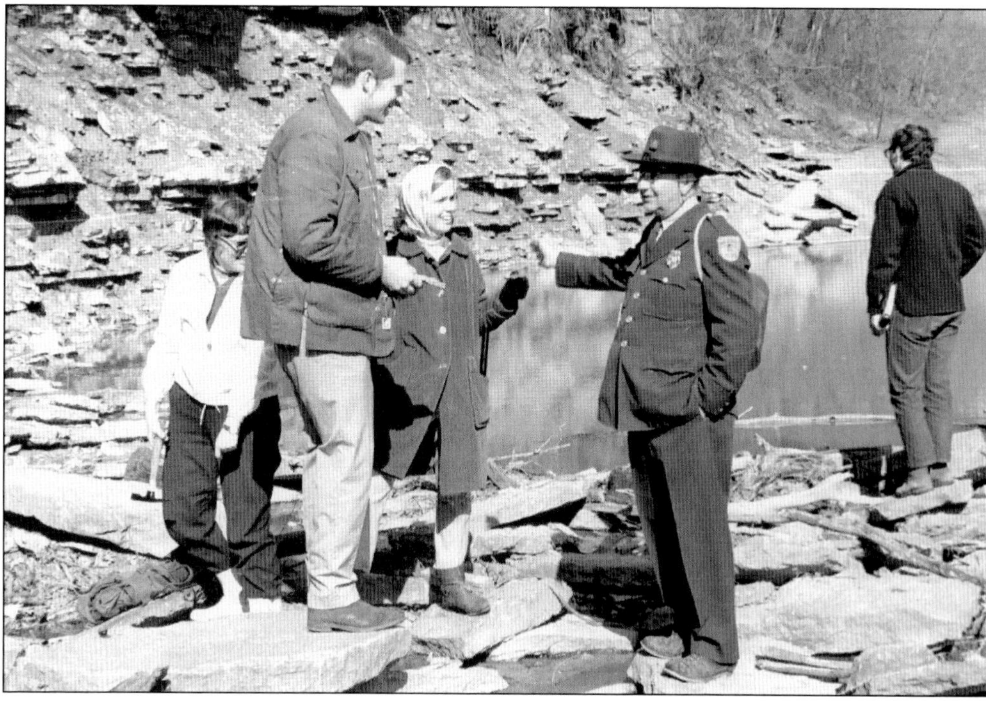

Fossil Hunt. Dr. Warren Huff (left), a specialist in clay mineralogy and paleovolcanology at the University of Cincinnati, chats with Herb Heger during a 1969 fossil hunt at Winton Woods.

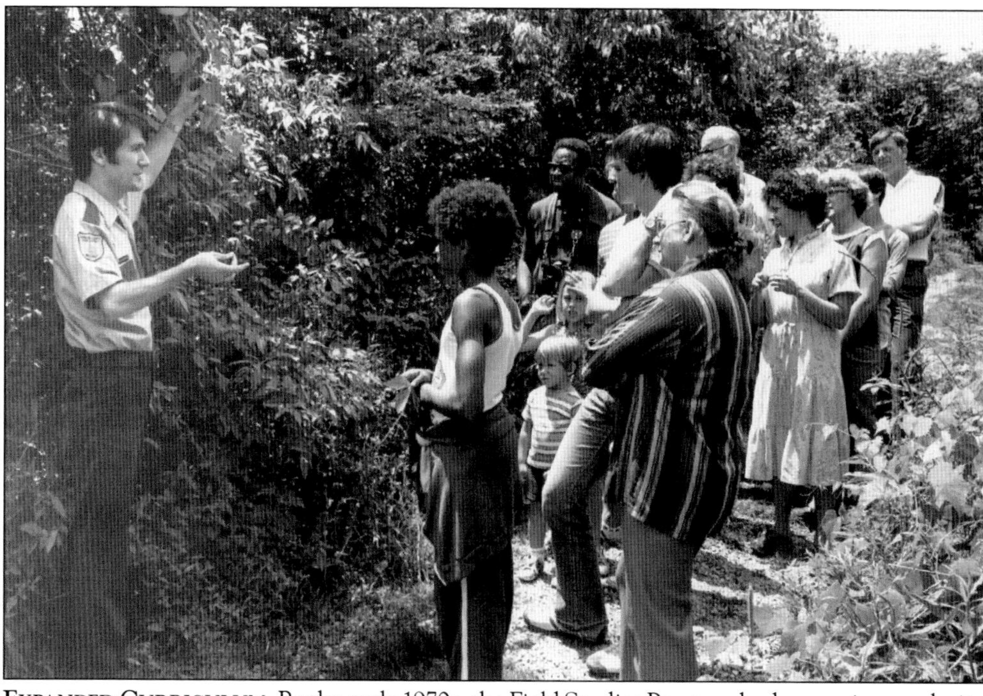

Expanded Curriculum. By the early 1970s, the Field Studies Program had grown in popularity. It also expanded the scope of its curriculum to include such topics as nature photography, nature sound recordings, and food chains.

Four

THE RECENT PAST

75 YEARS OF SERVICE AND MORE

Under the commissioners' quiet but determined leadership, the Hamilton County Park District continued to expand. By 1982, its 16 parks totaled more than 9,500 acres. Over the years, many generous gifts from individuals and area companies swelled the park district's total acreage to its present 14,500 acres. Certainly land acquisition and expansion were important to the park district's vision for future generations, but they represented only one facet of success that the park commissioners envisioned. The park district also faced many challenges in maintaining the exceptionally high quality in its existing parks that its visitors had come to expect. In the 1980s, for example, Sharon Woods Lake was closed to the public. Sedimentation and erosion produced a massive buildup of silt, which threatened the aquatic plant and animal life, as well as the lake's recreational activities. The park district drained the lake, dredged its bottom, and successfully restored the endangered area. The park district addressed similar issues a few years later when it closed Winton Woods Lake until it could be cleaned and restored.

While the parks have become safe havens of retreat and recreation for Hamilton County residents to hike, camp, golf, fish, or enjoy a picnic dinner, more than 80 percent of parklands have been returned to their natural state. Careful management of the parklands and their natural resources have led to impressive victories on the conservation front. The return of 120 acres of wetlands in Miami Whitewater Forest is only one notable example.

Finally, the park district has been adept at meeting the changing needs of its residents. Through partnerships with the Cincinnati Park Board and the Cincinnati Recreation Commission, the Hamilton County Park District has helped develop parks in areas of the county that have been underserved by the county.

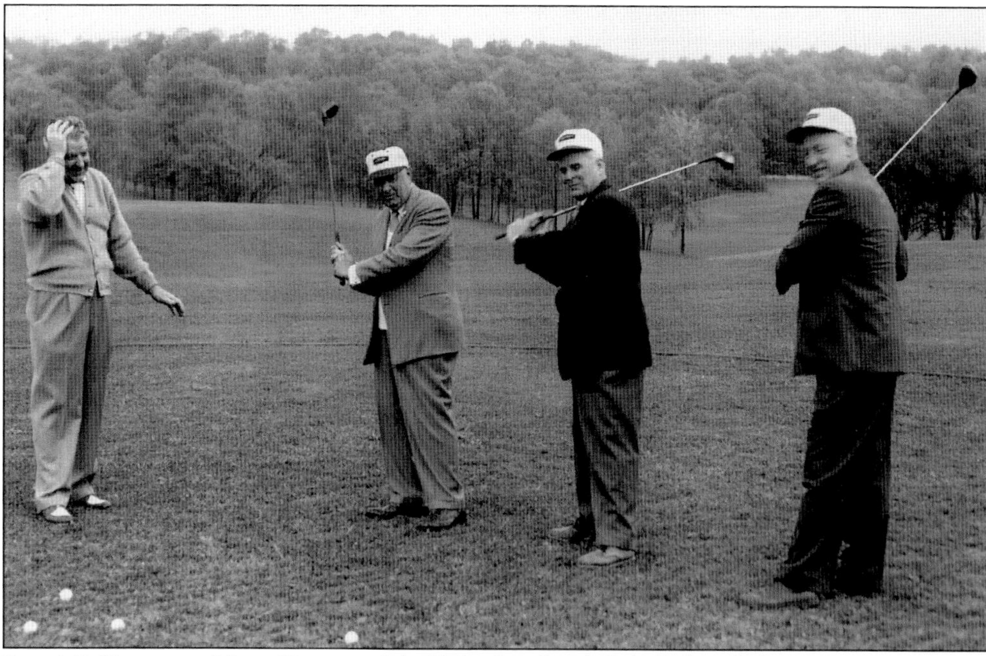

FORE! Golf manager Marty Kavanaugh holds his head in disbelief after all three Hamilton County park commissioners, Justin Rollman (left), Louis Nippert (center), and Sam Benedict dribble their tee shots a few feet. While this photograph shows a more playful side of the commissioners, they usually preferred to work behind the scenes and out of the public spotlight.

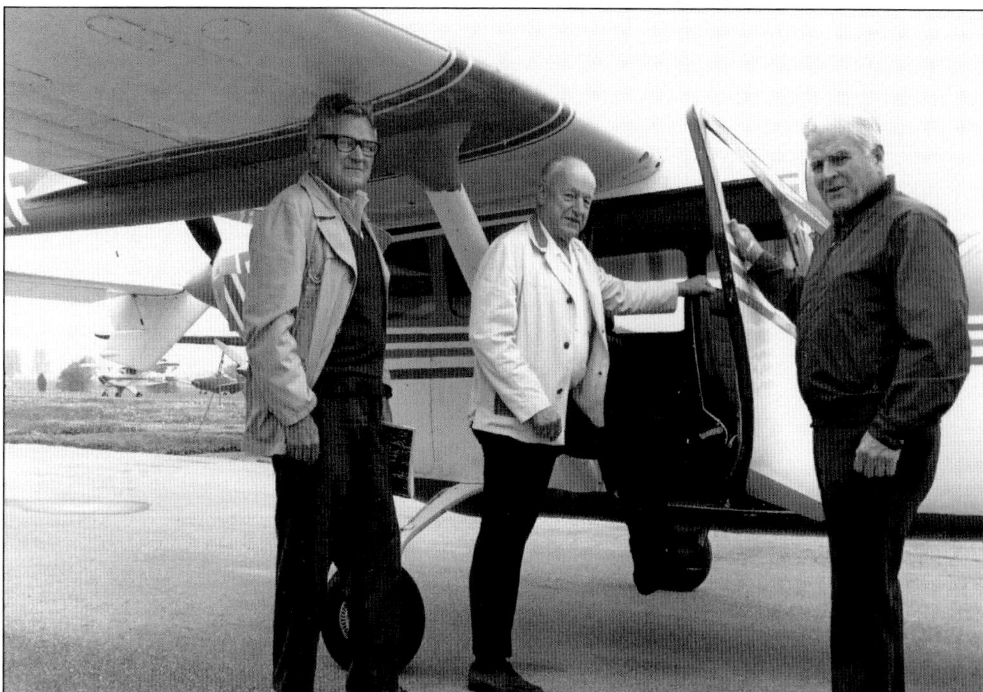

UP, UP, AND AWAY. In 1975, park commissioners took to the sky aboard a small airplane to conduct their annual inspection of the parks.

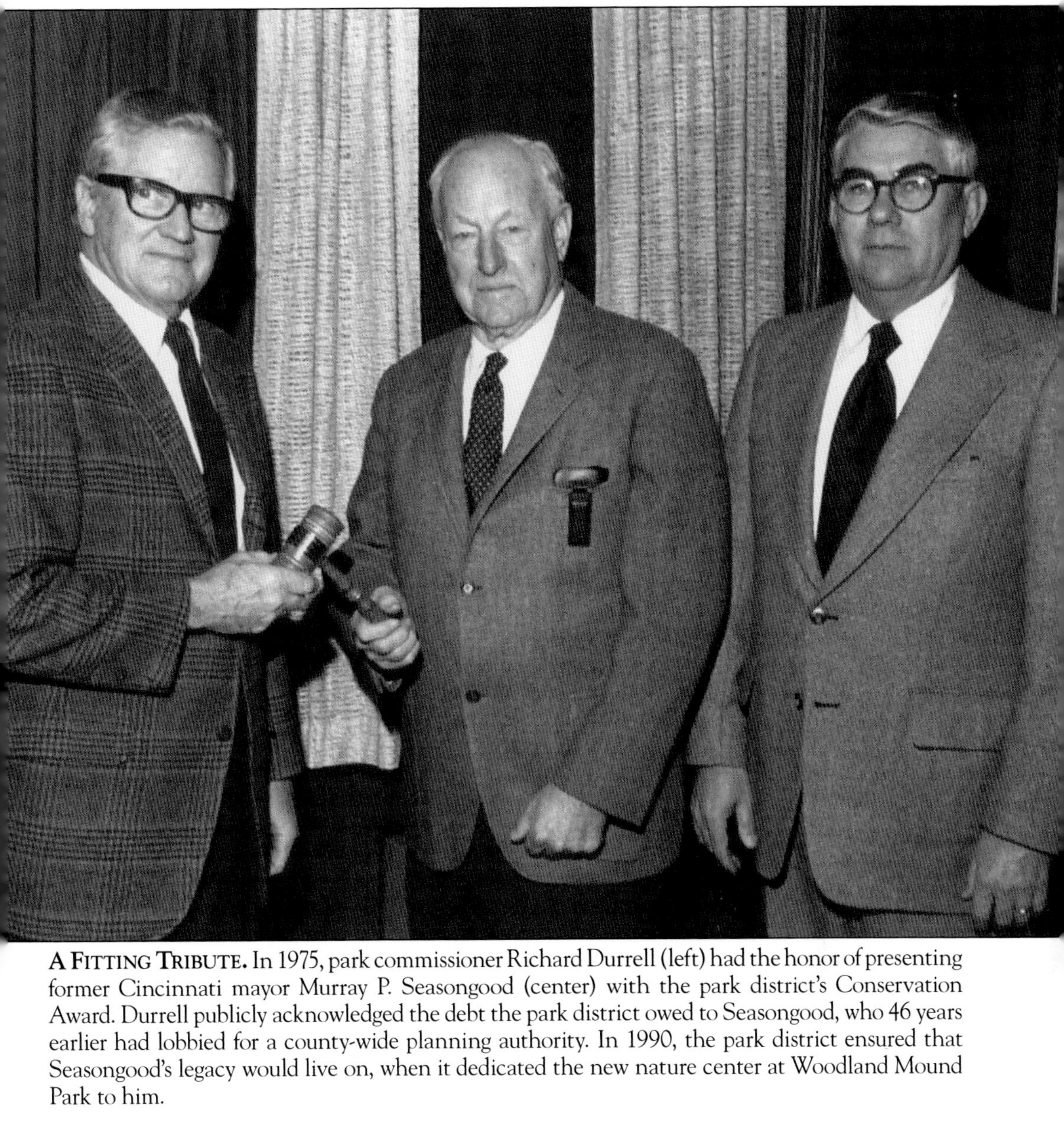

A FITTING TRIBUTE. In 1975, park commissioner Richard Durrell (left) had the honor of presenting former Cincinnati mayor Murray P. Seasongood (center) with the park district's Conservation Award. Durrell publicly acknowledged the debt the park district owed to Seasongood, who 46 years earlier had lobbied for a county-wide planning authority. In 1990, the park district ensured that Seasongood's legacy would live on, when it dedicated the new nature center at Woodland Mound Park to him.

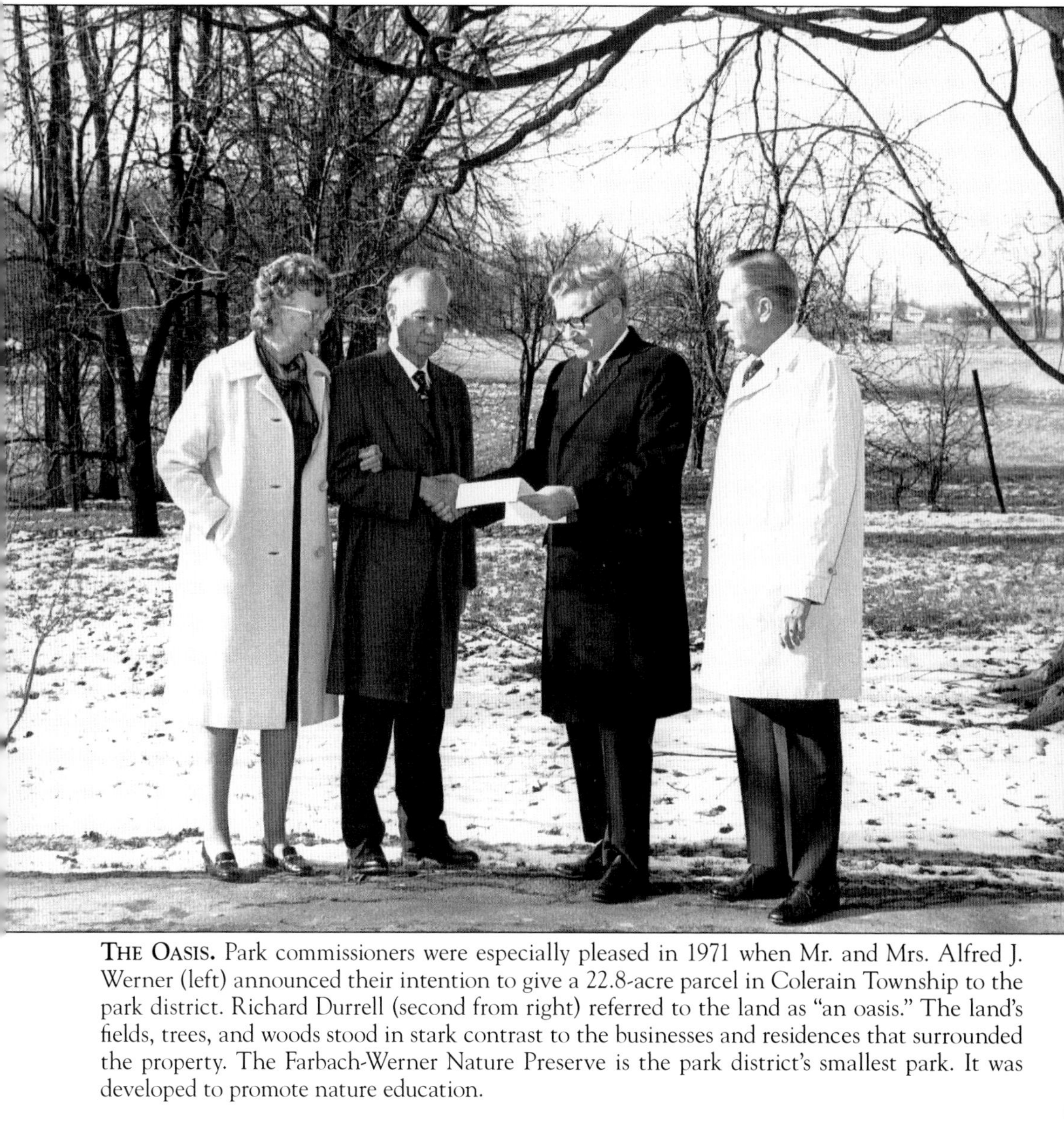

THE OASIS. Park commissioners were especially pleased in 1971 when Mr. and Mrs. Alfred J. Werner (left) announced their intention to give a 22.8-acre parcel in Colerain Township to the park district. Richard Durrell (second from right) referred to the land as "an oasis." The land's fields, trees, and woods stood in stark contrast to the businesses and residences that surrounded the property. The Farbach-Werner Nature Preserve is the park district's smallest park. It was developed to promote nature education.

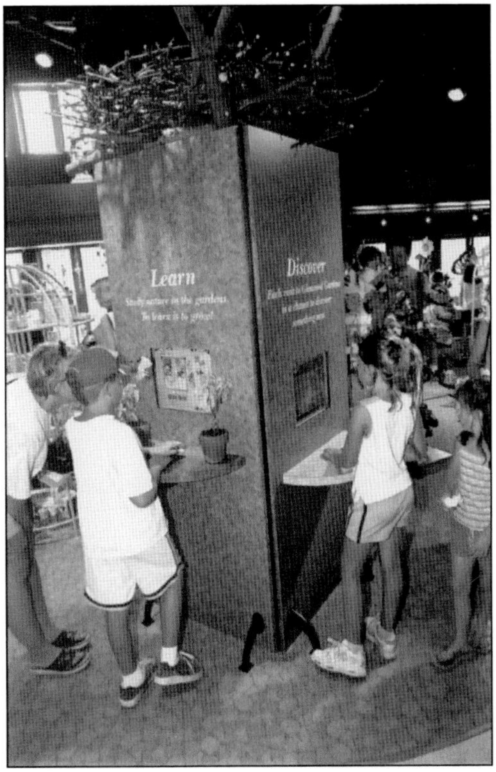

CAPTURING THE SENSES. Nature centers that educate and inform visitors of all ages are located at Woodland Mound, Sharon Woods, Winton Woods, and Miami Whitewater Forest (right). Park naturalists offer engaging, hands-on learning experiences.

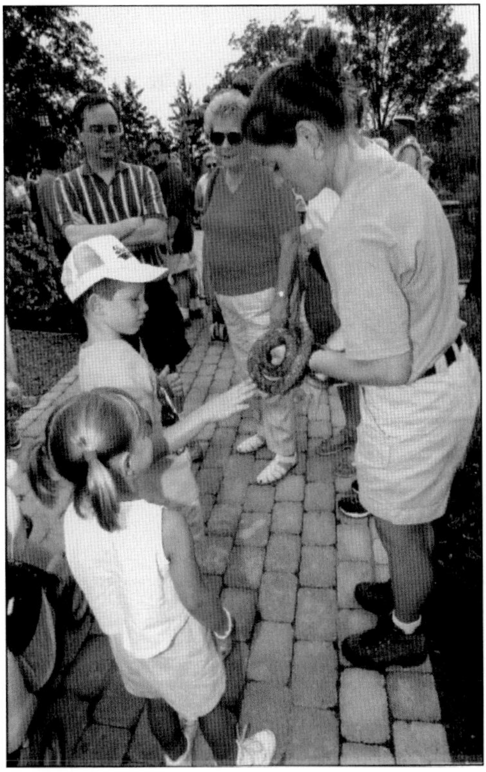

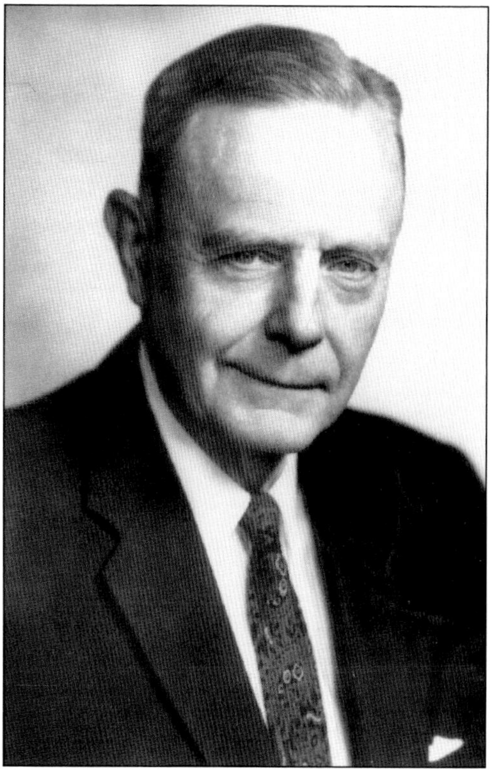

Preserving Nature's Legacy. Ann Richardson donated the 162 acres of this 265-acre preserve in 1978 in memory of her late husband, Dr. Albert S. Richardson (left). The Richardson Forest Preserve is located in Colerain Township. It is one of four conservation areas in the park district that are expressly designed to maintain natural habitats.

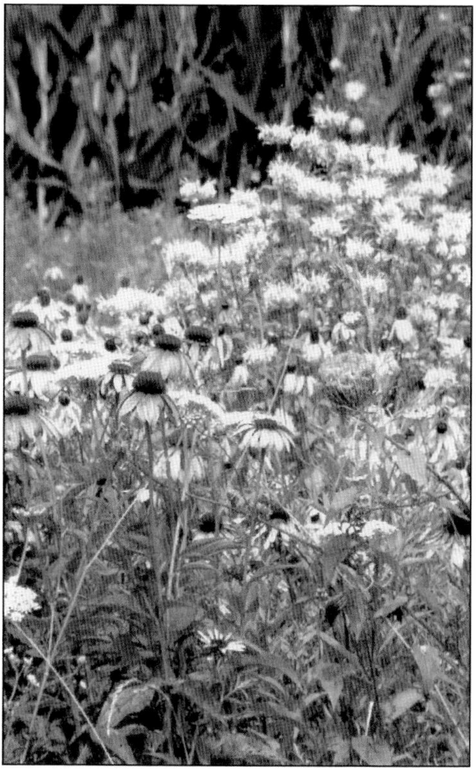

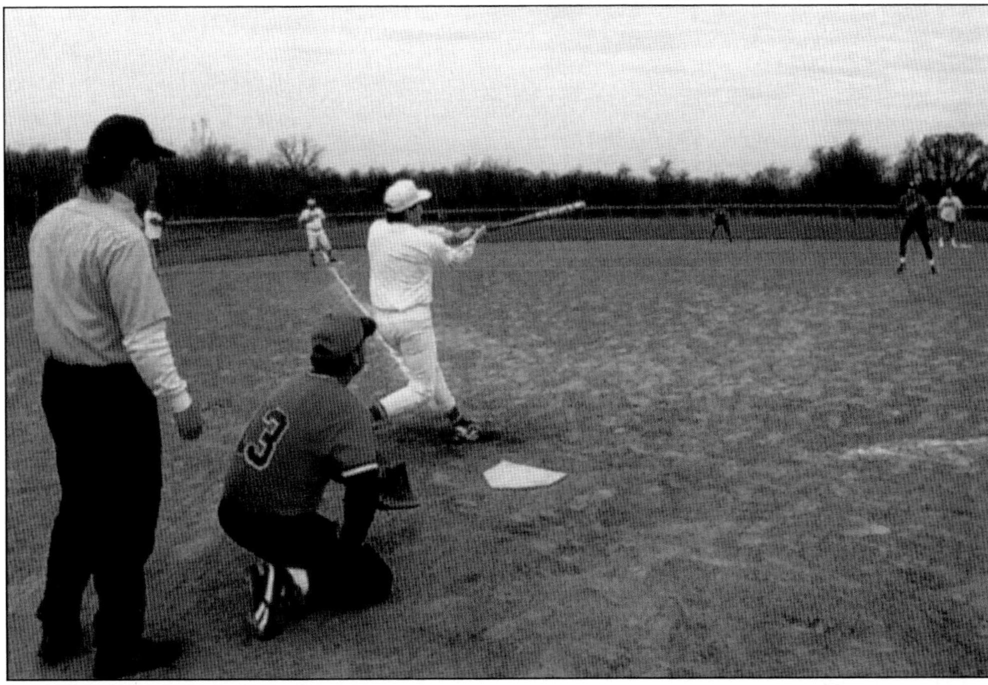

TRIPLE CREEK. This 177-acre park was created through a lease by the county commissioners in the 1970s. The park features four regulation ball diamonds and a parcours trail. Jack C. Murphy (below), of Murphy Homes, Inc., poses near the park sign. His company donated an additional 150 acres of land that was contiguous to the park.

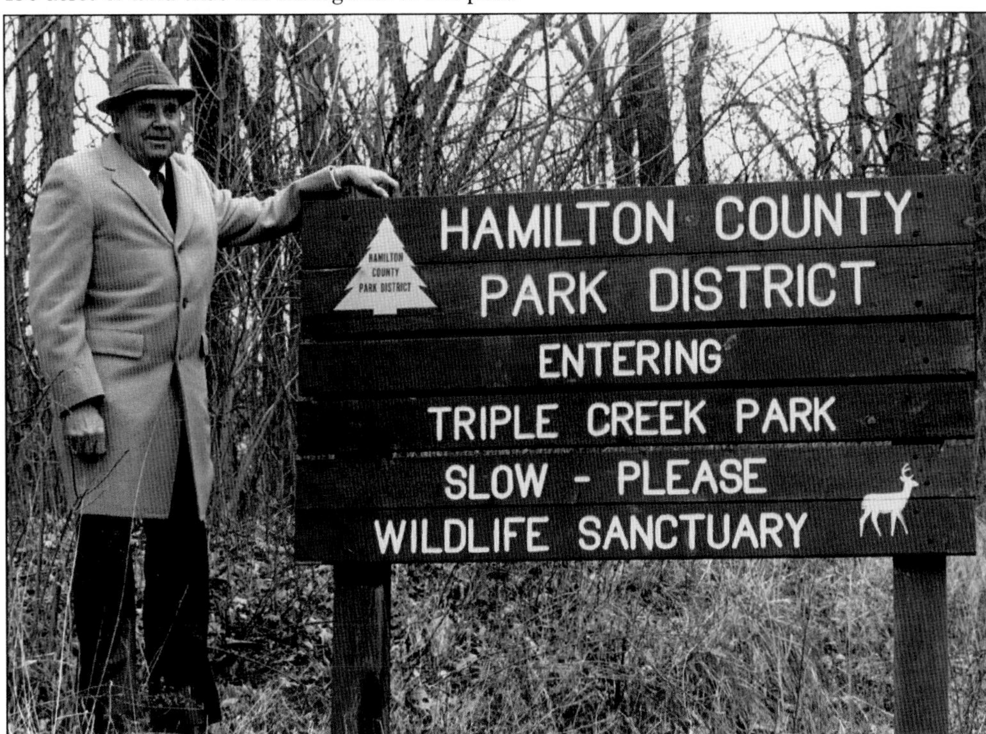

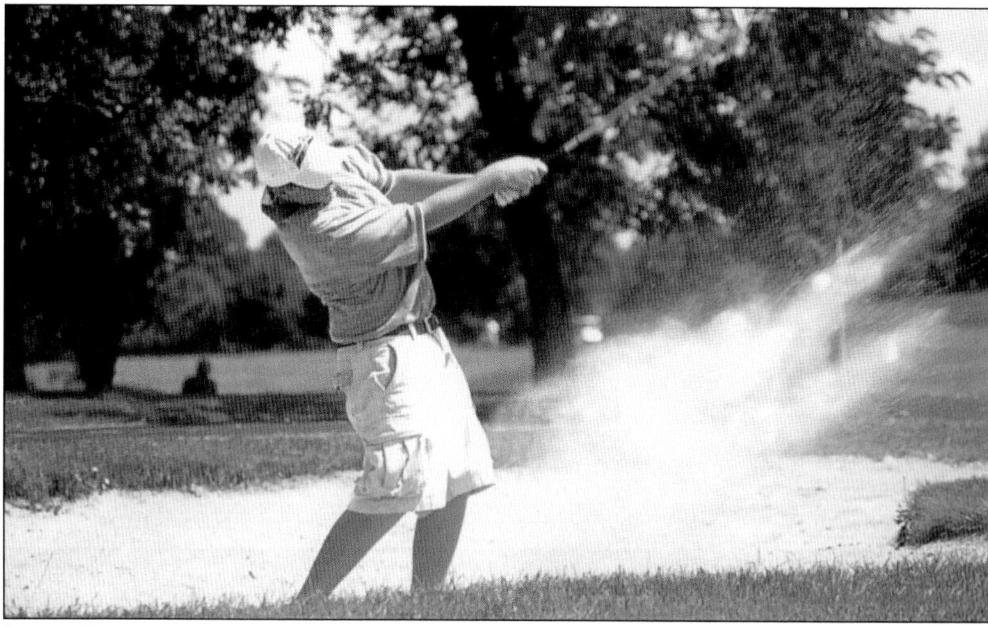

More Opportunities for Golf. In addition to the regulation courses at Sharon Woods, Winton Woods, Miami Whitewater Forest, and Shawnee Lookout, the park district opened a fifth golf course near Woodland Mound Park, called the Vineyard, in 1986. The Little Miami Golf Center, in Newtown, is the only par-three course. The Meadowlinks Golf Academy, also in Winton Woods, features a links-style course of par-three and par-four holes. Many county courses have junior leagues for youngsters.

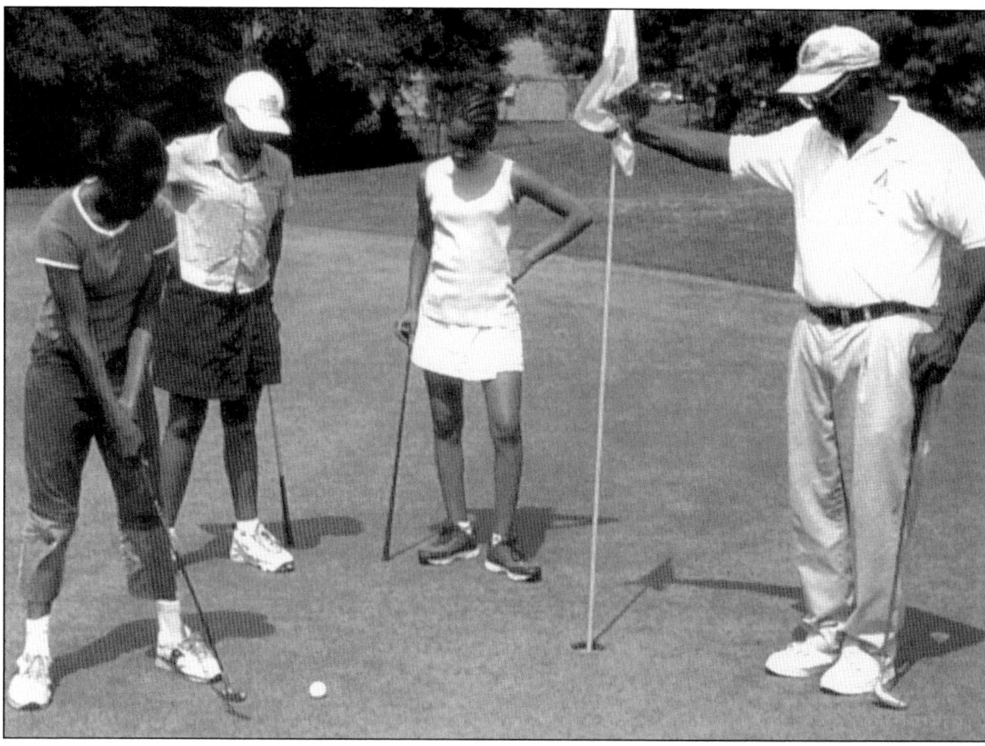

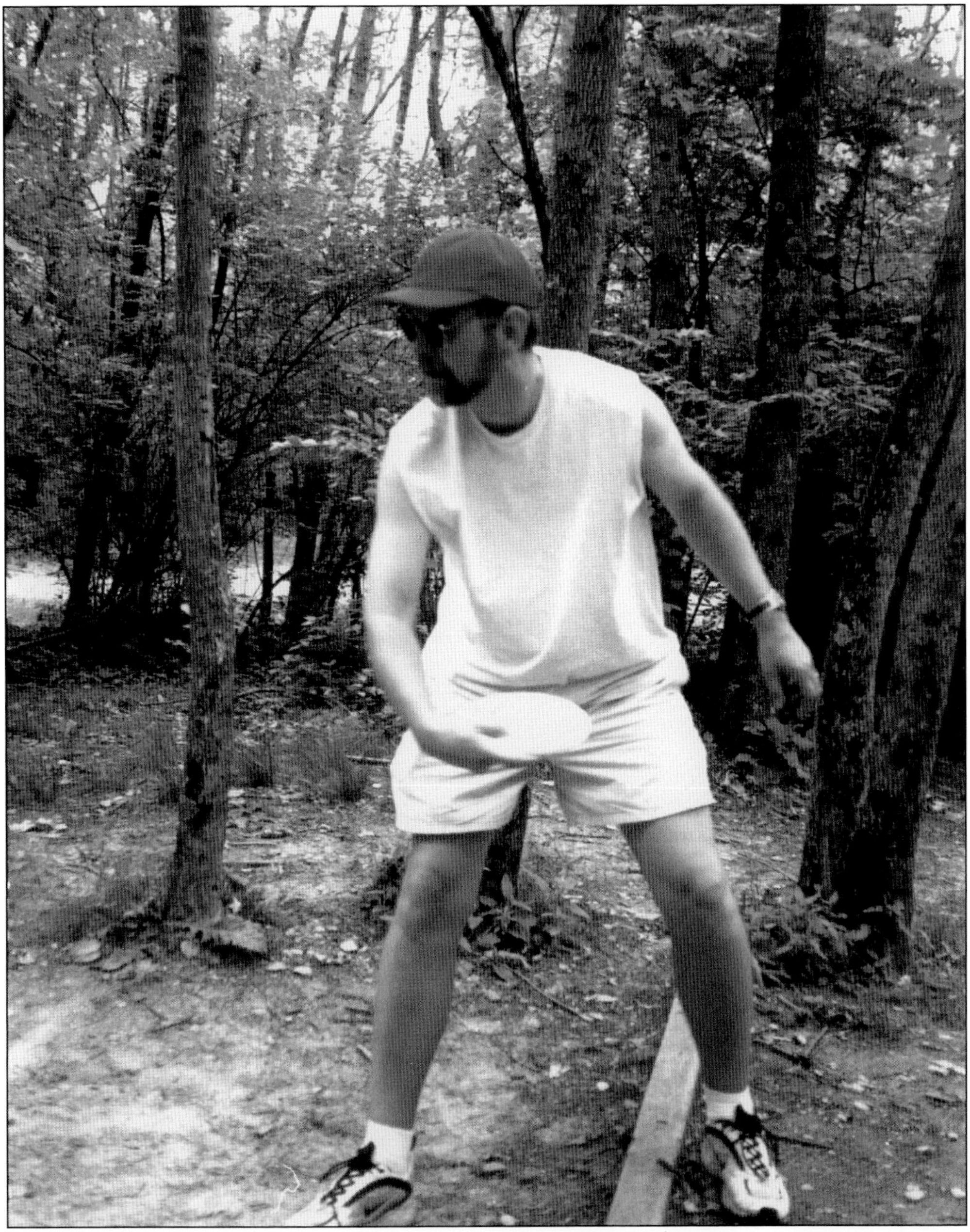

FRISBEES IN THE FORESTS. Miami Whitewater Forest and Embshoff Woods, in Delhi, both have nine-hole Frisbee golf courses. Hard-core disc golf enthusiasts can also tackle 18-hole courses at Winton Woods (above) and Woodland Mound.

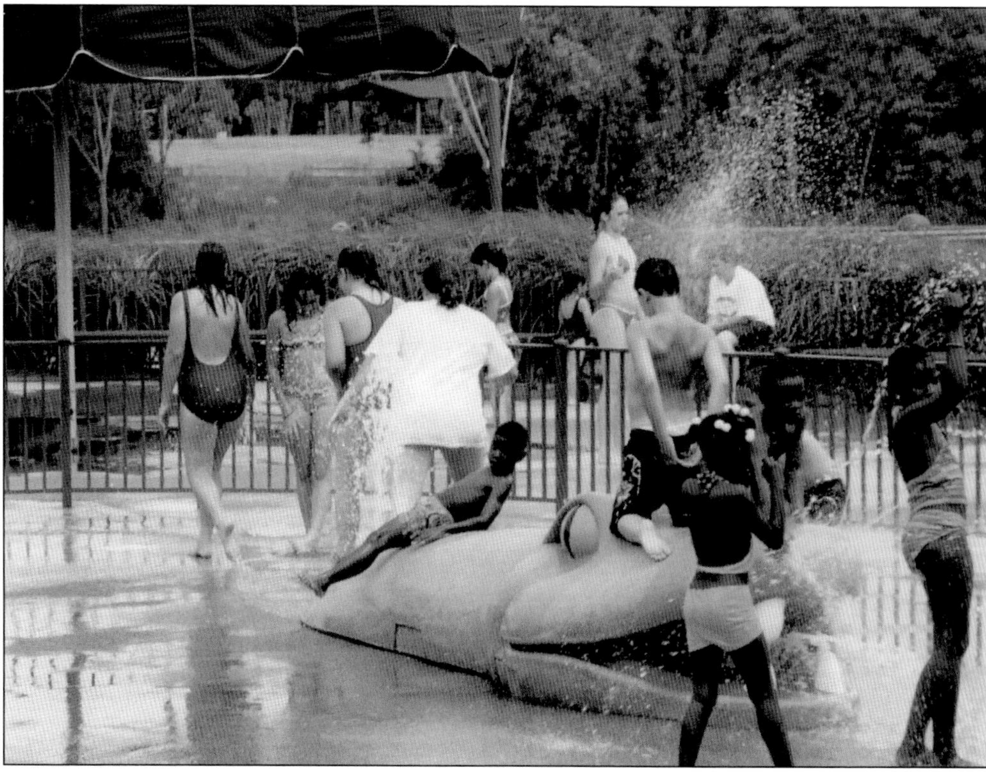

Wet Water Fun. The park district offers one solution to area children and their parents to combat hot summer days. Four parks contain wet playgrounds, with slides and stationary animal figures that spray water.

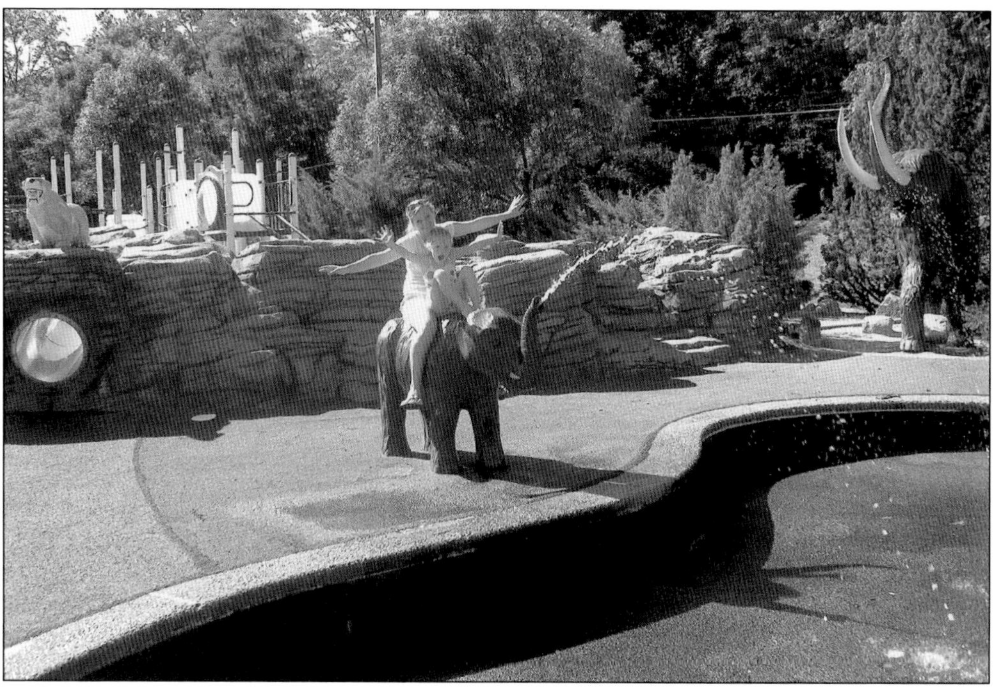

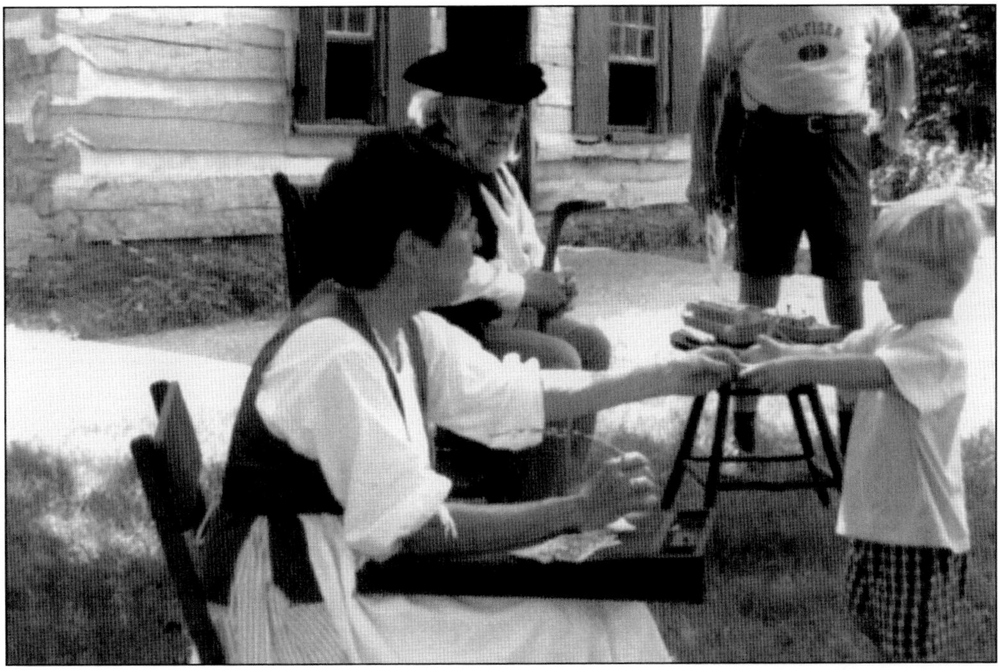

STEPPING BACK IN TIME. Citizens groups raised money to move two historical buildings, the old Springer Schoolhouse and a log cabin, to Shawnee Lookout. The structures were reassembled and restored. Today historical reenactors interact with guests, sharing insights about life in a bygone era.

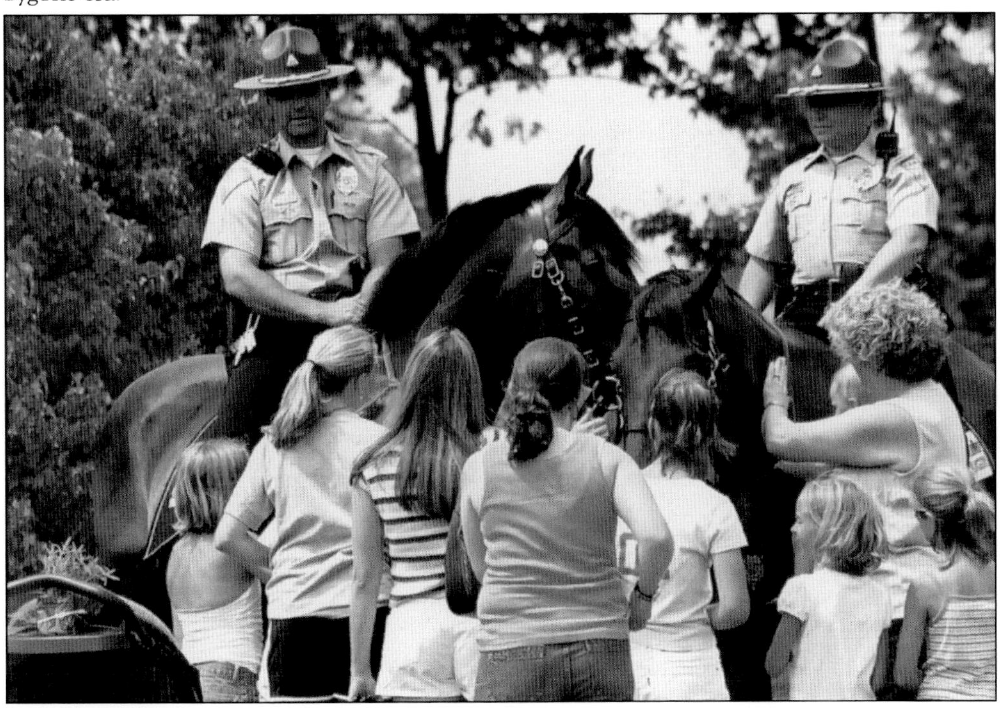

POPULAR WITH KIDS. Mounted park rangers usually draw a crowd when they make appearances at county parks.

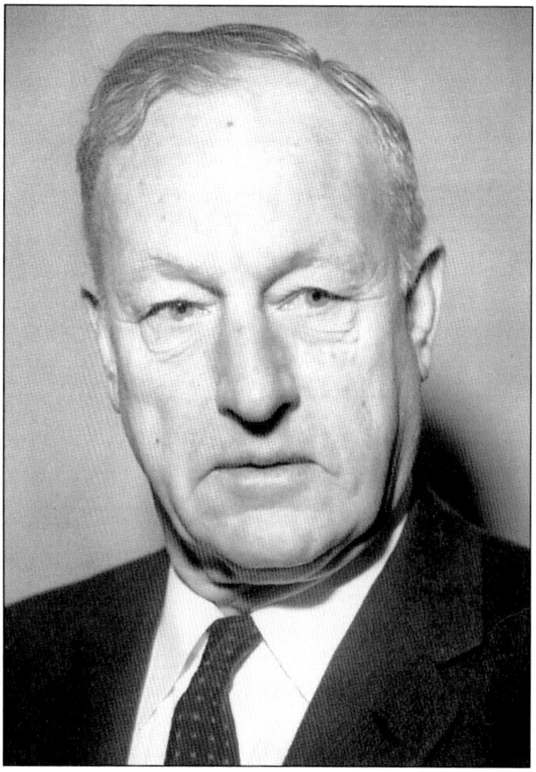

GLENWOOD GARDENS. In the 1960s, Hamilton County park commissioner Sam Benedict (left) and his wife Betty donated an 85-acre parcel of land, sandwiched between Glendale and Woodlawn, to the park district. In 1981, this parcel became Trillium Trails Wildflower Preserve. After the park district acquired an additional 239 acres from neighboring lands, it was able to develop Glenwood Gardens. This park offers a wonderful mix of walking trails that traverse wetlands and prairie growth.

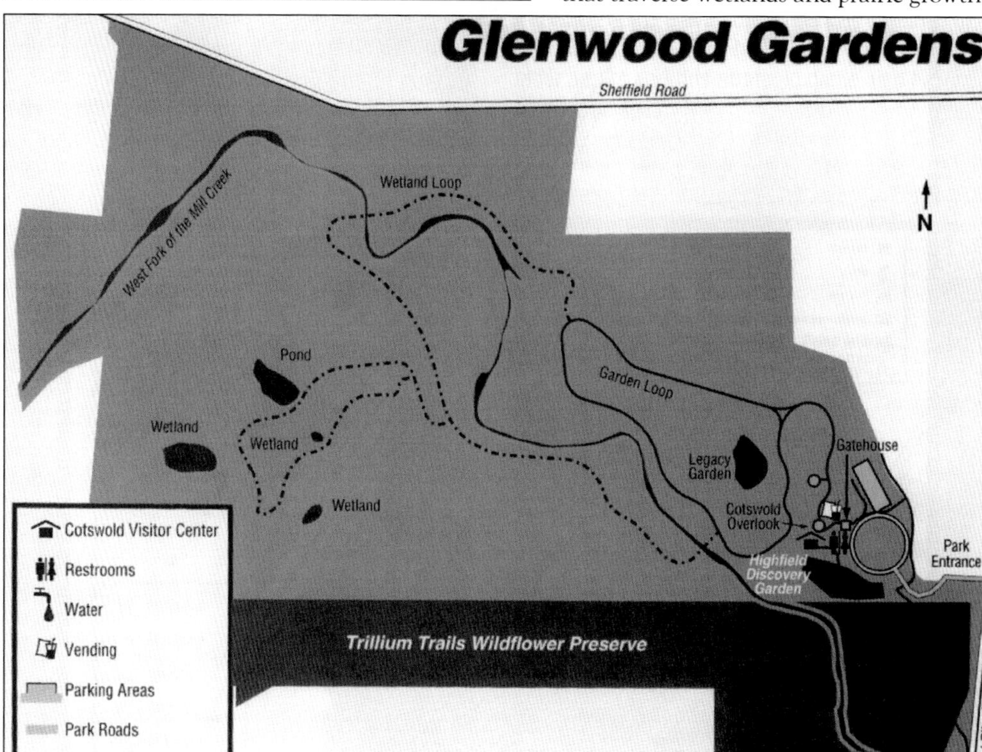

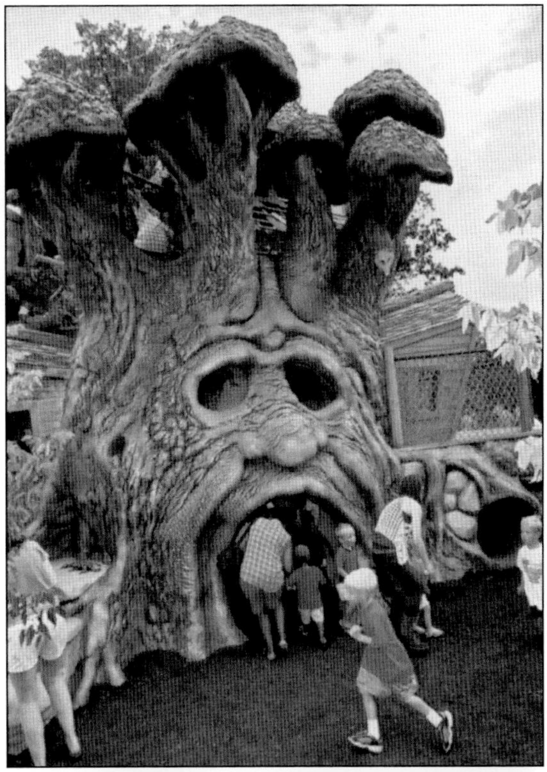

A Place for Kids. In 2004, the park district completed the final phase at Glenwood Gardens when it opened Highfield Discovery Garden. This child-oriented garden center features the 25-foot Discovery Tree and other interactive learning attractions.

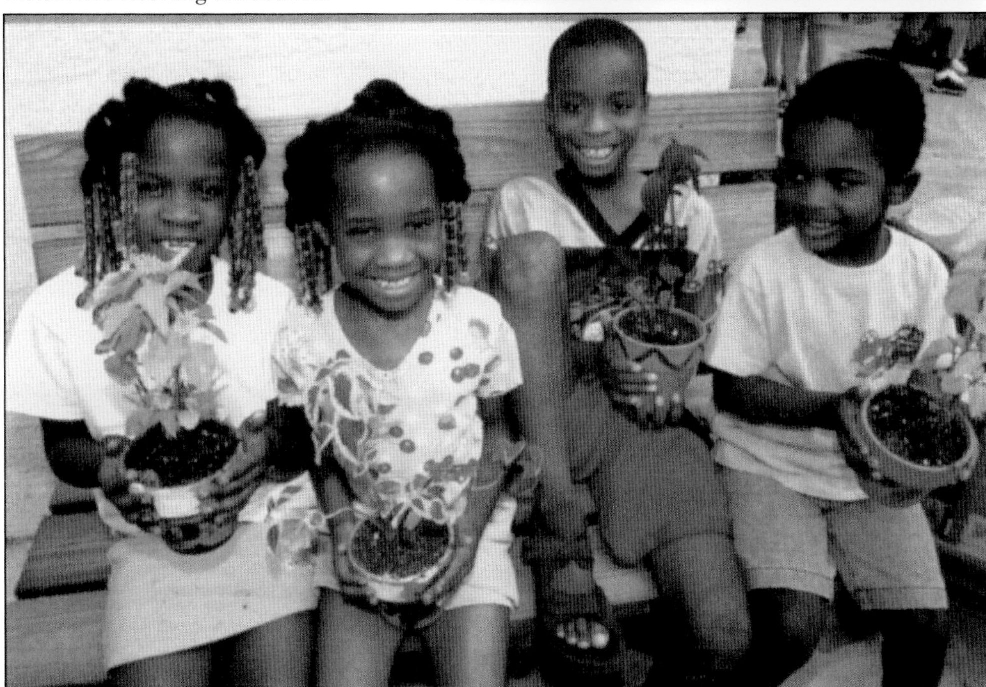

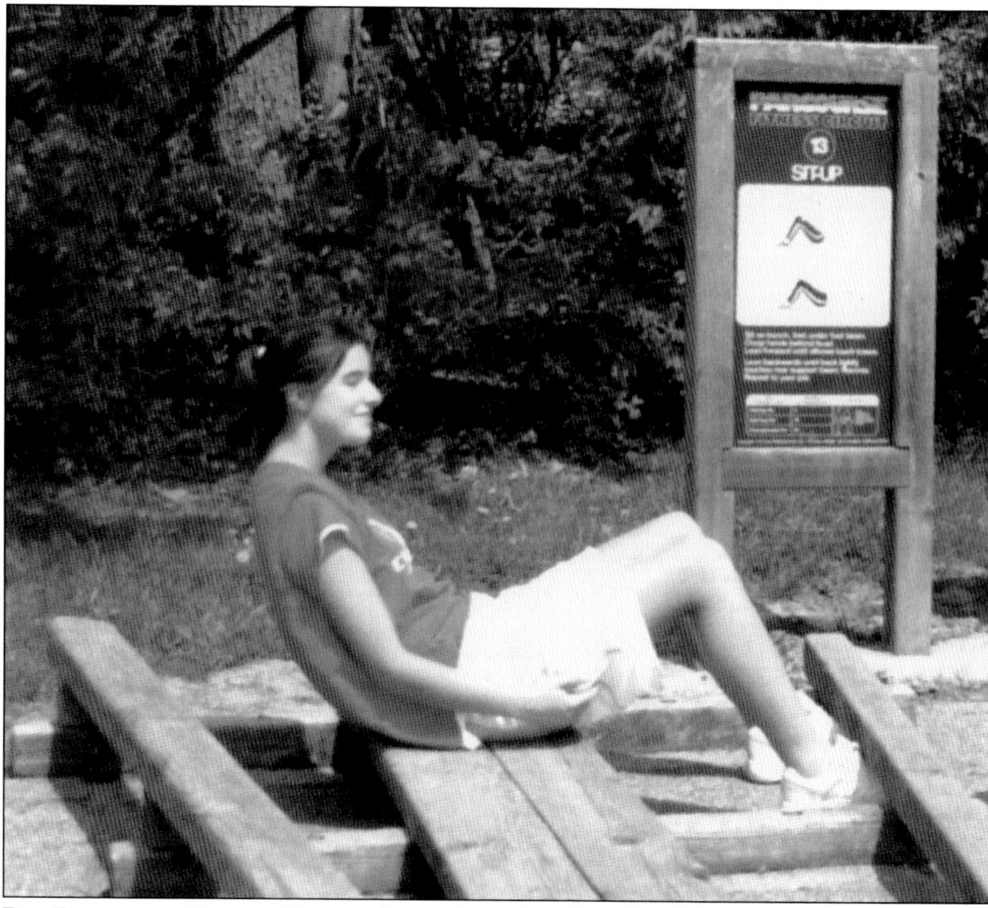

PAR COURSE, OF COURSE. Fitness aficionados and workout fanatics are frequent visitors at the park district's parcours fitness trails. The trails offer people a blend of calisthenics, isometrics, and cardiovascular exercises for a complete workout.

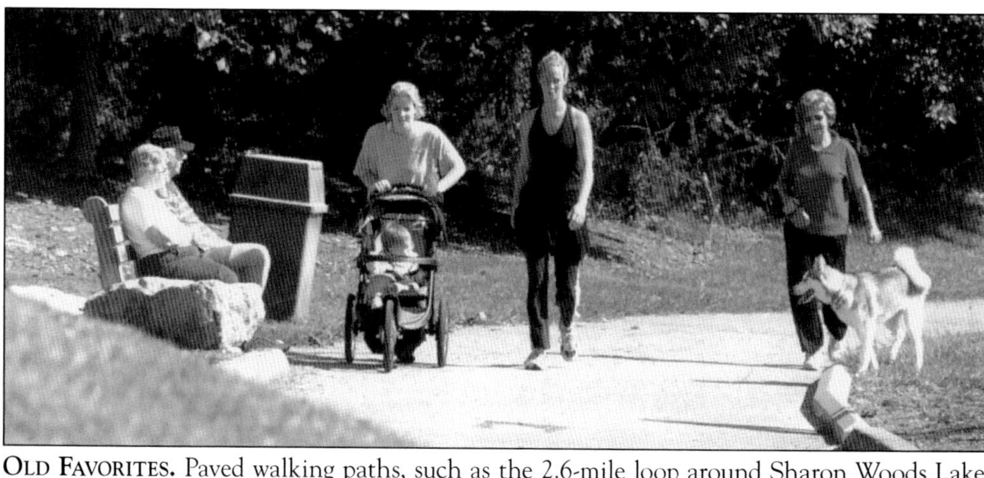

OLD FAVORITES. Paved walking paths, such as the 2.6-mile loop around Sharon Woods Lake, are popular destinations for moms with strollers, in-line skaters, cyclists, and joggers.

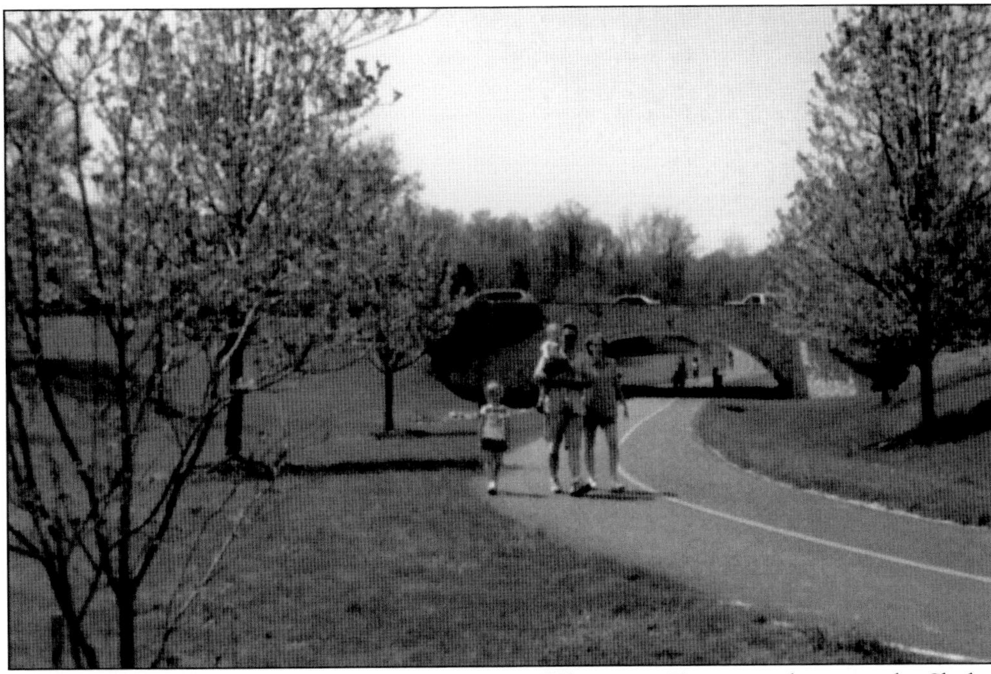

Shaker Trace Loop. Residents closer to Miami Whitewater Forest are drawn to the Shaker Trace Loop.

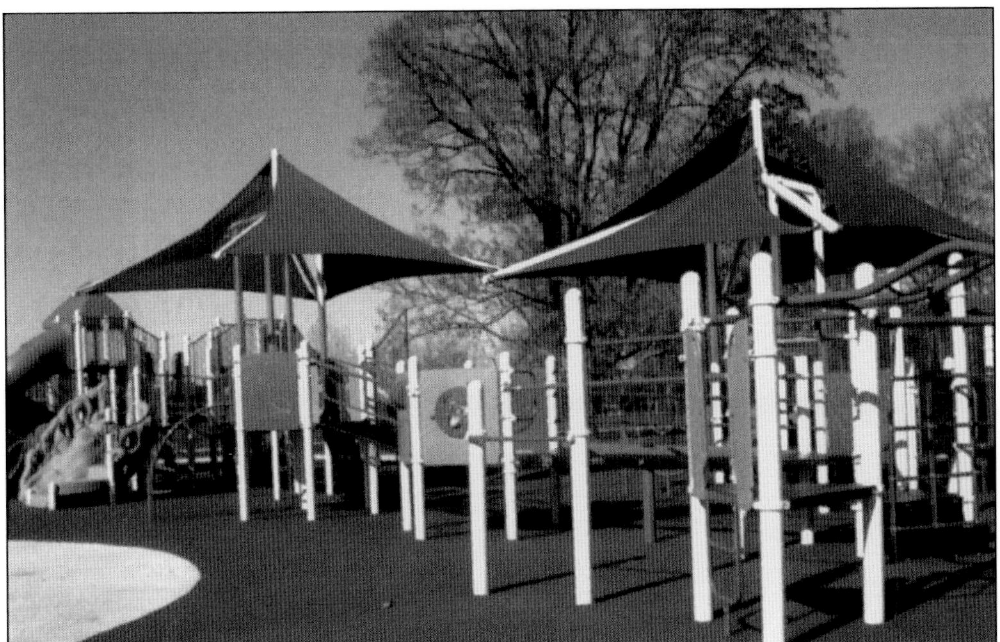

New Directions. Fernbank Park, located west of downtown Cincinnati along the Ohio River, had been designated for park purposes since the early part of the 20th century. In 2003, the park district embarked in a joint venture with the Cincinnati Park Board to revive the park. The newly renovated park boasts a state-of-the-art playground and a paved walking path.

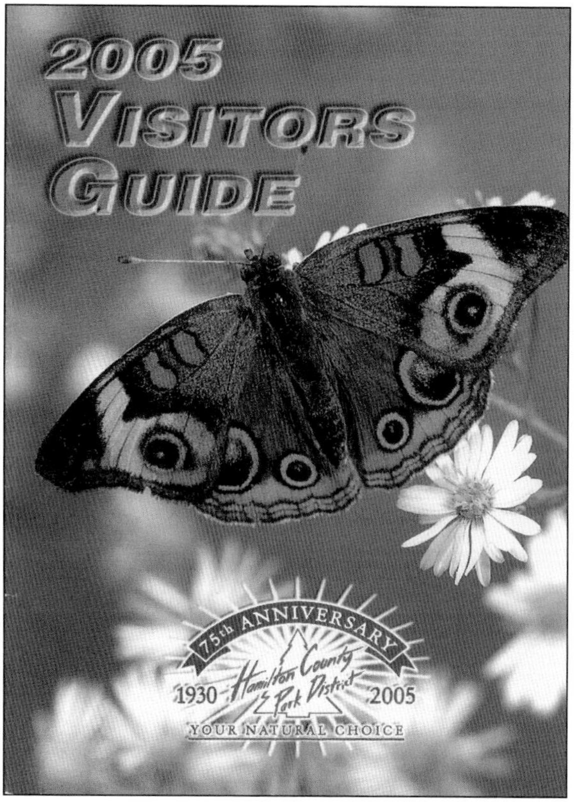

The Diamond Anniversary. Park officials commemorated the 75th anniversary of the park district throughout the entire 2005 season. The anniversary year map reflects the many changes that have taken place in the park district in its 75 years of service to the county.

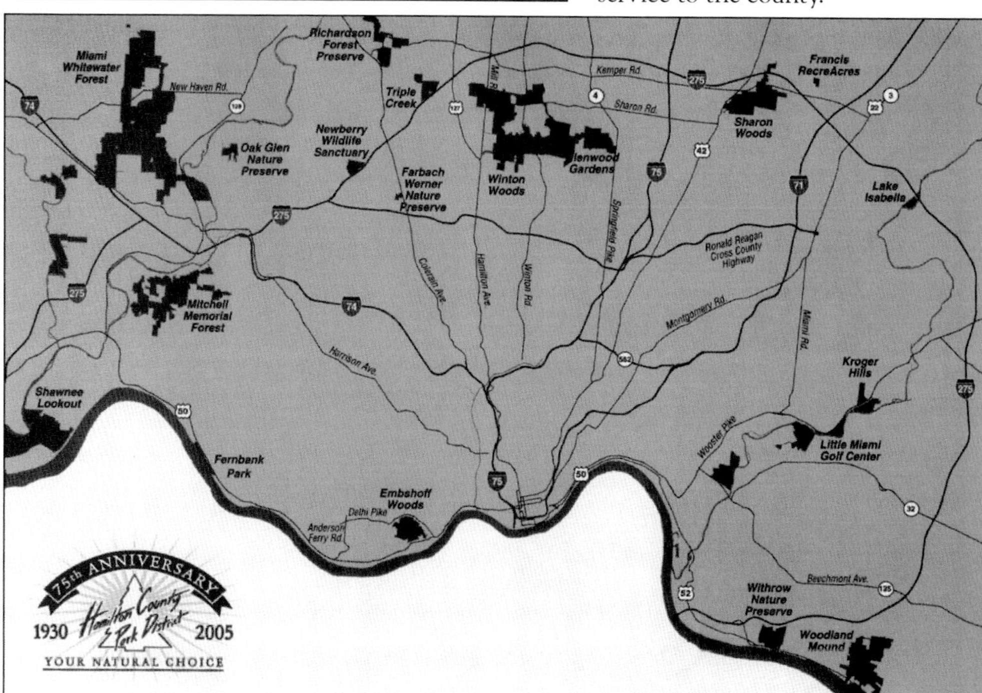

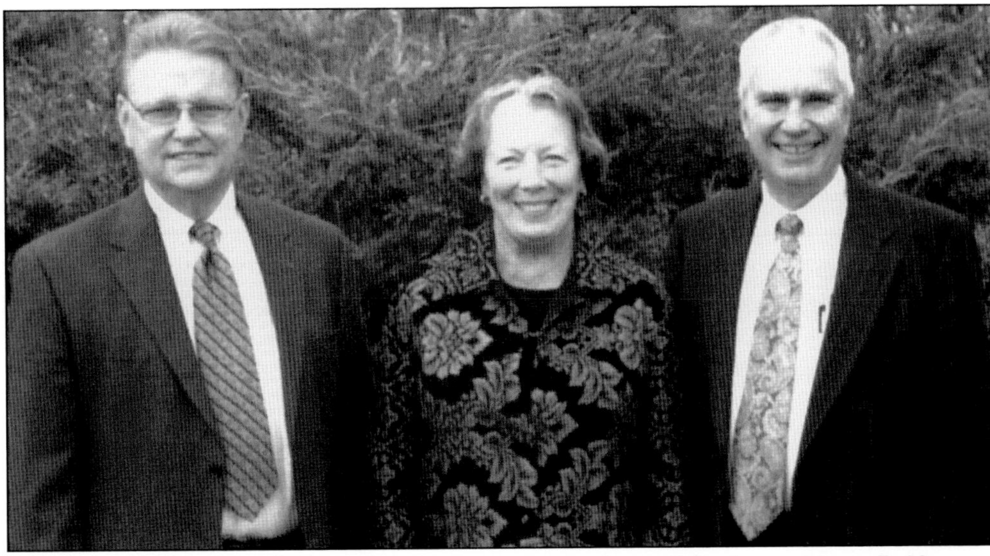

A WORK IN PROGRESS. The current park commissioners, James E. Bushman, Nancy R. Hamant, and Robert A. Goering Sr. (from left to right), are ready to face the challenges the park district faces in the 21st century.

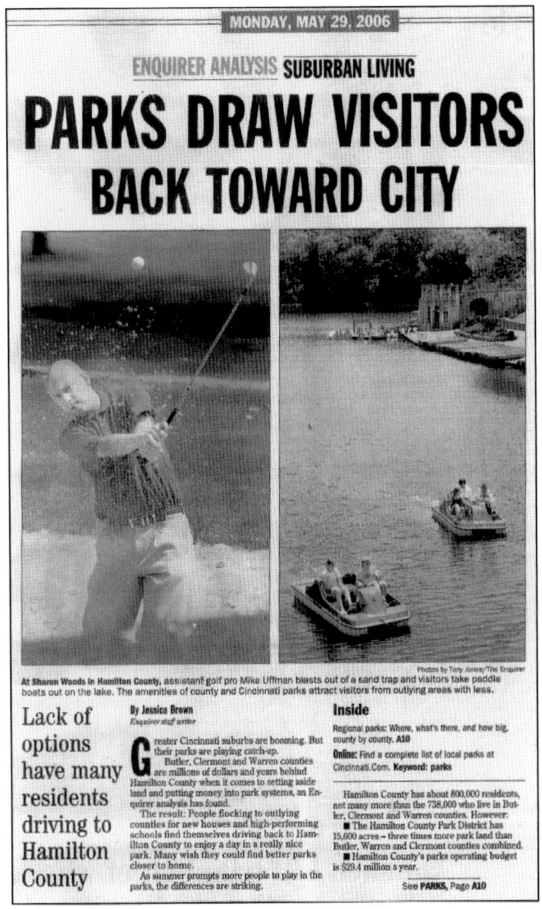

MONDAY, MAY 29, 2006

ENQUIRER ANALYSIS SUBURBAN LIVING

PARKS DRAW VISITORS BACK TOWARD CITY

Photos by Tony Jones/The Enquirer

At Sharon Woods in Hamilton County, assistant golf pro Mike Uffman blasts out of a sand trap and visitors take paddle boats out on the lake. The amenities of county and Cincinnati parks attract visitors from outlying areas with less.

Lack of options have many residents driving to Hamilton County

By Jessica Brown
Enquirer staff writer

Greater Cincinnati suburbs are booming. But their parks are playing catch-up.

Butler, Clermont and Warren counties are millions of dollars and years behind Hamilton County when it comes to setting aside land and putting money into park systems, an Enquirer analysis has found.

The result: People flocking to outlying counties for new houses and high-performing schools find themselves driving back to Hamilton County to enjoy a day in a really nice park. Many wish they could find better parks closer to home.

As summer prompts more people to play in the parks, the differences are striking.

Inside

Regional parks: Where, what's there, and how big, county by county. **A10**

Online: Find a complete list of local parks at Cincinnati.Com. **Keyword: parks**

Hamilton County has about 800,000 residents, not many more than the 738,000 who live in Butler, Clermont and Warren counties. However:

- The Hamilton County Park District has 15,600 acres – three times more park land than Butler, Warren and Clermont counties combined.
- Hamilton County's parks operating budget is $29.4 million a year.

See **PARKS,** Page **A10**

THE PRIDE OF HAMILTON COUNTY. Recent economic reports show a steady net population loss in Greater Cincinnati. This is especially true in Hamilton County. On Memorial Day, 2006, the *Cincinnati Enquirer* revealed that many people who move to neighboring counties in southern Ohio and northern Kentucky often return to Hamilton County parks. The Hamilton County Park District remains the crown jewel of parks in the region.

Consistent with our mission to preserve history on a local level, this book was printed in South Carolina on American-made paper and manufactured entirely in the United States. Products carrying the accredited Forest Stewardship Council (FSC) label are printed on 100 percent FSC-certified paper.